ADVANCE PRAISE FOR *A SOVEREIGN PEOPLE*

"Carol Berkin's path-breaking *A Sovereign People* highlights the way that high Federalists won the hearts and minds not only of the rich and powerful, but of ordinary people from all walks of life, leading them to look to the nation and the Constitution rather than to the states for the source of their identity. Her astute analysis of four foreign and domestic crises brings the critical decade of the 1790s to life, capturing the tensions, the hopes, and the fears of the people charged with creating the basis for a new and as yet untried nation. A tour de force."

> —Sheila Skemp, Clare Leslie Marquette Professor Emerita of History, University of Mississippi

"Carol Berkin has written a convincing reinterpretation of the four major crises of the 1790s. This essential book shows that the Whiskey Rebellion, Genet Affair, XYZ Affair, and Alien & Sedition Acts actually helped bind the nation together, increasing support for the government, a sense of American identity, and respect for the Constitution. Everyone interested in the history of this vital decade needs to have her book."

> —James H. Broussard, director, Lebanon Valley College Center for Political History

"With a masterful command of a complex history, Berkin uses her clear and concise style to help us rethink the founding of the United States. With powerful logic, and with an important timeliness, Berkin reveals how Americans discovered a shared national identity, and learned to love the new Constitution—despite often disagreeing with each other. A brilliant and important book."

> —Doug Bradburn, founding director, The Fred W. Smith National Library for the Study of George Washington at Mount Vernon

A SOVEREIGN PEOPLE

A SOVEREIGN PEOPLE

———◆·◆·◆———

The CRISES *of the* 1790s *and the* BIRTH
of AMERICAN NATIONALISM

CAROL BERKIN

BASIC BOOKS
New York

Published by Basic Books, an imprint of Perseus Books, LLC, a subsidiary of Hachette Book Group, Inc.

Books published by Basic Books are available at special discounts for bulk purchases in the United States by corporations, institutions, and other organizations. For more information, please contact the Special Markets Department at Perseus Books, 2300 Chestnut Street, Suite 200, Philadelphia, PA 19103, or call (800) 810-4145, ext. 5000, or e-mail special.markets@perseusbooks.com.

Designed by Amy Quinn

Library of Congress Cataloging-in-Publication Data

Names: Berkin, Carol, author.
Title: A sovereign people : the crises of the 1790s and the birth of American nationalism / Carol Berkin.
Description: New York : Basic Books, [2017] | Includes bibliographical references and index.
Identifiers: LCCN 2016047872 (print) | LCCN 2016049490 (ebook) | ISBN 9780465060887 (hardcover) | ISBN 9780465094936 (ebook)
Subjects: LCSH: United States—History—1783–1815. | Nationalism—United States—History. | Genet, Edmond Charles, 1763–1834. | Whiskey Rebellion, Pa., 1794. | XYZ Affair, 1797–1798. | Alien and Sedition laws, 1798. | Kentucky and Virginia resolutions of 1798.
Classification: LCC E310 .B345 2017 (print) | LCC E310 (ebook) | DDC 973.3—dc23
LC record available at https://lccn.loc.gov/2016047872

10 9 8 7 6 5 4 3 2 1

*To my
granddaughter,
Noa Grey Berkin*

CONTENTS

INTRODUCTION

WHEN PRESIDENT GEORGE Washington delivered his first inaugural address on April 30, 1789, he confessed that as a man of "inferior endowments from nature" who was "unpractised in the duties of civil administration," he feared his inadequacy to handle the challenges that lay ahead for the new federal government. Washington, however, was not the only man who felt the weight of those challenges. Along with the president, there were men who believed that the survival of the Republic rested on the Constitution and its government—and that the success of both depended upon them. The anxiety they shared with the president can be seen in the debates in Congress, in cabinet meetings, in newspaper articles, and in their private correspondence.

Like Washington, these men called themselves Federalists, but in spirit they were nationalists. They had written the Constitution or supported its ratification from a firm conviction that a strong government representing all the people of the Republic was the surest path to economic growth and prosperity, to civil law and order, and to winning the respect and recognition from foreign nations necessary to insure America's continued independence. They had met with fierce opposition at the ratifying conventions by men equally certain that the best way to protect the liberties and rights won in the Revolution was to keep power in the hands of the state governments. But the Federalists had won that hard-fought battle. And now, in 1789, the first president and the first Congress were preparing for the battles to come.

The stakes were high. If the federal government failed, and these men were well aware that it might, it would be their failure; if it succeeded, they hoped to be credited with that success. In short, Federalists tended to see themselves as the exclusive guardians of the federal experiment, the Constitution's true representatives and agents—and its only legitimate interpreters. They viewed anyone who opposed them, anyone who criticized them publicly or attacked their policies, as an enemy of the Constitution, of the federal government, and of the Republic.

There was opposition—in newspapers, in congressional debates, in memorials and petitions sent to the presidents, in outbreaks of open resistance and in challenges to the sovereignty of the United States by foreign powers. The laws passed by Congress and the policies set by the president were ignored by foreign representatives and resisted by citizens. Their policies were undermined by state officials protective of their own authority. And the Federalists in office were relentlessly accused of secretly plotting to destroy the Republic and create a monarchy in America. Federalists believed that this opposition would undermine their efforts to win the loyalty of the ordinary citizens to the Constitution and its government. Without the peoples' support, the Constitution was only a piece of paper.

Looking back from the twenty-first century, it is often difficult to imagine that the acceptance of the Constitution was ever contested or that the authority of the federal government was so widely doubted. But a closer examination of the decade after the ratification of that piece of paper reveals that attachment to the federal government grew slowly. As it did, a new identity emerged. Vermonters and New Yorkers and Virginians came to see themselves less as citizens of their home states and more as citizens of a nation. The Federalist economic and fiscal policies alone cannot explain this shift. Although Alexander Hamilton's economic plan ensured that entrepreneurs and commercial interests would have a vested interest in the survival of the federal government, it did not win the hearts and minds of ordinary citizens. The Federalists needed help to lay the foundation for a strong and enduring central government. They found it in the least expected places: crises of government legitimacy and sovereignty.

Some of these crises originated within the new nation's borders; others started abroad. In each instance, the Federalists resolved the crisis, and the process brought more Americans into the national fold. The central story of the 1790s is how patriotism came to be associated with this support for the Constitution and its government. If the Revolution freed the states and the Constitution linked them as never before, it was the Federalists in the 1790s, responding to one grave crisis after another, who established a nation on firm ground.

A Sovereign People tracks four of the crises of this founding era. It explores the context in which they arose, the nature of the challenge to the government, and how the Federalists chose to resolve the crisis. Unlike many accounts of these crises, this book does not focus on their role in the emergence of an opposition party led by Jefferson and Madison; instead, it scrutinizes the part these crises, and their resolutions, played in the emergence of American nationalism.

The first crisis was a domestic challenge to the legitimacy of congressional legislation. Known as the Whiskey Rebellion of 1792–1794, this was an armed resistance by western Pennsylvania farmers and distillers to an excise tax on the production and sale of alcohol. Frontier communities like these had a long history of resentment, first against the British and colonial governments and later against the state governments that they believed favored the more established eastern enclaves. In the early 1790s, Pennsylvania backcountry men nurtured a long list of such complaints, this time aimed at the new federal government. Chief among them was the government's failure to secure navigation rights to the Spanish-held Mississippi River that would have allowed them to ship their grain harvest to market before it spoiled. To preserve the value of their crop on the long haul across land, they distilled much of it into liquor. In 1792, however, the financially struggling federal government imposed a tax on the production and sale of this alcohol. The resulting rebellion is a reminder that the ghost of the American Revolution—with its call to citizens to rise up against tyranny—still haunted the land. The whiskey rebels, like the New England Shays' rebels of 1786, believed that they had a right to arm themselves and resist unfair legislation. And, like the Sons of Liberty and other radicals of the 1770s, they used intimidation and violence against the tax collectors and the members of their communities who dared to support the excise tax. Government failure to answer the whiskey rebels' challenge would set a precedent that made a mockery of its authority. The government's dilemma was how to end the rebellion, establish its legislative authority, and avoid fueling the public's fears of an abuse of power under the new Constitution.

The second crisis is known as the Genet affair. French ambassador Edmond Charles Genet arrived in America in the spring of 1793, armed with instructions from his country's revolutionary government to enlist US help in its struggle to spread an "empire of liberty" to other European nations. As the two republics in the Western world, France expected willing aid from the United States, just as France had aided the Americans in achieving their independence. Genet demanded that President Washington accept the French interpretation of the crucial 1778 Franco-American Treaty of Amity and Commerce and Treaty of Alliance, an interpretation that would allow French warships and privateers to make full use of American ports and territorial waters in its naval battle with England. Genet also enlisted Americans to man French privateers and to join in the invasion of Spanish and British territories in North America. In his enthusiasm to achieve these goals, Genet ran roughshod over American sovereignty, ignoring the president's Proclamation of Neutrality in the European war and flouting the policies in place to ensure that neutrality. In effect, Genet's actions would have turned the United States into a satellite of France rather than an independent sovereign nation. The government needed to assert its control over foreign policy without alienating the many Americans who continued to be grateful to the French for their aid during the Revolution and who hoped to see the French Republic victorious.

The third crisis, the XYZ affair of 1798, posed a diplomatic challenge to American honor and to its ability to sustain the policy of neutrality as the war in Europe continued to rage. In 1794, Washington had acted to ease tensions and avoid war with Britain by negotiating what was known as the Jay Treaty. In 1798, his successor, John Adams, hoped to do the same with France. Relations between the two countries had deteriorated since the Genet affair; privateering against American merchant ships had increased, and, in 1797, France had refused the credentials of an American ambassador. Adams sent three envoys to Paris to reestablish a cordial relationship between the two republics. Before any formal negotiations could take place, however, the French minister's agents demanded a bribe for the minister and a large loan toward the French war effort. The bribe was seen as an insult to American honor; the loan was likely to draw the United States into a war with Britain. The challenge facing President Adams was whether the situation called for a declaration of war against France or a second attempt at the negotiation of a treaty.

The fourth crisis involved the interpretation of the Constitution and the powers it granted the federal government. It began when the Adams administration tried to take advantage of the popularity it enjoyed for the handling of the XYZ affair. Federalists decided to pass legislation that would silence the partisan press supporting the Republican opposition as well as laws that would slow the growth of that party by imposing tighter immigration and naturalization laws. These Alien and Sedition Acts prompted both Kentucky and Virginia to pass resolutions that denied the authority of the federal government to legislate against free speech or to interfere with the power of state governments to control immigration. Both states suggested that allegedly unconstitutional laws could be declared null and void. And both states challenged the idea that the Constitution had created a "consolidated" or national government rather than a union of sovereign states. The government's task was to defend not only the constitutionality of its legislation as necessary and proper but to persuade the public that the citizens of America, not the states, were the source of authority for the Constitution and the federal government.

The Federalists made many mistakes in dealing with these crises. Yet we can see the arc of a rising nationalism as they navigated their way through each of them. The public's commitment to the Constitution and the federal government began as little more than a desire to honor and to express its trust in the Revolutionary War hero, George Washington. It slowly evolved into a respect for the office rather than the man. It grew stronger as citizens began to acknowledge the value of a federal government that would speak to the outside world with one voice and a united purpose. It deepened when once again the French showed contempt for America and declared that the people could be separated from their government. And it solidified as Kentucky and Virginia insisted that they could reject particular laws but made their argument within the context of acceptance of—and loyalty to—the Constitution and a federal government. The disagreement was not over whether the Constitution ought to be accepted and admired, but over whose interpretation of that near-sacred document was correct.

Modern Americans often assume that nationalism was an obvious and even automatic response to the transition from colonies to an independent country after the Revolutionary War. But this assumption misses the reality that the core of nationalism—loyalty to a country and its government and a shared identity as its citizens— was the result of the hard work of governance. The governments of Washington and Adams did not find perfect solutions to the crises facing their country, but over the course of their administrations Americans came to acknowledge that the federal government was the best-equipped institution to deal with critical domestic and foreign problems.

THE DECISIONS MADE by men like Washington, Hamilton, and Adams, members of an executive branch committed to a strong, active central government, ensured the survival of the young Republic during its critical first decade. Today, however, many Americans doubt the wisdom of what these eighteenth-century leaders called an "energetic government." We have seen an ebbing of confidence in government's capacity to play a positive role in our society. Nationalism has become closely associated with a call for limited government, and patriotism often takes the form of jingoism and empty chauvinism. A closer look at the 1790s will remind us that nationalism and patriotism once carried more positive meanings—and give us reason to believe they can do so again.

Part I

THE WHISKEY REBELLION

NONE OF THE seventeenth- and eighteenth-century rebellions by American farmers and slaves ended in success—except of course the American Revolution. The frontier participants in Bacon's Rebellion in 1676 failed to wrest power from the tidewater planters of Virginia. A New York slave revolt in 1712 ended with the brutal execution of many participants. North Carolina farmers were roundly defeated and their Regulator Movement crushed in 1775 when they rebelled against the policy of taxation without representation enforced by the colony's elites. The 1786 Shays' Rebellion, an uprising of New England farmers protesting unfair taxation and the threat of foreclosure on their farms, was easily squelched. Yet the impact of several of these uprisings could be felt long after the defeat of the men who embraced their cause. Former Regulators frequently joined Loyalist regiments to fight against planter revolutionaries in the war for independence, and Shays' Rebellion so frightened leading revolutionaries that it paved the way for the convention in Philadelphia that produced the Constitution. Thus, even the defeated played a critical role in shaping our national history.

The Whiskey Rebellion of the early 1790s is part of this tradition of influential failures, for it presented one of the first challenges to the authority of the new federal government. The Pennsylvanians and Virginians who resisted paying that government's first excise tax had several understandable, although not entirely defensible, reasons to resent the Washington administration and its imposition of a tax on their liquor and distilleries. Yet it would be a mistake to attribute high-minded or pure motives to these westerners. The whiskey tax was inconvenient, but it was far from oppressive. The decision by these men to defy a law passed by a representative legislature did not make them revolutionaries; it made them insurgents, citizens who resorted to violence against the men appointed to enforce the law and who engaged in intimidation of their neighbors who wished to obey it. Although some accounts of this rebellion portray them as heroic, a case can also be made that they were simply lawless and disgruntled.

In previous accounts of the Whiskey Rebellion, the focus has often been on whether these rebels were heroes or villains, whether their cause was just, and whether the government that mobilized to crush their revolt was simply eager to flex its muscles. But perhaps this focus obscures more than it illuminates. No matter how historians and their readers judge the whiskey rebels or the government that defeated them, it is important to realize that President George Washington and his allies had good reason to believe these westerners posed a serious threat to the survival of the federal government. To Secretary of the Treasury Alexander Hamilton, this rebellion, erupting at a moment when the affairs of the national government were not yet firmly established and the domestic enemies of that government were "as inveterate as ever," had created "a crisis in the affairs of this Country." Washington, too, believed the rebels' actions were "dangerous to the very being of government," and he saw it as his solemn duty "to check [the] daring & unwarrantable spirit" of the citizens of western Pennsylvania. These comments cannot be dismissed as empty political rhetoric, fear mongering, or elitist contempt for the common man; both men were truly devoted to and worried about the survival of the independent republic that had been placed in their care.[1]

To understand why the president and his secretary of the treasury decided to send troops to suppress the rebellion requires us to consider the context in which they acted. In the early 1790s, the power given to the federal government by the Constitution was still actively contested, challenged by influential former Antifederalist leaders in every state and by the many ordinary Americans, especially in the South, who shared their desire to restore the sovereignty of the individual states. The federal government Washington presided over was an untested experiment in sustaining the unity of a country of diverse economies, demographics, and forms of social organization through laws enacted by elected leaders. Under these fraught circumstances, the refusal to obey a law passed by Congress was, in effect, a denial of the authority and legitimacy of that federal government. To allow the rebels a victory would be to concede that other segments of American society could pick and choose which laws to obey and which laws to ignore. To men like Alexander Hamilton and George Washington, who had labored to forge a nation rather than a loose confederation of sovereign states, this challenge was at once a threat and an opportunity. The defeat of the whiskey rebels would provide dramatic proof of the government's readiness to enforce its laws. It would reassure its supporters and send a message to those who still opposed this embryonic national government that it would demand respect. In a sense, this crisis, like those that followed, was both a challenge and an opportunity; only by facing down such direct defiance of its authority was the federal government able to demonstrate its effectiveness and win the loyalty of the American public. Without these crises, it ran the risk of being ignored.

1
"The debt of the United States . . . was the price of liberty."
—Alexander Hamilton, January 1790

ON FEBRUARY 4, 1789, electors in eleven states cast their votes for the first president of the United States. Following the instructions set down in the Constitution, the state legislatures forwarded the ballots to Congress, where the House of Representatives was to tally the votes. It would be two months, however, before the results were reported, for neither the House nor the Senate had the quorum needed for their session to begin. It was true that winter snows had made travel to New York City, the seat of the new government, difficult, but this was not the sole cause of the delay. Many congressmen simply felt no urgency to leave their homes, plantations, farms, or legal offices to take their seats in a new, untested government that lacked the status of their more established local legislatures. The delay embarrassed those nationalists who hoped the Constitution marked the creation of what they called an "energetic" union of the states and who now found themselves prodding friends and colleagues to do their duty and make their way to New York. As Massachusetts representative Fisher Ames would lament as the delay dragged on, "The public will forget the government before it is born."[2]

At last, on April 1, 1789, the first session of the House of Representatives of the First Federal Congress was called to order. Five days later, the ballots for the presidency were at last counted. To no one's surprise, His Excellency George Washington, Esq., was unanimously elected. The news was greeted with a mixture of relief and delight, although Washington himself seemed more resigned and anxious than elated. He faced a task likely to prove as difficult—or perhaps more so—than the challenge of commanding the Continental Army.

In his April 30 inauguration speech, Washington made no effort to hide his trepidation. Nothing in his life, he declared, had filled him with greater anxieties than being summoned by his country to this new office. He confessed to doubts that he was up to the task ahead. Nature, he said, had given him "inferior endowments" and his experience as a military leader and a plantation owner had left him "unpracticed in the duties of civil administration." If he lacked confidence in his own skills, he expressed his certainty that the men of Congress would do the people's business without party animosities or local prejudices. He would soon have cause to revise this view.[3]

Washington may truly have doubted his own administrative abilities, but he did not doubt the magnitude of the responsibilities he had accepted. He believed the survival of the American experiment in republican government hinged on the success of the federal government. He saw clearly the problems facing him, as its leader: the embarrassing debt, the lingering opposition to the Constitution and to the powers it granted the federal government, and the challenge to demonstrate the legitimacy of a new, sovereign nation to the wider world. Daunting as these problems seemed, the president did not shy away from them. He quickly began to organize the executive branch. For his cabinet, he chose men of established talent and reputation, drawn from all regions of the country. But because he gave little weight to ideological consensus among his appointees, Washington brought the contest between nationalism and state sovereignty into this most intimate setting for decision making. His cabinet meetings would be contentious, and his cabinet members more given to conflict than to cooperation.

From the largest and richest of the southern states, he chose his fellow Virginian, Thomas Jefferson, to serve as secretary of state. It was a risky choice, for Jefferson had not supported the ratification of the Constitution. He had argued that the federal government it proposed was potentially as dangerous to liberty as George III and his Parliament had been, and he had urged his own state's ratifying convention to reject it. Despite Jefferson's known preference that power reside in state governments, Washington persuaded him that his diplomatic experience was needed in managing America's relationships with the other nations of the world. As secretary of war, Washington named the Massachusetts bookseller-turned–artillery expert, Henry Knox, an avowed nationalist, whose friendship the president valued and whose innate military genius he respected. Knox's primary duties would be establishing domestic law and order and protecting the country's borders. As attorney general, Washington once again drew on a Virginian, a former aide-de-camp, a distinguished lawyer, and a man with executive experience as governor of the Old Dominion, Edmund Randolph. Despite the fact that Randolph had presented the Virginia Plan at the Constitutional Convention, he fluctuated between a states' rights position and a commitment to the authority of the national government. But it was the president's choice of thirty-four-year-old Alexander Hamilton of New York to serve as secretary of the treasury that reflected Washington's own ardent nationalism. Hamilton was an unabashed nation builder, eager to see the United States gain a seat at the table among the greatest European powers.

Unlike Jefferson, Hamilton did not fear that a strong national government would increase the threat of tyranny. Instead, he saw the greatest danger to America's survival in the jealous protection of the states' prerogatives. In the years following the Revolution, Hamilton had seen the results of political provincialism—the competition among the states that hindered economic recovery, episodes of social unrest and the continuing threat of slave revolts, and the inability to secure the country's borders. For him, the creation of a strong and active national government was the remedy to America's ills; state autonomy was the disease.

Washington appointed Hamilton on September 11, 1789. It would fall to him to set the nation's floundering finances in order and establish its public credit. Anyone who knew the brilliant and brash New Yorker was certain of one thing: he did not lack for confidence in his ability to set the country on the path to fiscal stability. He would soon be given the opportunity to prove himself, for less than two weeks after Hamilton took up his portfolio Congress directed him to evaluate the country's finances and prepare a plan to pay the country's staggering debts. No one was certain how great those debts were, to whom the money was actually owed, or, for that matter, which debts were the responsibility of the new government. There were loans outstanding from foreign allies; there were promissory notes, or "Continentals," given to Americans who had contributed supplies to the army and to soldiers in lieu of pay. Then there were states that had not repaid their Revolutionary War debts. Were these debts to be included in the federal government's burden? And, finally, where was the revenue to come from that would allow the government to honor its debts?

Hamilton had answers to all these questions. With truly remarkable speed, he completed an exhaustive report on strategies for handling the public credit. The report was Hamilton at his best, relentlessly and closely reasoned, offering several alternative plans for payment of the foreign and domestic debts, every paragraph reflecting the urgency he felt to set the country's financial reputation aright. There were three key elements of Hamilton's plan: the federal government would fund its debt, setting aside a specific portion of all revenue to ensure regular payment installments; it would assume responsibility for the remaining Revolutionary War debts of the states;

and it would pledge to repay this consolidated domestic debt to current rather than original note holders.[4]

Hamilton's proposals created a firestorm within the House of Representatives. The more astute congressmen realized that the secretary's goal was grander than the establishment of the US public credit. With his *Report on Public Credit,* and other reports that would quickly follow, Hamilton intended to bolster the importance of the federal government and to set a commercial trajectory for the new nation's political economy. What came to be known as the Hamiltonian system would give shape to much of the political controversy in the early Republic, and it would spur the emergence of an anti-administration party.

There was much to protest in Hamilton's report—and members of the House were skilled at protesting. Representatives like Maryland's Michael Stone saw the assumption of state war debts as a move to tip the balance of power between the states and the federal government in favor of the latter. Like most eighteenth-century men, Stone was well aware that the power to raise revenue and decide its uses was the sine qua non of any government. If the states were relieved of their outstanding war debts, they would have no justification for raising taxes. This was a consequence devoutly desired by a nationalist like Hamilton but just as devoutly opposed by states' rights men like Stone. At the same time, representatives from states that had retired their war debts balked at shouldering the burden of their less fiscally responsible neighbors.

Representatives from southern states saw other, serious dangers in Hamilton's report. They opposed his proposal to pay off the domestic debt to current certificate holders rather than to the original creditors. Because the majority of current domestic debt holders were speculators from the northern states, southern representatives were quick to label Hamilton's plan a brazen move to create a political economy favoring northern businessmen over southern agriculturalists. They were correct about Hamilton's long-term goals if not his immediate intentions. In October 1789, he would boast to the British ambassador George Beckwith that the United States was "a young and a growing Empire, with much Enterprize and vigour," but he would also concede that Americans were now "and must be for years, rather an Agricultural, than a manufacturing people."

For Hamilton, the future belonged to manufacturing, trade, and industry—not to farming—and it would take careful planning and government encouragement to move the country in what he believed was the right direction.[5]

For other representatives, including Hamilton's old ally, James Madison, Hamilton's proposal to pay off government certificates to current rather than original holders raised serious moral issues. Many of these certificates had first been issued to soldiers and to private citizens who had supplied the army during the war. But they had changed hands since the peace, as farmers, widows, and veterans grew weary of waiting for repayment and became fearful that the Confederation government would never have the resources to honor its debts. These ordinary citizens had sold their certificates to speculators for whatever they could get. For men like Madison, Hamilton's willingness to reward speculators was unethical.

On January 28, 1790, as Congress began to discuss the report, the hotheaded, combative Georgian James Jackson expressed his disgust that the mere rumor of this proposal to pay current creditors had ignited "a spirit of havoc, speculation, and ruin." His soul, Jackson declared, "rises indignant at the avaricious and immoral turpitude which so vile a conduct displays." No one in the House doubted that the targets of Jackson's indignation were northern speculators and businessmen. Although less given to dramatic declarations than was his fellow southerner, Madison shared Jackson's concern about the consequences of Hamilton's proposal. The only moral path, Madison concluded, was to seek out the original creditors and to discriminate in their favor when payments were determined. Hamilton considered this an impractical, if not impossible, demand. It was beyond the resources of the federal government to follow the trail of sale and resale back to the original certificate holders. This profound disagreement between Hamilton and Madison, between the practical and the moral path, severed the alliance between two men who had, together, orchestrated the Constitutional Convention. Perhaps nothing reflected the emerging divisions between entrepreneur and planter, commerce and agriculture, North and South more than the abrupt move by Madison into the anti-administration camp.

2

"There is perhaps nothing so much a subject of national extravagance, as these spirits."
—Alexander Hamilton, *Federalist 12*

ALTHOUGH ASSUMPTION, FUNDING, and the payment to current debt holders were the key elements of the report, they were not the only proposals to spark controversy. Hamilton had stressed that the costs of establishing public credit could not be covered by duties on imports alone. There was a limit to how much these could be raised without strangling American trade. Thus, some form of domestic taxation was necessary. Hamilton knew that no one in Congress would dare support direct taxation; the only option therefore was an excise tax. He proposed to lay that tax on wines, spirits, including those distilled within the United States, teas, and coffee.

Anyone who had read Hamilton's *Federalist 12* and *21* would not have been surprised at this suggestion—or of his recommendation that the tax should fall on alcohol. He had pointed out the merits of taxing consumable commodities in *Federalist 21:* "It is a signal advantage of taxes on articles of consumption that they contain in their own nature a security against excess." In other words, consumption would simply decline if the rates were set too high. To ensure against this decline, and to guarantee that the revenue collected was adequate, the government would be careful not to set an unreasonable or oppressive rate.[6]

In *Federalist 12,* Hamilton had pointed to the advantages of sizeable duties on imported alcohol. First, consumption of foreign spirits was high enough to ensure solid revenue. "The whole quantity imported into the United States," he wrote, "may be estimated at four millions of Gallons; which at a shilling per gallon would produce two hundred thousand pounds." Second, a tax on the purchase of alcohol promised to have social and moral value as well, for "if it should tend to diminish the consumption of it, such an effect would be equally favorable to the agriculture, to the economy, to the morals and to the health of the society. There is perhaps nothing so much a subject of national extravagance, as these spirits."[7]

He made these moral and health arguments in his January report on public credit, confident that no one could deny that eighteenth-century Americans *did* consume a troubling amount of alcohol. On the eve of the Revolution, New York City boasted more taverns than churches, and drunkenness was common enough that Benjamin Franklin once amused himself by collecting more than two hundred terms for excessive drinking, ranging from "addled" and "afflicted" to "boozy," "cracked," and, a local Massachusetts phrase, "halfway to Concord." Wealthy drinkers preferred imported products—French wines, Portuguese Madeira, port, and Caribbean rums. But domestic breweries turned out their share of beer, cider, and rum for the ordinary American's consumption. By 1770 there were more than 140 rum distilleries in the colonies, producing about 4.8 million gallons each year. Domestic rum was so cheap that the average adult male may have consumed three pints each week. And, after the Revolution, the production of domestic whiskey soared. Altogether, it is estimated that by the 1790s an average white American over the age of fifteen drank almost six gallons of absolute alcohol each year.[8] (In 2015, the World Health Organization declared that the United States ranked twenty-fourth in national consumption of alcohol, with an estimated 2.43 gallons a year.)

HAMILTON WAS NOT alone in worrying about his fellow countrymen's drinking habits, especially the consumption of hard liquor, or "ardent spirits." Before independence, John Adams had denounced the many colonial taverns serving hard liquor as "dens of iniquity." And in 1774, the Philadelphia Quaker Anthony Benezet had published a damning critique of Americans' excessive drinking. In his *The Mighty Destroyer Displayed,* Benezet condemned distilled liquor as unhealthy, degrading, and immoral. By 1784, Methodists were urging their congregations to abstain entirely from hard liquor. That same year, the respected Philadelphia revolutionary Dr. Benjamin Rush published *An Inquiry into the Effects of Ardent Spirits on the Human Mind and Body.* In it, he asserted that liquor could be addictive and could lead to death.[9]

Hamilton wove these themes and arguments into his call for an excise tax on alcohol. "The consumption of ardent spirits," he wrote, "no doubt very much on account of their cheapness, is carried to an extreme, which is truly to be regretted, as well in regard to the health and the morals, as to the economy of the community. Should the increase of duties tend to a decrease of the consumption of those articles, the effect would be, in every respect desirable." Despite a concern about the terrible effects of these "pernicious luxuries," Hamilton did not lose sight of the practical benefits of a tax on alcohol. Raising the duties on foreign alcohol, he argued, would benefit American agriculture because domestically produced cider and malt liquors would slowly replace imported distilled spirits. Of course, Hamilton did not actually expect the decrease in consumption to be so great that no revenue would be raised. "Experience has shewn," he conceded in his report, "that luxuries of every kind, lay the strongest hold on the attachments of mankind, which, especially when confirmed by habit, are not easily alienated from them."[10]

Hamilton anticipated many of the concerns his call for a tax on alcohol would raise—and managed to turn them to his advantage. He conceded, for example, that the collection of the new, higher duties on foreign alcohol would be difficult, and he predicted "extensive frauds," even if customs collectors were vigilant and penalties were high. His solution to this problem was to establish a second tier of inspection once the goods were delivered to the merchants and dealers. Honest merchants would be eager to report any irregularities reflected in the delivery of the products, and a second inspection would make fraud far riskier for dishonest importers.

This was a bureaucratic solution, but, as usual, Hamilton's agenda went beyond mere efficiency. In fact, there was a third motive for introducing all these new taxes, a motive more political than fiscal or moral. Throughout his public career, Alexander Hamilton was ready to seize any opportunity to expand federal power at the expense of state power, for he believed that only a strong, active national government could unlock the productive capacities of America and make it equal in prosperity and influence to the great nations of Europe. By establishing a federal excise tax on liquor, he would effectively cut off a potential revenue source for the states. And, by introducing a system of internal customs inspection, he would expand the federal government's reach and authority. Like his proposed assumption of the states' Revolutionary War debts, these policies would bolster the authority and power of the nation and diminish the power of the states.

Having made his case for the new taxes, Hamilton proceeded to lay out the duties he recommended Congress impose. For imported alcohol, the duties should range from thirty-five cents a gallon on higher-quality Madeira to twenty-five cents on sherry and twenty cents on other wines. The strength of the imported ardent or distilled spirit determined the tax on each item. Hamilton introduced a sliding scale of duties on other imported stimulants as well; thus, the elegant hyson tea was to be taxed over three times more than bohea, and coffee, less popular than any variety of tea, would bear only a five-cent tax.

Hamilton then turned to domestically produced spirits. He carefully distinguished between spirits distilled from "Molasses, Sugar, or other foreign materials" (rum) and those distilled from materials grown or produced within the United States (grain whiskeys), yet this proved a distinction without a difference, as the fees he recommended for the two were nearly the same. He also distinguished whiskey produced on farms for local or home consumption from whiskey produced for the market, yet he made it clear that both should be taxed. To ensure that home brew did not escape the excise, he placed an additional tax on stills not located in a city, town, or village.

Hamilton anticipated the likely objections to this part of his plan. He knew that memories of British customs abuses were still raw in the minds of many Americans, and he took pains to assure Congress that misconduct by revenue collectors would not be tolerated. He pledged that criminal charges would be brought against any customs man guilty of abuse and stipulated that even when seizures of goods were made with probable cause, a distiller or a seller found innocent of an infraction would be compensated.

The secretary of the treasury's report—long, detailed, and with multiple moving parts—left representatives the task of figuring out how all the elements of his proposed program fit together. Doubts about the need for an excise tax soon surfaced. Without the assumption of state debts, some argued, an excise tax would not be necessary. Others expressed doubts that a tax on alcohol would bring in enough revenue to make a dent in the government's fiscal obligations.

Yet, by May 1790, many representatives had reluctantly conceded the inevitability of a federal excise tax. On May 25, one of Hamilton's strongest allies, the gifted orator Fisher Ames of Massachusetts, summed up their dilemma: "What revenues are left you if the excise is rejected?" No one had an answer to his question.[11]

The second session of Congress ended in August, leaving Ames's question hanging in the air. Before adjourning, the House asked the secretary of the treasury to submit another report on public credit. On December 13, 1790, Hamilton delivered a second report on the subject of an excise tax. This time, he was less focused on a justification for the excise and more concerned with defending his proposed method for its collection. There were, he said, only two possible approaches: the first, to make the security of the revenue depend chiefly on the vigilance of the public officers; the second, to make it depend upon the integrity of the individuals who would be interested in avoiding payment of the duties imposed. Hamilton put his confidence in the former. He trusted Congress would do the same.[12]

Hamilton urged Congress to pass legislation based on his report as soon as possible. Congress, which was proving itself disinclined— or unable—to rush passage of any legislation, moved remarkably quickly. The debates, which began on January 5, 1791, took less than a month, although they were as lively and colorful as others that dragged on for much longer. Southerners were the most vocal opponents of the bill, for they were rarely producers of liquor or wine. As consumers of these "pernicious" but widely desired luxuries, southern gentlemen would pay a high price for their continued enjoyment.[13]

In the end, the most compelling argument against the excise tax was that it would be deeply unpopular with most Americans. Timothy Bloodworth, a representative from North Carolina, worried that public disapproval of the tax could lead to violence. How would the government handle such an uprising? "Suppose," he asked, "the people should not consent to the law, is one part of the people to be marched against another?" His concern was genuine, and, as it turned out, it was prescient.[14]

Despite the impassioned pleas of opponents like James Jackson, the bill passed the House by a vote of 35 to 21 on January 27, 1791. The nay votes were primarily sectional, coming from Virginia, the Carolinas, Georgia, and Maryland. But hints of a second division, this one on an east-west axis, could be seen in the three negative votes from Pennsylvania's representatives. After some amendments by the Senate, the statute was recorded on March 3, 1791.[15]

An Act Repealing, After the Last Day of June Next, the Duties Heretofore Laid upon Distilled Spirits Imported from Abroad, and Laying Others in their Stead, and Also upon Spirits Distilled within the United States and for Appropriating the Same was as lengthy as its title suggests, with sixty-two separate sections, detailing, among other things, the items to be taxed, both foreign and domestic, the scale on which the fees would be set, the mechanisms for collection, and the penalties for failure of compliance. Despite its formal title, the act quickly became known simply as "the whiskey tax." Just as quickly, it became apparent that there were men willing and eager to defy the federal government and its new excise law.[16]

Hamilton had been prepared to protect against evasion of the duties on foreign spirits by smugglers. He had been careful to add a second ring of inspectors to ensure that merchants could not defraud the government. But the challenge to the federal government did not come from the shippers of foreign wine or the sellers of New England rum. It did not come from tavern keepers or middlemen who sold the Madeira and Caribbean rum that entered through the port cities along the Atlantic. It did not come from the urban working men and women who saw the price of their domestic rum or whiskey go up so much that a gallon consumed a full day's wages. Instead, it came from the West, from the Pennsylvanians across the Allegheny Mountains and from settlers in the region of Virginia soon to become Kentucky. These farmers mounted the first major domestic challenge to the authority and sovereignty of the new federal government.

3

"The law is deservedly obnoxious to the feelings
and interests of the people."
Minutes of the meeting at Pittsburgh,
Pennsylvania, September 7, 1791

HAD HAMILTON BEEN too sanguine about compliance by American whiskey producers? Perhaps he might have anticipated a problem if he had known more about the circumstances of life on the frontier. He had assumed that the farmers of western Pennsylvania, like all other producers of spirits, could pass along the cost of the excise taxes to the consumer. But in the Pennsylvania counties of Westmoreland, Fayette, Allegheny, and Washington and in the Virginian interior of Kentucky, that was not an option. These frontier farmers faced problems and complications that set them apart from eastern producers.

Grain was the primary crop of the region, but getting it to market in its natural state was expensive and risky—virtually impossible—because the nearest major overland market, Philadelphia, was almost three hundred miles away. No water route was available because the Spanish refused to open the Mississippi River to Americans. This was a source of intense frustration to backcountry farmers, who had pressed both the older Confederation government and the new federal government to negotiate a treaty with Spain that would open navigation of the river. Yet, as of 1791, no real progress had been made. With little firsthand knowledge of diplomacy, westerners had seen the failure as nothing more than a neglect of their needs. Bowing to the reality that their grain could not easily reach a market, these Pennsylvanians had turned to the production of whiskey from their harvests. These distilled spirits were not just marketable. Unlike grains, they did not spoil but improved with age, and they could be carried overland to Pittsburgh and on to Philadelphia in jugs on the backs of mules. Despite the costs of transportation and competition from foreign liquors, farmers who chose to produce whiskey for the market could make a profit. Many farmers, however, chose not to pursue distant markets but settled instead for using their whiskey locally to pay for their dry goods or farming supplies. By the time Hamilton proposed his tax on both the distilleries and the whiskey they produced, whiskey was well established as the major medium of exchange in this region that rarely saw cash. It was used to celebrate weddings and bring solace to mourners, but it was also used to pay off debts, the minister's salary, and the farmer's rent. The farmers who used their whiskey as a substitute for currency would not be able to pass the cost of running their distilleries along to consumers.

Whether they were commercial or noncommercial whiskey producers, western Pennsylvania farmers resented the new tax and the circumstances that had prompted it. What, they asked, would they gain from compliance? Why should they support a government that did not fight for navigation rights to the Mississippi? Why support a government that did not rid their landscape of hostile Indians? Why accept a tax imposed so that the government's creditors could profit from the payment of the public debt? After all, few if any of those creditors were their neighbors.

Even those who might accept the need for the tax were likely to resent its many requirements. It was not simply that, in their mind, the duties were too high. It was not just that those duties had to be paid *before* the liquor left the distillery, an upfront expense that weighed heavily on cash-poor westerners. Nor was it that the law required every distiller, even those who were illiterate, to keep a daily record of production and to make his account available to inspectors. It was not even that the law gave unfair advantage to large-scale urban distillers who were to be taxed according to proof as well as quantity and who were capable of producing high-proof whiskey, which was taxed at a lower rate. It was the insult added to all these injuries: the law forbade the payment of the tax in the only ready resource they had, whiskey.

These frontier farmers considered the penalties for infractions draconian. If a distiller was caught with a cask of spirits that lacked an inspection certificate, he would lose more than the liquor. The fine or penalty imposed on him might end up costing him his horses, cattle, carts, and tackle as well. And if he failed to pay the annual tax of sixty cents per gallon of still capacity, he could be forced to sell all his personal goods to pay the fines. An arrest for any of the many infractions meant a trial, and by 1792 that meant attending a court in Philadelphia rather than a local one. The expense of a trip to Pennsylvania's capital city almost equaled the value of the average westerner's farm.[17]

The farmers watched with resentment as the jobs of inspectors of the stills and collectors of the whiskey tax were filled through social connections and outright nepotism. When an old friend of the president and the secretary of the treasury, Edward Carrington, was made supervisor of revenue for the state of Virginia, he wasted little time appointing Colonel Thomas Marshall, a family connection, as the chief revenue officer for the region of Virginia that would soon become Kentucky. In Pennsylvania, one of the wealthiest distillers,

General John Neville, was appointed as inspector of federal revenue for the Western District. Neville had been popular in the Allegheny County community despite his background as a Federalist, an Episcopalian, and a transplanted Virginian, but affection for him cooled as he began to appoint members of his family to excise-related posts. Neville went from being a respected neighbor to a highly visible target for anger against the whiskey tax.[18]

Western Pennsylvanians wasted little time mobilizing resistance to the excise tax. Their fellow distillers in Kentucky, however, took a completely different tack: they chose to simply ignore the tax. Here in what was still western Virginia until June 1792, local distillers simply refused to keep the required records and did not bother to register their stills. Their passive resistance was helped by the fact that no one was willing to serve, as John Neville had done, as a revenue collector. It was helped even more by the refusal of local courts to acknowledge the existence of the federal excise law. Despite the almost universal evasion of the excise, the local federal prosecutor did not bring a single action to the courts. It was just as well, for grand juries showed no interest in charging anyone with breaking this law. When the prosecutor resigned in 1792, no one came forward to replace him. The excise was so universally rejected that not a single lawyer could be found to take up the government's cause.[19]

Both Hamilton and his assistant secretary of the treasury Tench Coxe were aware of—and embarrassed by—the situation in Kentucky, but neither was certain what to do about it. They made a few efforts to see the offenders punished in the courts. Coxe, for example, tried authorizing Colonel Marshall to offer generous fees to any private attorneys willing to prosecute the lawbreakers. But no one volunteered. The Treasury then tried a carrot-and-stick approach, offering to forgive all arrears for the past period if Kentucky distillers promised to pay the taxes in the future. No one accepted the offer. Hamilton finally made a far more radical concession, proposing that the distillers be allowed to pay their taxes by providing whiskey to the federal government's western army. That, too, failed. All Hamilton could do was hope news of the Kentucky resistance did not become widely known.[20]

The Washington administration was clearly frustrated by the situation in Kentucky, but it viewed the organized protests and the eruption of violence in Pennsylvania far more seriously. Washington, Hamilton, Adams, and their fellow Federalists understood that a nation born in revolution carried a collective memory that violence was sometimes justified. The 1786 Shays' Rebellion, led by a veteran of the war for independence, had frightened those who hoped that the creation of a representative government would make a resort to arms an unacceptable means to redress grievances. Even the Revolution's most celebrated radical, Samuel Adams, had called for the execution of the Shays' Rebellion leadership, insisting that citizens of a republic had no justification to rebel. The fear that the revolution was not, and might never be, over meant that few political leaders shared Thomas Jefferson's acceptance of occasional rebellion.[21]

The worries of the president and his colleagues were founded not only on memory but on the whiskey rebels' use of techniques a rebel like Samuel Adams would immediately recognize. On July 27, 1791, they organized a planning session at Redstone in Fayette County. Soon committees had formed in Washington, Fayette, Westmoreland, and Allegheny Counties. On August 23, the Washington County committee passed a series of resolutions strongly censuring the tax. More ominously, its resolutions included a warning: any person who accepted an excise office would be considered inimical to his neighbors. In the interests of alliance building, the Washington County committee deputized three members to meet with delegates from the other three counties on the first Tuesday of September. And, finally, it arranged for its resolutions to be printed in the *Pittsburgh Gazette*. Suddenly Timothy Bloodworth's scenario seemed more reality than rhetoric.[22]

By September 1791, the revolt against the whiskey tax had escalated. Protestors were no longer simply issuing resolutions; they were engaged in acts of physical intimidation and violence. On September 6, about twenty men armed themselves and donned disguises. Some, it was reported, put on women's dresses, perhaps in homage to the tea party members who boarded British ships in 1775 dressed as Indians. Their target was Robert Johnson, the newly appointed collector of revenue for Allegheny and Washington. In the tradition of prerevolutionary protests, they tarred and feathered Johnson, cut off his hair, and took his horse so he would have to ignominiously walk to get help.

Throughout the rest of the year, delegate meetings and vigilante violence operated in tandem. While the delegates, including a number of influential men like the novelist H. H. Brackenridge and the Swiss-born supporter of the nascent Jeffersonian Republicans Albert Gallatin, issued resolutions and sent petitions to Congress, gangs of disgruntled farmers and distillers tarred, feathered, and inflicted burns and bruises on anyone foolhardy enough to work as a revenue collector or inspector.

The intensity of the resistance in these western counties had its desired effect, causing most local government officials to lose heart in their missions. The experience of the deputy marshal of the District Court of Pennsylvania was illustrative. In October 1791, he traveled to Allegheny County to serve processes against several men accused of breaking the law. But his nerve failed him by the time he reached Pittsburgh. He concluded that the western part of the state was in tumult and that his own life was in danger. Certainly the man he recruited to serve the processes would have agreed. Slow-witted and possibly senile, the hapless John Conner was seized, whipped, tarred and feathered, robbed of his money and his horse, and left tied up in the woods, hoping for rescue. No further efforts would be made in 1791 to serve warrants in Allegheny.[23]

Even the suspicion that a man represented the federal government seemed enough to set off violence in Allegheny, as one Robert Wilson tragically learned. Wilson was delusional and believed that he was an agent of Washington's government. When he began snooping around farms and stills, others began to believe it too. Dragged out of bed, burned with a hot iron, and tarred and feathered by local whiskey rebels, Wilson refused to promise his tormentors that he would stop spying on them. He also refused to denounce the government or renounce the tax. Although his connection to the Treasury was entirely illusory, Wilson almost died clinging to the belief that he was a loyal officer of his government.[24]

Thus, only a few months after the excise law went into effect, the Washington administration realized it faced a dire challenge. With Kentucky distillers flouting the law by ignoring it, sporadic outbreaks of violence against it in South Carolina, and petitions demanding its repeal making their way to the House, the government began to look impotent. Rumors spread of a plan between the Pennsylvania rebels and the Kentuckians to secede from the United States and create their own independent country. Although the idea went no further than an agreement to name the new country Westylvania, it was enough to convince at least one member of the Washington administration, Alexander Hamilton, that the western communities were tinderboxes of social and political anarchy.

4

"What occasion is there for such violent and
unwarrantable proceedings?"
—Chief Justice Thomas McKean,
November 8, 1792

EVERY DAY THAT whiskey distillers failed to pay their taxes meant the loss of much-needed revenue. Far worse, every day they openly resisted the law, the embarrassment of the government deepened. In July 1791, Washington had optimistically written to David Humphreys, his former aide-de-camp, now serving as the US ambassador to Portugal, that "each days experience of the Government of the United States seems to confirm its establishment, and to render it more popular—A ready acquiescence in the laws made under it shews in a strong light the confidence which the people have in their representatives." Yet by the fall of the year, he found himself searching for an explanation of this western challenge to federal authority. He believed it arose from a moral and intellectual weakness of ordinary citizens. Western farmers, the president concluded, had proven susceptible to manipulation by unscrupulous and ambitious demagogues who told them their liberties and livelihoods were in danger. This trope of demagogues and deluded followers, which had once explained the origin of the Revolution to King George and to his American Loyalists, would appeal to the supporters of government throughout the Whiskey Rebellion.[25]

The secretary of the treasury did not care as deeply as did the president about who pulled the strings—if strings there were—in the revolt against federal law. Hamilton believed the growing insurgency revealed the weakness of the federal government. As early as April, writing to Washington, he declared, "It is to be lamented that our system is such as still to leave the public peace of the Union at the mercy of each state Government. This is not only the case as it regards direct interferences, but as it regards the *inability* of the National Government in many particulars to take those direct measures for carrying into execution its views and engagements which exigencies require." For Hamilton, the resistance to the excise was a warning that could not be ignored; the federal government must equip itself to enforce its laws, or it was no real government at all.[26]

In his message to the House on October 25, 1791, Washington tried to downplay the impact of the opposition to the whiskey tax. On the whole, he wrote, "enlightened and well-disposed Citizens" recognized the necessity for a revenue law. But, he conceded, in the vague and general language he frequently resorted to, that "the novelty . . . of the tax, in a considerable part of the United States, and a misconception of some of its provisions, have given occasion, in particular places to some degree of discomfort. But it is satisfactory to know that this disposition yields to proper explanations and more just apprehensions of the true nature of the law." The president expressed his confidence that opposition would "give way to motives which arise out of a just sense of duty, and a virtuous regard to the public welfare." Washington would return often, in his correspondence and in his public statements, to this notion that duty and a belief in the public welfare must triumph over irresponsible opposition to the law.[27]

In November 1791, the House turned to Hamilton for the "proper explanations" the president trusted would turn protest into compliance. They asked the secretary of the treasury to report on the nature of the complaints against the excise tax and to give his opinion on whether, or how, to modify the law to address those complaints. In response, Hamilton submitted a lengthy report on March 5, 1792. In it he frankly conceded that strong opposition to the tax existed, citing the many petitions he had received demanding its repeal or, at the very least, its modification. The criticisms in these petitions ranged from claims that the whiskey tax controverted the principles of liberty to the notion that it injured morals, interfered with the business of distilling, and oppressed those who did not pay or who did not follow proper procedures with heavy and excessive penalties.[28]

One by one, Hamilton refuted these charges. His responses were typically thorough and tightly argued. He only occasionally revealed his annoyance at some of the accusations and requests. For instance, he found the charge that an excise tax was "inconsistent with the genius of a free Government" absurd. Free or not, all governments needed revenue, and the only alternative to an excise tax was far more drastic: a tax on land and other property. He was equally dismissive of complaints from distillers that keeping a daily account of the quantity they produced was burdensome. Hamilton, a lawyer and a man of letters, could not imagine how it could be onerous to sit down each evening and enter the required information in a book the Treasury had provided. And he flatly rejected westerners' claims that they were cash poor and thus needed to pay the tax in whiskey. Other complaints he rejected on practical grounds. Although he sympathized with distillers who found it hard to pay the duty first and then recoup the expense from the consumer, he saw no practical way to ease this burden. Collecting from the distiller's many consumers would be far more costly than taxing the liquor at its source.

Hamilton ended his lengthy report with several sensible suggestions for amending the law, including a proposal that distillers be allowed to register their stills at a central office in each county rather than face an inspection on their property. He also supported a change in the way the duty was calculated so that a man had to pay only for the time he actually worked his still.

Hamilton's arguments were sound, his suggestions practical, and his calculations accurate. His mistake was to assume that a protest born of frustration and a sense of abandonment could be laid to rest by a recitation of fact and an insistence on logic and reason. In every sense, the greatest virtue of his vision—its expansiveness—was also its greatest weakness. He was devoted to building the nation he believed America could, and should, become, and he had a plan to ensure it would achieve greatness. But his vision, however patriotic, did not easily tolerate opposition, compromise, or alteration. Law and order, stability, productivity—these were the pillars he believed were needed to sustain the Republic. There was simply no room for violence or even protest, which he believed would lead only to anarchy or tyranny.

Throughout March and April 1792, the House discussed Hamilton's report, debated the merits of the westerners' demands, and argued over what it, as the legislature, should do. There were numerous acerbic exchanges, but the whiskey tax was not always the source of these disagreements. The revenue issue seemed to bleed into others, including sectional tensions. When Fisher Ames of Massachusetts suggested that unanswered requests for more vigorous military protection from Indian attack lay at the heart of western discontent and violence, Pennsylvania's William Findley angrily corrected Ames's use of the term "requests." The people of the frontier do not desire protection as a favor, he declared, "they demand it as a right; they know that protection and allegiance are inseparable; that if they are not protected, their connexion with the Government is dissolved."[29]

Southern resentment against northern advantages also made its way into the discussions. North Carolina representative John Steele began a speech on the floor of the House with a rousing defense of all opponents of the excise tax. He said the refusal to obey the law did not arise, as some of his colleagues were suggesting, from "a restless and disorderly spirit among the people." Rather, he declared, it was born of "an aversion which freemen . . . ever will have to this mode of taxation." Having defended resisters wherever they might be, he narrowed his concern to the men of his own region. Southerners, distilling alcohol for home consumption, were required to pay an excise tax, while New Englanders, producers of rum, could export their alcohol without any duty charged. And this disparity was not unique. He lamented that all southerners, as farmers rather than manufacturers, were disadvantaged, for they had to pay high duties on essential imports like salt, shoes, and nails. Wherever Steele looked it appeared the laws of the federal government favored the North over the South, just as wherever Pennsylvania's Findley looked he saw the East oppressing the West.[30]

April ended with little consensus on what to do to appease the distillers—or whether they should be appeased at all. The only thing the House could agree on was that steps ought to be taken to protect the country if a full-scale insurrection developed.

On April 26, the legislature passed a bill making it legal for the president to call out the militia if needed "to execute the laws of the Union, suppress insurrections, and repel invasions." If this was the stick, on May 5, as the session of Congress was closing, the House offered the carrot. It passed a bill decreasing the tax rate on domestic spirits made from domestic grains. This effort to accommodate the whiskey rebels went much further than Hamilton had suggested or thought wise. There was nothing to do now but wait to see whether this concession would have the desired effect.[31]

5

The *"great* and *real* anxiety is . . . the ability to preserve the national government."
—Alexander Hamilton, May 1792

IT WAS CLEAR that the cost of the apparent failure of the excise tax, and the debates it engendered, had to be measured in more than dollars and cents. The revenue issue was entangled with too many others, some of them centered on Hamilton's fiscal policies, others on emerging conflicts over foreign affairs, and still others on negotiations over navigation of the Mississippi that affected Kentucky and western Pennsylvania so acutely. Most ominously, the debate over the revenue issue exposed the tensions between agriculture and commerce and between coast and interior. In April 1792, John Steele of North Carolina had bluntly pointed out where the fault line lay: "This, sir, may not improperly be termed a struggle between two classes of citizens whose interests are and will be for some years, dissimilar—the agricultural and manufacturing parts of the United States." Steele saw little hope for a peaceful resolution of this conflict. "It will not be difficult," he declared, "to predict how it will terminate."[32]

By 1792, sectional tensions had splintered the coalition of nationalists that had produced the Constitution. Madison, Hamilton's most important ally at the Philadelphia convention, had joined his fellow Virginian, Thomas Jefferson, in transforming the anti-administration concerns of men inside and outside of Congress into an organized opposition party. Their success meant increased criticism of Hamilton's policies in the press and on the floor of Congress. Damaging but unfounded rumors of corruption on the part of the secretary of the treasury were also surfacing, rumors used by Jefferson and his supporters in an attempt to alienate the president from Hamilton.[33]

Hamilton resented the polarizing role his policies were playing in American politics. On May 26, while he waited to hear whether the accommodations made to the distillers had produced positive results, he poured out his anger and frustration to his friend Edward Carrington. The target of that anger was Thomas Jefferson, who had, Hamilton reported, "thrown censure on my *principles* of government and on my measures of administration." The tale Jefferson and his allies have spread of a monarchical party bent on "the destruction of State & Republican Government" was, he assured Carrington, pure fabrication. The "*great* and *real* anxiety is not the destruction of state governments, but the ability to preserve the national government." The "language of my heart," he confided to his friend, spoke for the success of the American experiment in republican government. Yet he feared that success was uncertain. "It is yet to be determined by experience whether [republican government] be consistent with that *stability* and *order* in Government which are essential to public strength & private security and happiness." For Madison and Jefferson, the possibility of a monarchy and the ascent of one segment of society over others were the most pressing domestic threats; Hamilton, by contrast, pointed to the danger of national financial instability and the emergence of social anarchy.[34]

The crowning of an American king did not seem imminent as the summer of 1792 began, but the threat of social anarchy did appear to be a very real possibility—and not only in western Pennsylvania and Kentucky. In some areas of North Carolina, for example, the revenue could not be collected. Hamilton was ready to use force, but he was uncertain whether North Carolina's militia would cooperate. Writing to his friend Carrington once again on July 25, the secretary asked whether Virginia's militia could be counted upon to restore order in North Carolina. The query pointed to the central problem of enforcement: the only acceptable military forces available were the state militias, because the use of the federal government's western army would provoke serious opposition. But would a militia act in support of a federal law—and in another state, no less? And could a governor be counted on to call out his militia if the president made the request? No one, including Hamilton, knew the answer to these questions.[35]

Pockets of resistance in the lower South might not turn into open rebellion, but no one in Washington's administration could be hopeful about the situation in the West. There, residents were preparing for a guerrilla war against the federal government. In Pennsylvania's Washington County, some five hundred men met to form an organization they called the Society of United Freemen. The society, which quickly became known as the Mingo Creek Association, had a pedigree that stretched back to the Confederation era. Like the men who had joined Shays' Rebellion, many members of the society had been active irritants in the postwar years, disrupting debt cases in the courts and interfering with the sale of foreclosed property. They had also been boosters of the local economy, protecting local production of whiskey by enforcing boycotts on liquor brought in from the East.[36]

By late August 1792, the society had succeeded in recruiting the local militia company, led by Colonel John Hamilton, to spearhead armed resistance to the government. Colonel Hamilton had proven his loyalty to the resistance in 1791 by participating in the attack on Robert Johnson. Now, the society was eager to take on a bigger target: General John Neville, the inspector for the entire Western District of Pennsylvania. They began by attempting to prevent Neville from operating out of rented office space in the home of one William Faulkner. The society threatened to burn down Captain Faulkner's house and tar and feather its owner if he did not withdraw his offer to assist Neville. When Faulkner refused to be intimidated, the society ramped up its tactics. First, it placed an anonymous ad in the Pittsburgh paper, calling for a convention. The forty delegates who attended issued a set of radical demands, including a demand that the federal government repeal the excise tax and replace it with a tax on the wealthy. Two days later, thirty armed men attacked Faulkner's home and his tavern. They fired their guns at the tavern sign, which featured a head of President George Washington. They ransacked Faulkner's home and refrained from burning it down only out of fear that the fire would spread throughout the community. Faulkner had had enough; the next day, the *Pittsburgh Gazette* carried his notice that he would remove Neville's office from his home.

News of the attack reached Philadelphia by September 1. Although Hamilton was ill at the time, he immediately instructed his assistant secretary to send George Clymer, the federal revenue inspector for the entire state of Pennsylvania, to the western counties on a fact-finding mission. Hamilton no doubt knew Clymer as a quiet, unassuming man, a philanthropist and a devoted Federalist who had attended the Constitutional Convention and supported ratification. But Clymer was hardly the man to take the pulse of the western counties; he was a wealthy businessman, born in Philadelphia and living just outside the city—and, as the chief revenue inspector, he had a vested interest in quelling opposition to the whiskey tax.

Not surprisingly, Clymer had little success. He was frankly frightened of his reception in the western counties, and this led him to take drastic, and foolish, measures. He decided to present himself as the secretary of war, Henry Knox; when the ruse was discovered, he resorted to a new alias, calling himself Mr. Smith. Arriving in Pittsburgh, he refused to venture far from the town or the protection of the local fort. Thus, he could not discover who had menaced Captain Faulkner or learn who was armed and ready to obstruct the law or gather the names of the delegates to the Mingo Creek convention. Nor was he able to act as Hamilton hoped, as an emissary of law and order, persuading citizens of the western counties to obey the excise.[37]

Clymer was stymied even in the actions he did take. When he asked a local judge, Alexander Addison, to take depositions that would reveal the names of those who attended the Pittsburgh convention, his request was rejected. Like Clymer, Addison had been a strong supporter of the federal Constitution, but he was openly sympathetic to the protests against the excise tax. He reminded Clymer that he was a judge of Pennsylvania *state* courts, not a federal judge, and made clear he had no intention of becoming an active participant in a federal investigation. Clymer's cool reception, combined with the refusal of local officials to assist him, led him to the unshakeable conclusion that westerners held both the state and federal government in contempt. In his reports, he expressed little hope that the insurgents would comply with the law.[38]

Yet Hamilton had already come to the conclusion that the government had a major crisis on its hands. The dilemma was clear: to concede an inability to enforce laws passed by Congress would be fatal to the new government, while to issue idle threats would be as damaging to the government's reputation as surrendering to the demands of lawbreakers. For Hamilton, then, the question was not, should the government do something, but what was the most effective thing it could do? He had reached out for advice to his friend and coauthor of the *Federalist* essays, John Jay, in early September, declaring, "There is really, My Dear Sir, a crisis in the affairs of the Country which demands the most mature consideration of its best and wisest friends." The options Hamilton asked Jay to consider revealed the direction of his own thoughts. Should Washington issue a presidential proclamation that denounced the Mingo Creek convention as a criminal act and warned westerners to abstain from further acts of resistance? Would such a proclamation have any meaningful effect? Or was force necessary? And if so, should the president himself lead a military expedition? Hamilton's own answers to these questions were obvious: the best and most effective response to the crisis was the speedy suppression of the rebellion by the military. The longer the rebellion continued and the more organized it became, the more difficult it would be to restore law and order.[39]

The president also recognized the situation for what it was: a challenge to the sovereignty and legitimacy of the federal government. Writing to Hamilton on September 7, Washington voiced his indignation at the refusal of westerners to obey the law. "Such conduct in any of the Citizens of the United States, under any circumstances that can well be conceived, would be exceedingly reprehensible; but when it comes from a part of the community for whose protection the money arising from the Tax was principally designed, it is truly unaccountable, and the spirit of it much to be regretted." Washington's claim that the revenue from the whiskey tax was earmarked for the military protection of the western settlers was probably an attempt at justification; the tax was imposed to ensure that the interest on the public debt could be covered. This did not diminish the seriousness of the crisis. The president, like Hamilton, knew that contempt for the federal government, if left unchecked, would erode the government's fragile authority. It was time, he agreed, to "check so daring & unwarrantable a spirit." He had approved Hamilton's preliminary step of ordering Clymer to survey conditions in the western counties. And he assured his treasury secretary that he would not hesitate to "exert all the legal powers" invested in him as president to see the laws executed. Thus far, he conceded, the government's policy of forbearance had not had the desired effect. In fact, the hope that these rebels "would recover from the delirium & folly into which they were plunged" had only served to increase the disorder.[40]

But Washington was far more cautious than Hamilton. The president thought it wise to pursue all legal means to deal with the insurgents before sending in troops. He would ask Attorney General Edmund Randolph to rule on the legality of the recent Mingo Creek convention and on whether those who attended it were indictable. If the answer to both questions were yes, Washington would have the matter brought before the circuit court at Yorktown that October. Angry as the president may have been at the westerners' "daring & unwarrantable spirit," he realized a resort to force before all other remedies had been exhausted would be a political mistake. He had no wish to strengthen the voices of anti-administration critics who warned of the federal government's potential for oppression and the dangers inherent in a strong executive branch.[41]

John Jay had also favored political and legal steps over military intervention. In his answer to Hamilton's request for advice, he suggested the president do nothing drastic until Congress reconvened in October. Washington could address the crisis in his message to the legislature and gauge its support by its reply. Without congressional backing, strong measures might well suggest an overreach of executive powers and thus "render the operations of the administration odious." Yet, like the president, Jay did not entirely rule out the use of force if further outrages were committed. If another attack on the dignity of the government occurred before Congress met, Washington must leave "nothing to Hazard."[42]

In the meantime, Washington and his cabinet decided to reach out to state officials and the general public through a presidential proclamation. He turned, as he often did, to Hamilton to draft the document. On September 11, Hamilton delivered his draft, along with a cover letter commenting on the recent good news that a court in the eastern county of Chester, Pennsylvania, had indicted and convicted several people for an assault on an excise officer. According to Attorney General Randolph, the jury rendering the verdicts had declared, "It was not a question with them, whether the law was good, or bad; but that they would never countenance an opposition to laws in such a form." Hamilton considered this to be such good news that he ordered his assistant to publish the account of the case in Philadelphia's *Gazette of the United States*.[43]

The Chester County convictions were heartening, but they did not persuade Washington that a public warning was unnecessary. Thus, on September 15, 1792, he issued his proclamation on the rebellion against the excise tax. He began by stating that "certain violent and warrantable proceedings" had obstructed the operation of federal laws, making it necessary for him to "admonish and exhort all persons whom it may concern to refrain and desist from all unlawful combinations." He then charged the courts, magistrates, and other officers to do their duty and urged all persons concerned with "the just and due authority" of their government and the preservation of the public peace to aid and assist in enforcing the law. On Hamilton's suggestion, Washington forwarded this proclamation to all the state governors. At Hamilton's urging, he included a brief note expressing his confidence they would use their influence to promote due obedience to the law.[44]

Privately, Washington expected little cooperation from the governor of Pennsylvania in prosecuting anyone indicted for criminal activity. His doubts were fueled by his personal history with the man in the governor's seat, Thomas Mifflin. Early in the Revolutionary War, Mifflin had served as an aide-de-camp for Washington and soon after was appointed quartermaster general for the Continental Army. Washington's friend Richard Henry Lee believed Mifflin was a man of "real merit and public virtue," but Mifflin also showed a "warm temper" and frequently quarreled with fellow revolutionaries. By 1777, he had become a vocal critic of Washington. He resigned his position and joined the "Conway Cabal," a group hoping to replace Washington as commander in chief with Horatio Gates. This explains why, on October 1, 1792, Washington ordered Attorney General Edmund Randolph to personally travel to Yorktown to see that the court business was conducted properly. The president hoped, he told his fellow Virginian, that the presence of the country's highest-ranking legal officer would give the proceedings "a more solemn & serious countenance aspect." No one knew better than Washington how important symbols of authority were when that authority was new and not yet firmly established.[45]

6

"Where the law ends, there tyranny begins."
—Chief Justice McKean, 1792

THE PRESIDENT MAY have genuinely hoped that indictments and an appeal to citizens' patriotism would quell the resistance. When a Methodist congregation in Fayette County sent him assurances of its support, he expressed his pleasure that the opposition to the excise tax was not as universal in the western counties as he had been led to believe. He was, he wrote in reply, happy to learn that the congregation intended to use its influence to "inculcate the necessity & advantage of a peaceable compliance with that law." But Washington was practical enough to begin preparing for the use of military force if legal action and moral suasion proved inadequate. He was also enough of a realist to know how dangerous military force could be.[46]

Unlike Hamilton, whose particular genius was in policy rather than politics, Washington understood the possibly disastrous consequences of calling out the regular army. He was well aware that the anti-administration forces were coalescing around Madison and Jefferson, and he wanted to ensure that the use of force did not provide grist for the opposition's propaganda mill. The president knew that the opposition press in Philadelphia (where the federal government had moved in 1790) was always ready to stoke the public's fear of Federalist plots to destroy the people's liberties, whether through physical force or political aggrandizement. If a federal army marched against Pennsylvania's western counties, Washington told Hamilton, the critics would shout, "The cat is let out. . . . We now see for what purpose an Army was raised."[47]

Governor Mifflin's response to the president's proclamation came on October 5. It would do little to calm Washington's fears. Mifflin readily admitted that the law had been broken, but he noted with satisfaction that the culprits in Chester County had been indicted, convicted, and fined by state officials. The same "regular process" had been followed in the case of several Allegheny County men engaged in violent opposition to the law. To emphasize that he intended to enforce law and order, Mifflin enclosed a copy of a letter he had issued to the judges of the Pennsylvania Supreme Court and the members of the Courts of Common Pleas. In it, he requested officials take every opportunity to "inculcate the indispensable duty of obedience to the acts of Congress." In essence, Mifflin was sending the president a message: Pennsylvania would handle its own affairs.[48]

George Clymer, whose reports to Hamilton had become increasingly grim, would have dismissed Mifflin's claims as an empty assurance. On October 10, Clymer offered his own assessment of conditions in the four western counties, and he left little doubt that lawlessness reigned. Washington County, he wrote, "is the most repugnant to the law and furnishes the most examples of violence." The leaders there were David Bradford, a lawyer, and James Marshall, a former county lieutenant. The county's justices of the peace and clergy were equally complicit in the rebellion. Clymer considered Fayette County scarcely more moderate, though the rebels here, led by state assemblyman John Smilie and Congressman Albert Gallatin, had as yet committed fewer acts of violence. Westmoreland County, under the leadership of the former Antifederalist, Congressman William Findley, was "engaged in the general opposition." Clymer referred to Findley as "the father of all the disturbances of the Western Country." In Clymer's estimation, the heart of the problem was the degenerate character of these westerners. What could be expected from them when "the duties of Citizenship are but poorly understood, or regarded, [and] where the moral sense is so greatly depraved as it is in this Country, by the intemperate use of the favourite drink"?[49]

There were some Pennsylvania justices who supported strong measures against those who did not obey the laws of Congress. On November 8, 1792, the state's chief justice Thomas McKean issued a stern charge to the Philadelphia grand jury. McKean, who had abandoned his support of the federal government over Hamilton's fiscal policies, nevertheless found the increasingly violent resistance inexcusable: "It is strange that a people, but just rescued from the galling yoke of foreign bondage, having just got rid of a despotic government, will not submit to one free and equal." The revenue tax, he declared, was small; it promoted industry, and it restrained the excessive consumption of alcohol that made men "restless and impatient." There was a remedy available to those who believed the whiskey law bore too heavily upon them: present their case to the legislature they elected. Any alternative was unthinkable, for "where the laws end, there tyranny begins." Despite McKean's vigorous defense of law and order, few indictments were brought across the state for riots or breaches of the peace connected to the revenue act. When indictments came down, as in the case of the men who attacked Robert Wilson, charges were often dismissed. James Brison, the Pennsylvania official reporting the proceedings in the Wilson case, seemed eager to categorize the attack as an act of violence against a private individual. "The indictment," he noted, "only states the Riot, assault, battery and burning, without mentioning anything of the Revenue law." This allowed Brison to claim that he did not need to forward the details of the case to the governor or the federal authorities.[50]

On November 6, 1792, Washington sent his message to the new session of the Second Congress. He assured the legislators that contentment with the excise law was growing, although he admitted there were still pockets of resistance. After the usual lengthy debate, the Federalist-dominated House of Representatives responded with a declaration of its support for the measures the president had taken and an expression of its collective regret that "symptoms of opposition . . . have manifested themselves." "No particular part of the community," the representatives agreed, "may be permitted to withdraw from the general burdens of the country." If this was less than a rousing endorsement, it was nevertheless a pledge of support.[51]

Meanwhile, in what was surely a cynical step, Governor Mifflin asked the purported leader of the rebellion, William Findley, to report on the mood of western Pennsylvanians and the role influential men might be playing in the resistance to the whiskey tax. Findley responded on November 21, providing the governor with an evaluation that perfectly fit Mifflin's own public position on the matter. The leading citizens of the western counties, Findley declared, had no "disposition to maletreat [sic] the public officers or to make a riotous opposition to the execution of the Excise law." Any misconduct that had occurred was rare and had been "too much magnified," for it involved a very small part of the district. Findley assured the governor that the guilty men had been severely punished by local courts and expressed his confidence that the federal courts would meet with no interruption as long as they did not attempt to transport the accused out of their home counties. Findley could not resist citing what he termed a miscarriage of justice: two respectable citizens of Washington County had been indicted upon the oath of a "hostler of low character." This sort of reliance on disreputable witnesses, he warned, was "pregnant with dangerous effects."[52]

Armed with Findley's report, Governor Mifflin issued his own annual message, assuring Pennsylvanians that the instances of outrage were few and the offenders had been prosecuted. What Mifflin conveniently failed to convey was Findley's doubts that the western counties would, under any circumstances, comply with the excise law. On this issue, Findley spoke frankly and no doubt with some pride: "The execution of the law, even conducted with the greatest discretion, has some serious difficulties to encounter. It is well known that in some Counties, as well of Virginia as of Pennsylvania, Men have not, and cannot be induced by any consideration to accept of the Excise offices. . . . Whatever method may be adopted to carry the law into effect, though I hope that riots will be prevented, yet the assistance of the people to support the officers, I presume, is not to be expected." Of all the statements in William Findley's report, this alone rang true.[53]

7

"It is the duty of the general government to protect the frontiers."

Resolutions of a meeting at Lexington,
Kentucky, May 24, 1794

AS 1793 BEGAN, the violence in the western counties became sporadic. But as General Neville knew, and reported to the government, this did not mean that the resistance had dissipated. The Mingo Creek Association remained strong, and, with the support of local militias, it was slowly seizing control of governmental functions. In an effort to make some progress in enforcing the law, Neville looked to Benjamin Wells, deputy collector for Fayette and Westmoreland Counties.

Wells was determined and persistent, owing to his overwhelming desire to profit from his commissions and from the rewards he could collect by turning in unregistered stills. Taking his cue from the man who created a familial network known as the "Neville Connection," Wells had placed his son Charles in a quartermaster's office in a Maryland fort. He was grooming a second son, John, as a future collector of revenue. Wells let little deter him; when a still owner's son knocked him out for snooping around the family's mill, Wells picked himself up and continued the search. Throughout 1793, despite numerous physical attacks, he doggedly sought out tax evaders. Even when his excise office was stoned and its windows smashed, even after men threatened his wife with violence, Wells persisted. Not until November 1793, when his home was invaded and his life threatened, did he turn over his record books and his excise commission and agree to publish his resignation in the *Pittsburgh Gazette.* Wells was broken but not bowed. He persuaded Neville to give his son John the excise commission. The senior Wells then became a courier of sorts, traveling from the western counties to Philadelphia, carrying the names of tax-evading distillers to the Treasury Department and the names of his attackers to the Justice Department in hopes of provoking a military campaign against the whiskey rebels.

However, a series of diplomatic crises distracted the federal government. Algerian pirates had ramped up their seizures of American merchant marine vessels; the French revolutionaries had guillotined their king; and Edmond Genet, the French ambassador to the United States, was trying to turn America into a subsidiary of his nation. Then, in late August 1793, yellow fever broke out in the nation's capital city.

There were few diseases more dreaded in eighteenth-century America. Yellow fever took its name from one of its symptoms, the yellowing of the victim's eyes and skin. No one, neither doctors nor government officials, was certain how the disease was spread. Although the actual culprits were infected mosquitoes, some experts, including Dr. Benjamin Rush, blamed rotting vegetables and other garbage. Others blamed the flood of French refugees seeking asylum from political upheavals in the Caribbean for bringing the disease to their city. Everyone agreed, however, that this was a disease to be feared. The first deaths had come in July. Soon the number of people suffering the telltale yellowing grew, and more deaths quickly followed. By late August, as the death toll rose, Dr. Rush declared that the city was in the midst of an epidemic.

No one had a cure. On August 27, the College of Physicians advised Philadelphians to avoid anyone displaying symptoms, and Rush urged anyone who could to flee the city. Some 20,000 people left Philadelphia, including the president and his family, Secretary of State Thomas Jefferson, and Secretary of War Henry Knox. Alexander Hamilton had already contracted the disease before he fled to the safety of Albany; he was among the fortunate few who recovered. The federal government had shut down. As the fatalities rose to more than a hundred a day in October, civility also fell victim to the disease. Friends avoided one another, and, at the first sign of the fever, family members were banished from their homes. Parents deserted their own children. There was such a rush to get infected people out of the city and into the cemetery that one resident, seeing a coffin loaded with a body, wondered how many people had actually been buried alive. Relief did not come until the end of October when the first fall frost stemmed the spread of the disease. On October 31, the city hospital hoisted a white flag, a sign that no yellow fever patients remained within its walls. The epidemic was over, but as many as 5,000 men, women, and children had died before the city returned to normal.[54]

Government officials slowly filtered back into Philadelphia that fall, although Washington and Jefferson took up the government's business from the safety of Germantown until late November. To the administration's relief, the determined resistance of the distillers of Pennsylvania's western counties seemed to have diminished; no reports of serious violence were waiting for Washington or Hamilton when they returned to the capital. Hamilton no doubt hoped that a new policy he had initiated that summer was having the desired effect. He had decided to relent and to allow the army to buy whiskey from both Virginia and Kentucky distillers. He was gambling that Pennsylvania whiskey makers would choose to comply with the law in order to benefit from sales to the military. At the very least, the lure of a military market for their whiskey might shatter the unity of these westerners in their opposition to the tax.[55]

But, at the start of 1794, it became obvious that the apparent peace of the last months of 1793 would be only temporary. In January, a mysterious but charismatic leader called "Tom the Tinker" cut a swathe of destruction and intimidation throughout the Pittsburgh area. Tom, who many suspected was not a single individual but a group of men, published threats in the *Pittsburgh Gazette* aimed at anyone supporting the excise. He then made good on those threats with a rash of barn burnings, targeting men who had dared to register their stills.

News of Tom the Tinker's violence did not immediately reach the president, but Washington had received reports of the November attack on Benjamin Wells. The news moved the president to change his approach; he would abandon leniency in favor of firm threats of punishment. This decision led him to issue a second proclamation on February 24, 1794, entitled Proclamation on Violent Opposition to the Excise Tax. It detailed the attack on Wells, and, to demonstrate the administration's determination to bring the perpetrators of violence to justice, it offered a reward of $200 to anyone "who shall first discover and give information" on the unknown assailants to a judge, justice of the peace, or other magistrate.[56]

Within Washington's inner circle, the new fear was that a general disregard for the authority of the federal government had reached the highest levels of some state governments. Not only was the Pennsylvania governor showing his contempt for Washington, the governor of the recently created state of Kentucky was mocking the administration. On March 10, Washington had found it necessary to convene his cabinet to discuss Governor Isaac Shelby's refusal to suppress the French recruitment of American citizens to invade Spanish Louisiana. In 1793, Shelby had stubbornly denied Thomas Jefferson's report that Revolutionary War veteran George Rogers Clark had joined forces with French minister Edmond Genet in a plot to seize Louisiana. He continued to stonewall the new secretary of state, Edmund Randolph, in 1794. His message was clear—and disturbing: as governor, he could ignore the federal government's diplomatic alliances if and when he chose to do so. Shelby's defiance forced the president to issue yet another proclamation on March 24, 1794, warning citizens "to refrain from enlisting, enrolling, or assembling themselves for such unlawful purposes." Offenders would face severe punishment. But it was only Minister Genet's shortage of funds that finally put an end to this crisis.[57]

By April 1794, even if they were no longer signing up for an invasion of Louisiana, Kentuckians showed little evidence that they were any more loyal to the federal government. In fact, that May Kentucky's original response to the excise tax—ignoring it—gave way to active protest. Hundreds of distillers and their supporters held a mass meeting in Lexington, where the agenda quickly moved beyond the call for repeal of the whiskey tax. The thirteen resolutions they passed were a litany of western disappointments and frustrated demands. The protesters condemned the federal government for failing, "through design or mistaken policy," to provide them free navigation of the Mississippi River. They criticized the government's failure to force British forts out of the Ohio Valley. And they expressed outrage at the government's failure to protect its citizens from Indian attack.[58]

Washington would not have denied the serious challenges to the prosperity and safety of western residents. But these were not the only challenges his administration was struggling to address. With limited military and financial resources, the president was doing his best to deal with a host of domestic and foreign questions facing America daily. He could not meet unrealistic demands for a quick resolution to western grievances. But patience did not prevail among those westerners who felt thwarted by "design" or incompetence. The Lexington resolutions reflected the depth of resentment among men unable to appreciate the often delicate nature of treaty negotiations with foreign countries and uninterested in the number and complexity of problems facing the federal government.

Not only that, but the number of angry westerners seemed to be growing. In July 1794, news would reach the cabinet that a second down-and-out Revolutionary War hero, General Elijah Clarke, had led a movement of Georgians determined to secede and create a new republic on Creek Indian lands. Unlike Westylvania, the Georgia plot went beyond mere talk. Clarke's followers constructed forts in Indian territory and established a settlement. Although the Georgia militia stepped in to thwart the secessionists, Clarke's actions endangered the peace negotiations the federal government was conducting with the Creeks at the time.[59]

The violent resistance to the whiskey tax in Kentucky and Pennsylvania, the Genet and Clark plan to recruit Americans for an invasion of Louisiana, the Lexington resolutions that accused the federal government of intentionally ignoring western safety and incompetence in securing western economic needs, and the Georgia secession movement—each reinforced the administration's conviction that anarchy and instability were spreading. It would not take much more to persuade the president that drastic measures were necessary.

8

"Finding the opposition to the revenue law
more violent than I expected . . . "
—Collector of revenue, Robert Johnson,
July 1794

THE FINAL IMPETUS for military action came from Pennsylvania. Despite Tom the Tinker's barn burnings early in 1794, Governor Mifflin continued to insist that he had taken all the action required to stem the resistance to federal law. He had, after all, sent a circular letter in March that urged acquiescence. The response, he was pleased to report to the president, had been patriotic. As proof of his success, Mifflin enclosed extracts from letters attesting to the return of law and order. These came from none other than Judge Alexander Addison and David Redick, a lawyer who regularly attended insurgent meetings. Addison assured Mifflin that he had heard of no criminal behavior since the rioters of Allegheny County had been brought to justice. He laid any lingering problem—small though he insisted it was—squarely on Hamilton's choice of revenue collectors, especially Benjamin Wells. The men Hamilton had appointed, Addison lamented, lacked both spirit and discretion. The people understandably had no confidence in them. Redick too placed the blame for the resistance on the men chosen to collect the tax. Because citizens he talked to feared "a vindictive spirit" in collector Robert Johnson, Redick believed a change in personnel "would have very happy effects." On Hamilton's advice, Washington did not reply to the governor's letter, agreeing with his treasury secretary that nothing he said would force the governor to admit he had a dangerous rebellion on his hands.[60]

Congress, like Hamilton, was no longer willing to placate the insurgents of western Pennsylvania. On June 5, after only a month of debate, the legislature passed An Act making further provisions for securing and collecting the Duties on foreign and domestic distilled Spirits, Stills, Wines and Teas. This law empowered the president to create new districts and surveys and to alter older ones in order to make enforcement of the excise tax easier. The president was also given the authority to appoint new supervisors and inspectors of stills and ports. Penalties for noncompliance were increased: any spirits not entered at an office of inspection were liable to seizure and forfeit. Congress's intent was clearest in section 8 of the bill, which stipulated that an owner or worker of a licensed still must attest to distilling only during the period his license indicated, or else he could not ask for its renewal. Hamilton was delighted with Congress's decisive action, telling John Jay that the legislative session had proven "much better than I expected."[61]

The new regulations and the expansion of the revenue bureaucracy were unlikely to have a calming effect on the distillers of Allegheny, Fayette, Washington, or Westmoreland Counties. In fact, while Congress was crafting the new law, the insurgents were tightening their grip on these western Pennsylvania communities, once again borrowing many of the techniques the colonial radicals had employed during the 1760s and 1770s and that the members of Shays' Rebellion had turned to in the following decade. In May, the rebels erected liberty poles throughout the region, a frontier tribute to the Sons of Liberty two decades earlier. Where once committees of safety had demanded loyalty oaths from men hesitant to join the Revolution, now Tom the Tinker and his allies demanded that hesitant westerners publish statements of loyalty to the resistance in the local press.

Revenue officers like General Neville began to prepare for the worst. They did not have long to wait. The first target that summer was John Wells, son of the beleaguered Benjamin Wells. When the younger Wells took over the position of collector for Westmoreland County, he opened his office in the home of Philip Reagan. In June, a force of almost 150 men surrounded Reagan's house and took him hostage. They then moved on to Wells's own house and burned it to the ground. Reagan managed to escape, but no excise office would be set up in his home again. Similar attacks soon followed on other excise offices. Any man foolish enough to rent space to revenue collectors was tarred and feathered, and efforts to serve summonses on noncomplying distillers were met with violence.[62]

In July, as Marshal David Lenox and General Neville traveled through Allegheny County to serve summonses, they barely escaped a mob that ambushed them. A few days later, the much-awaited showdown between Neville and the rebels finally took place. On July 16, the Mingo Creek Association sent some thirty men, armed with rifles and clubs, to arrest the marshal, who was staying at Neville's home. Gunfire was exchanged, and five attackers were killed. The next day, six hundred men gathered and issued two demands: all writs in Neville's possession must be handed over, and Neville must resign. When this insurgent army marched to the Neville homestead, it found Major Abraham Kirkpatrick of the US military and ten of his soldiers there to defend the revenue collector. Kirkpatrick tried to negotiate with the rebels but failed. Neville's outlying buildings were burned, and his home was once again attacked. The marshal was captured, though later released. General Neville, who managed to escape, wisely fled to the safety of Pittsburgh.[63]

It was no longer possible for any reasonable person to insist on the general peacefulness of the four western counties. On July 18, Major General John Gibson summarized the situation around Pittsburgh for Governor Mifflin. "I am sorry to have to inform your Excellency that a civil War has taken place in this county." Major Thomas Butler, commander at Fort Fayette, Pittsburgh, echoed Gibson's judgment in his letter to Secretary of War Henry Knox. "Sir, I feel extreme pain in communicating to you the lawless and disorderly state of this western country at this period." Like most supporters of the federal government, Butler laid the blame for the trouble on "designing men" who had persuaded "the deluded inhabitants" to oppose the excise law. "Deluded" would be the most common adjective assigned to those who followed leaders like Tom the Tinker and the lawyer David Bradford.[64]

On July 19, the insurgents struck again, intercepting the US mail carrier and taking several letters addressed to government officials. Their goal was to discover who in their counties was asking for federal help. The robbery suggested that, for the first time, the insurgents were worried that support was waning among the more influential men of the region. The concern was justified; the recent escalation of violence had led a number of leading citizens to wonder whether the whiskey rebels had finally gone too far.

Yet Tom the Tinker and Bradford believed the insurgency had not gone far enough. A few days after the battle at the Neville home, a meeting was called at the Mingo Creek Church. The mood was tense, given the recent violence and the deaths of a number of their fellow rebels. Bradford managed to rally them by reading a defiant and provocative—and stolen—letter written by Colonel Neville's son. The young Neville boasted to his friend of his wealth, declaring that he did not care whether the rebels burned his home too, for he had plenty of other property. The meeting's main purpose, however, was not to shore up support for the resistance among the farmers present. It was to test the loyalty of certain specific—and prominent—supporters of the rebellion by soliciting their opinions on the attack on Neville and the destruction of his property. Attention quickly turned to the man most suspected of apostasy: the frontier lawyer and novelist, Hugh Henry Brackenridge.

From the beginning, Brackenridge's support of the whiskey rebels had been a surprise. He had begun a career in politics with his election to the Pennsylvania assembly in 1786, but his staunch defense of the Constitution led to his defeat for reelection. Although he ran to be a delegate to the Pennsylvania ratifying convention in 1787, his neighbors in Allegheny County preferred to send the uneducated William Findley to represent them. Brackenridge promptly satirized the ignorance of these ungrateful backcountry constituents and abandoned politics for literary pursuits. It is unlikely that many western Pennsylvania residents would read his novel *Modern Chivalry* when it came out in 1792 and 1793, but if they had, they would not fail to perceive the author's contempt for uneducated men aspiring to public office.

When Tom the Tinker challenged Brackenridge's continuing commitment to the cause, Brackenridge hedged. Hoping to appear the voice of caution and reason, he commented that it might have been morally right to burn down Neville's house, but it was still illegal. In fact, he said, it was actually an act of treason that would carry dire consequences. In assaulting Neville and the marshal, the rebels had provided the president with the right to call out the army against them. Brackenridge hastened to assure the meeting that he doubted

Washington wished to wage war against citizens of his own country. He was confident, he said, that the president would grant everyone amnesty if only the rebels promised to obey the law.

Although he had no real authority to speak for the president, Brackenridge was offering the rebels a way out of the dilemma their attack on Neville had created. But they decided to follow a different tack: further escalation. They resolved to rally the region and instruct militia commanders to arrest the men who had dared to request the federal government's help. What had started as a revolt against the excise tax had now effectively become a war of secession.

Brackenridge was not the only leading citizen to decide things had gone too far. When armed militias converged on the town of Washington, a number of the local elites in the resistance called for moderation. Even John Hamilton, the commander of the Mingo Creek militia, tried to prevent his men from marching against the federal government. William Findley, a fierce opponent of Alexander Hamilton and his fiscal programs, began to soften his rhetoric and play the role of peacemaker. It was all to no avail.[65]

On July 28, Bradford and six other leaders of the resistance issued a circular letter to the militia officers in the western counties. "You are called upon as a citizen of the western country to render your personal service, with as many volunteers as you can raise to rendezvous at your usual place of meeting on Wednesday next, and thence you will march to the usual place of rendezvous at Braddock's Field . . . on Friday the first day of August next." To Bradford's satisfaction, the militiamen answered his call. As August began, nearly 7,000 came together at the appointed spot.[66]

9
"The crisis is now come, submission or opposition."
—David Bradford, August 1794

PRESIDENT WASHINGTON, TOO, had been gathering his forces, but for the time being these remained legal and political rather than military. He still refused to call on General Anthony Wayne and the federal army to suppress the rebellion, but he was now ready to clear the path for an expedition composed of state militias. To this end, he had written to Supreme Court justice James Wilson, asking for certification that civil and judicial authorities were unable to restore law and order in the western counties. While he waited for Wilson's reply, Washington began to accumulate evidence to support the argument that military intervention was necessary. Hamilton contributed to the effort on August 1, when he took a deposition from Frances Mentges, a colonel in the Pennsylvania militia. Mentges confirmed the earlier accounts of the attack on Neville's home and warned that a convention of the four western counties, plus neighboring Virginia counties, had been called for August 14. The colonel's deposition ended with an assertion that "it is intirely [sic] impracticable to execute the laws . . . by the means of civil process and Judiciary proceeding."[67]

Events now moved rapidly. On August 2, 1794, the president called a meeting with Governor Mifflin. The federal government was represented by Secretary of State Edmund Randolph, Secretary of War Henry Knox, Secretary of the Treasury Alexander Hamilton, and Attorney General William Bradford; the Pennsylvania officials accompanying Mifflin were Secretary of the Commonwealth Alexander Dallas, Chief Justice Thomas McKean, and Attorney General Jared Ingersoll. Washington was unusually blunt: we all know the subject of this meeting, he said; we all know the circumstances that prompted it. Edmund Randolph read aloud the most damning evidence that the western insurgents had struck "at the root of all law and order." When he finished presenting the letters from General Neville, his son Presley Neville, Marshal David Lenox, and the commandant of Fort Fayette, as well as the deposition from Mentges and one from the post rider whose mail had been raided, Washington addressed Mifflin directly. He asked the governor to demonstrate his cooperation by taking some preliminary steps while they waited for James Wilson's letter of certification. Everyone present understood that Washington wanted the governor to call out the state militia.

Washington's request was greeted with silence from the Pennsylvania delegation. Randolph stepped in and read the act of Congress under which the president was proceeding. When Mifflin and his associates said nothing, Randolph attempted to buttress the president's request by citing a Pennsylvania act of 1783 that authorized mobilizing the militia for sudden emergencies. This prompted Alexander

Dallas to speak. He waved the argument away, declaring that this law had been repealed. Randolph then tried another approach. He asked Dallas for his legal opinion: Did the governor have the authority to call out the militia? Dallas refused to answer officially, saying only that, as a private citizen, he would support the governor's use of the militia if it were necessary. But Chief Justice McKean immediately declared that there was no necessity to act. Nothing, he insisted, had shaken his confidence that the judiciary was capable of handling the situation. The use of force, he added, would be as bad as anything the rioters had done; it would be equally unconstitutional and illegal. Hamilton was appalled by this comment. The government's authority, he said, must be maintained. Opposition to that authority and to the Constitution itself could be seen in the rebels' demands for navigation of the Mississippi; in threats to create a new, independent country in the West; and in violent resistance to the excise tax. An immediate resort to military force was indeed necessary. The moment had come when it must be determined whether the government could maintain itself. The rioters must be quelled; the officers of the union must be protected in the execution of their duties; obedience to the laws must be compelled. To this Alexander Dallas replied that Judge Addison had warned that even those westerners who were peaceable would join in opposition to any effort to force them into submission. Hamilton retorted that nothing Addison said could be trusted, for the judge was a promoter of the opposition in western Pennsylvania. What was said after this exchange is lost, for the record of this meeting abruptly ended.[68]

Mifflin's intransigence posed a serious problem for the president. The immediate use of the Pennsylvania militia was impossible absent the governor's support. Later that day, Hamilton offered advice to Washington. Regardless of what Mifflin might say, regardless of what he might do or not do, it was obvious that military force was necessary. If Pennsylvania would not provide that force, other states surely would. "The very existence of Government demands this course," Hamilton wrote; the military suppression of the rebels was "a duty of the highest nature."[69]

To Hamilton, the central questions were no longer legal or political; they were tactical. How many troops were needed to put down the rebellion, and from which states should these militia units

be drawn? Hamilton, who wanted a powerful show of force, recommended an army of 12,000 men, 9,000 of them on foot, 3,000
mounted on horseback. Because the governor of Pennsylvania had
insisted his own state militia was inadequate to the task, Hamilton
proposed that Pennsylvania be held responsible for only 6,000 men,
with the remaining 6,000 drawn from the neighboring states of New
Jersey, Maryland, and Virginia.[70]

The following day, Washington received the official certification
from Justice Wilson he had desired. Wilson's opinion was brief and
to the point: Hamilton was right; Addison was wrong. Military force
was necessary. The only obstacle now was whether the governor of
Pennsylvania would agree to cooperate. On August 5, Washington
got his answer: no. Governor Mifflin informed the president that
the Pennsylvania militia would not be called out, as he remained
convinced that the judicial process was working. It was doubtful, the
governor added, that the men called out to the militia in one county
of Pennsylvania would agree to suppress men of another. He was certain he was not authorized to make them do so.[71]

And anyway, Mifflin assured the president, he had already taken
appropriate action. Even before their August 2 meeting, he had instructed Attorney General Dallas to send a letter to every judge, justice, sheriff, and brigade inspector in the western counties, requiring
them to "exert all your influence and authority to suppress, within
your jurisdiction, so pernicious and unwarrantable a spirit" as the
men who attacked Neville had shown. In the meantime, Mifflin suggested that the president appoint a commission of three respectable
men to negotiate with the rioters, an idea first suggested by General John Wilkins to Pennsylvania marshal Clement Biddle. Wilkins,
who had warned that "some of the most respectable people in the
country" were engaged in the rebellion, thought that a commission
would lead to "the happiest consequences." Mifflin believed these
commissioners could restore peace by promising the insurgents that
the state of Pennsylvania would forgive all past transgressions if the
rioters promised to obey the law in the future.[72]

Mifflin's defiance of the president and his rejection of Wilson's
ruling were insulting but unsurprising. The governor's loyalties lay
elsewhere, with the anti-administration Republican Party of Jefferson and Madison. But his warning that the Pennsylvania militiamen

would balk at suppressing their fellow citizens could not be ignored. Washington realized he would have to find ways to rally public opinion, especially in Pennsylvania, to avoid the dire outcome Mifflin predicted. Adding to the problem, there were some in Washington's own cabinet who were inclined to agree with the governor's view that a military intervention was unwise.

No cabinet member denied that the insurgents posed a challenge to the authority of the new, untested federal government. No one doubted that the stakes were high. If the government's laws were not respected, if the officials charged with administering them were not safe, what would the future hold? But in the face of Hamilton's call for immediate military action, Edmund Randolph urged patience and negotiation. On August 5, the president received letters from both men, each forcefully arguing his case. The letters demonstrate Hamilton's eagerness to exert the power of the Executive Office and Randolph's wariness at how such a demonstration of power would be interpreted by the opposition party. Hamilton's first thought was how to defend the authority of the federal government; Randolph's was whether the resort to military force would mean the end of the Federalist Party as well as the Whiskey Rebellion.

Hamilton's letter repeated the arguments he had made in defense of military action. To drive home his point, he offered a long and thorough chronology of the events leading up to the current moment of crisis. It was a catalogue of acts of intimidation and bloodshed, treasonous plots, and public disrespect for federal law and authority. The president had no choice, he concluded: he must send in an army to end the rebellion. Randolph devoted his letter to a litany of problems a military solution would generate. Chief among them was the political advantage it might offer the Republican Party. "It is a fact," he wrote, "that the parties in the U.S. are highly inflamed against each other." There were some within Washington's circle—and here Randolph clearly meant Hamilton and Knox—who "court the shining reputation, which is acquired by being always ready for strong measures," but he believed that Jefferson and his supporters understood the working of the popular mind far better than these Federalists. The Republicans would be quick to capitalize on voters' outrage and alienation if citizens did not believe conciliation had been genuinely sought. "Some gentlemen"—and here again, he meant Hamilton and

Knox—"believed that reconciliation should be offered with one hand and terror held out with the other." But overtures of peace by a commission while an army was forming would be mistrusted not only by the insurgents but also by the rest of the world. There would be suspicions that the commissioners were sent only to gloss over inevitable violence, or as a ruse to measure the strength of the insurgents, or as a tactic to discover the most culpable and mark them for punishment. Others might suspect that the commission was designed solely to stall until General Wayne's western army could turn its attention to the slaughter of American citizens rather than "savages." The president's wisest course, Randolph insisted, remained diplomacy and negotiation. Should the peace commission fail, as Randolph feared it must, Washington lost nothing by waiting for its report. The option to send in troops would remain. His message, so different from Hamilton's, was equally clear: delay would cost nothing and patience might gain much.[73]

In the face of this disagreement between his current secretary of state and his treasury secretary, the president chose a compromise between the urgency of one advisor and the caution of another. He would send a peace commission, but he would not delay the assembling of a military force. Washington's decision reflected his political intelligence, for he understood that broad public support would depend on the appearance that all peaceful efforts to end the crisis had been made.

The president quickly assembled the peace commission. As his emissaries to the insurgents, he wisely chose three Pennsylvanians: Attorney General William Bradford, Senator James Ross, and Pennsylvania Supreme Court justice Jasper Yeates. He directed Randolph to immediately send instructions to these commissioners. They were given broad latitude to negotiate with "any bodies of men or individuals" they thought represented the rebels, and they were free to assess how best to proceed once contact was made. But they were to present the situation in these unambiguous terms: the president was extremely upset; the government considered the obstruction of its laws to be dangerous; the president has been given the power to call out the militia, but he preferred a negotiated peace. Finally, the commissioners were to hold out no false promises of repeal of the tax, for the Constitution did not give the president the authority to nullify a law passed by Congress. He did, however, have the power to grant amnesty if the obstruction of the law ceased and the men subject to prosecution were not sheltered. And if the duties were paid that year, all past failures to do so would be ignored. These instructions reflected the firm but conciliatory approach Randolph had so fervently desired, but the final instruction left no doubt that Hamilton had won a victory, too. The commissioners were told to issue this warning: the militias would be ready to act if negotiations failed.[74]

Probably to remind the president of the sovereignty of Pennsylvania, Governor Mifflin decided to send his own commissioners to treat with the insurgents. On August 6, he appointed the state's chief justice Thomas McKean and General William Irvine to negotiate on behalf of the state. Like Washington, Mifflin left much to the discretion of his commissioners, but he did urge them to impress upon the insurgents the "folly of a riotous opposition to . . . laws, which were made by the spontaneous authority of the people." They were to exhort the "deluded Rioters" to return to their duties as law-abiding citizens.[75]

On the same day that Mifflin gave his instructions to the Pennsylvania commissioners, David Bradford was urging the residents of Monongahela, Virginia, to join his whiskey rebels at their next general meeting at Parkinson's Ferry. "The crisis is now come," Bradford told them, and the choice before them was "submission or opposition." Pennsylvania's insurgents had made their choice: "We are determined in the opposition."[76]

10
"Such disorder can only be cured by copious bleedings."
—Samuel Hodgdon, August 1794

ON AUGUST 7, Washington issued another presidential proclamation, this one drafted by both Hamilton and Knox. Although addressed to the insurgents, it was designed to persuade the American public more broadly that the challenge to the federal government in western Pennsylvania was a genuine crisis. The proclamation began with the multiple charges the government leveled against the whiskey rebels, including subverting the just authority of government and the

rights of individuals, holding meetings that encouraged further opposition to the law, misrepresenting the laws to render them odious,
and committing numerous acts of intimidation and violence against
revenue officials. It followed with evidence that the government had
responded to the rebels' complaints not only by lowering the duties
but also by "explanations, by forbearance and even by particular accommodations." Yet acts of treason continued, and the war against
the government of the United States had intensified. If Pennsylvania
refused to call out its militia, the president could do so himself, having been granted that power by Congress. He could also call other
state militias into the field. This the president said he had done, with
"deepest regret" but "the most Solemn conviction, that the essential
interests of the Union demand it, that the very existence of Government and the fundamental principles of social order are materially
involved in the issue." The proclamation ended with the president's
command that the insurgents disperse by September 1 and return
peaceably to their homes.[77]

Washington had committed to negotiating but begun preparing
to use force. Thus, as the federal peace commissioners headed west
to negotiate with the leaders of the insurgency, Secretary of War
Henry Knox sent orders to the governors of Pennsylvania, New Jersey, Maryland, and Virginia to put their militias on standby. Knox
then requested and received permission to travel to Maine to look
after his land holdings there. Alexander Hamilton took over the co-
ordination of military operations.[78]

Washington had not forgotten Governor Mifflin's refusal to cooperate. He waited until the proclamation had been issued, the state
governors had been called upon to organize their militias, and the
instructions had been sent to the commissioners. Then he instructed
Edmund Randolph to reply to Thomas Mifflin's defiant August 5
letter. The result was a stinging rebuttal of the governor's justifi-
cations for refusing to muster the Pennsylvania militia unless the
president directly ordered it. Mifflin had pursued an independent
course, which might have been acceptable, Randolph wrote, "if there
were no federal government, federal laws, federal judiciary, or federal officers"—a notion Federalists feared might still be desirable
to many Americans. But the federal government did exist, and although Mifflin was free to disagree with the president's handling of

the whiskey rebels, he was not free to withhold cooperation. "Not to do what must be done to execute the laws," Randolph declared, now sounding much like Hamilton, would endanger "the Constitution, the Government, the principles of social order, and the bulwarks of private right and security." If, as Mifflin maintained, he could not guarantee sufficient numbers from his state's militias, the president was preparing to assemble men from neighboring states to join whatever men the governor could provide to create an army of 12,000–13,000. At the same time, Randolph informed Mifflin, the president had sent a commission to the western counties to make a last effort to appeal to the reason, virtue, and patriotism of their citizens.[79]

Mifflin soon replied, beginning his letter with a fervent if defensive denial that he intended any disrespect or disobedience. "I thought," he declared in a long letter addressed directly to Washington, "I had manifested the strongest sense of my federal obligations . . . and . . . expressly recognized the subjection of [Pennsylvania's] individual authority to the national jurisdiction." But what began as an apology for any misunderstanding segued quickly into another spirited defense of his actions. He could not be expected to adopt the preliminary measure the president had desired under a Pennsylvania act that had been repealed. He had no irrefutable evidence when he and the president met that the Pennsylvania courts were unable to enforce the laws; indeed, the only evidence to the contrary were "the hearsay of Colonel Mentges and the vague narrative of the post rider." Before closing, Mifflin shifted from a defensive to a decidedly aggressive stance, expressing his concern that the president might be planning to abuse his authority. He hoped, he wrote, that the military force the federal government was assembling would be used solely to quell the rioters, not to enforce the excise tax as well.[80]

Mifflin's stubborn insistence that force was unnecessary did not matter. For on August 7, the same day that Washington issued his proclamation, the president instructed Henry Knox to order Mifflin to "forthwith . . . issue your orders for organizing and holding in readiness to march at a moment's warning, a Corps of the Militia of Pennsylvania." Mifflin, now convinced he had no choice but to comply, moved to ensure that the Pennsylvania assembly would share the responsibility for calling out state militia to march against its fellow citizens. It is likely that the expected arrival of thousands of troops from states loyal to the Union, far more than any respect for the president's authority, had prompted Mifflin's surrender.[81]

On August 8, an unexpected emissary arrived in Philadelphia from the West. Hugh Henry Brackenridge had come to bear witness to the bleak prospects facing both the government and the rebels. He spoke with the authority of one who had been part of the resistance movement from its inception. It was true, he confessed to Hamilton's undersecretary, Tench Coxe, that he had continued to attend the meetings and conventions held by the insurgents even after the violence against Neville, but only to urge moderation rather than armed resistance. Although he and other moderates had managed to save Pittsburgh from an attack by the burgeoning rebel army, Brackenridge warned that the insurgents were now far more dangerous because they were entirely irrational. He hastened to add that the targets of their abuse were equally irrational. Presley Neville, for example, suffered under the delusion that Brackenridge was a rebel warlord himself.

By August, Brackenridge said, he had become frantic, equally fearful of being punished by the whiskey rebels as a traitor to the cause and arrested by the authorities as a traitor to his country. He was under no illusions about how large and powerful the resistance movement had grown. The rebels, he told Coxe, had won over the majority of the people of the four western counties and of three Virginia counties as well. This whole tramontane region was on the brink of seceding from the Union and creating an independent country of its own. The root cause of the discontent was not the excise tax alone but the entire Hamiltonian system, from assumption, to the creation of a bank, to the failure to distinguish the original holders of the debt from speculators. "There is a growing, lurking discontent at this system," he declared, and it was "ready to burst out and discover itself everywhere." If the government attempted to suppress these people, "the question will not be whether you will march to Pittsburgh, but whether they will march to Philadelphia, accumulating in their course and swelling over the banks of the Susquehanna like a torrent, irresistible and devouring in its progress."[82]

Whether Brackenridge's dire—and highly dramatic—prediction of civil war and secession would prove true depended, in part, on the success or failure of Washington's peace commission. The prognosis was not good. On August 14, a rebel congress representing five western Pennsylvania counties and Ohio County, Virginia, met at Parkinson's Ferry. More than two hundred delegates, both radical and moderate, attended. A body of 250 armed men also came as observers. The meeting was thus so large that it had to be held outdoors. The mood was decidedly defiant, as the liberty poles erected in the area demonstrated. The rebels had created their own flag, its six stripes of alternating red and white representing the unity of the counties at the congress. To the surprise of everyone present, word arrived on August 15 that members of the president's federal peace commission were nearby.[83]

The commissioners were eager to meet with the rebels but not optimistic about the outcome of deliberations. Attorney General William Bradford had sided with Randolph in urging a delay in the use of military force but like Randolph, he had seen the delay as a political move unlikely to result in any actual progress. When the peace negotiations inevitably failed and the insurgents' unreasonableness was revealed, he was certain the public would rally in support of the president and his turn to military action.

Bradford's reports to Randolph, even before negotiations began, had been consistently negative. His pessimism was reinforced by conversations along the route to the rebel congress with men like General Neville and Marshal Lenox that convinced Bradford the violence and intimidation of revenue officers was spreading. In a letter of August 15, he told the secretary of state that a force of some two to three hundred insurgents had recently descended upon the home of the collector for Bedford County. Neighbors prevented the destruction of the man's property, but he was captured and forced not only to resign his office but also to tear his commission to pieces and trample on it. As Bradford and his fellow commissioner Yeates traveled west, they heard other disturbing stories and rumors, including that Governor Mifflin's proclamation urging obedience to the law had been ridiculed and that the western counties had already declared independence.[84]

Writing to Henry Knox on August 17, Isaac Craig seconded Bradford's pessimism. Given all they had seen and heard already, Craig told Knox the commissioners could not help but be "Pritty [sic] well Convinced that the powers they are vested with will have but a small effect in bringing the Misguided multitude to a sence [sic] of their duty as Citizens of the United States." Craig's sentiments were echoed in the commissioners' report that same day. Despite a firm belief that their peace mission was quixotic, Bradford and his fellow commissioners prepared a letter to be presented to the insurgents. Soon afterward, they met in Pittsburgh with a small special committee appointed as negotiators by the rebel congress. This committee included Brackenridge, who had returned home after his Cassandra-like testimony, and was now back in the good graces of the rebels. The remaining committee members were the moderate Albert Gallatin and two of the most radical leaders of the resistance, David Bradford and James Marshall.

At the meeting, the commissioners described their mission as "frankly and sincerely" as possible to the special committee. The president, they said, was eager for a peaceful resolution to the crisis but was ready to take military action if necessary. The rebels must provide full assurances that the people will obey the law in order to avoid that action. And they must act quickly. Their authority to negotiate would end on September 1; after that, "no indulgence will be given to any future offence against the United States."[85]

The commission's quid pro quos had been stated. On August 22, the special committee asked whether the pardons proposed depended on individuals keeping the peace or on the whole region doing so. Does an individual who is granted amnesty lose it if the community breaks the peace? The committee members then frankly admitted that, though they thought acceding to the law was the best idea, they could not promise that the people would follow that decision. A flurry of notes back and forth followed, with clarifications of terms by the commissioners and additional requests by the rebels' committee. The commissioners received an encouraging letter from Cook, saying the committee approved of the terms offered and promised to report those terms faithfully to the people. Some tension arose when the rebels asked that members from Virginia's Ohio County also be covered by the promise of pardons, but the commissioners explained that their instructions covered only the four Pennsylvania counties. The Virginians made an effort to save face, declaring that they were cutting off all negotiations "untell we Consult our Constaituents & the Cometee of Safety [sic]."[86]

There was little more the commissioners could do but wait until their next meeting with the insurgents on September 2. In Philadelphia, meanwhile, the president and his cabinet were finalizing preparations for military action. On August 24, Washington had called Randolph and Hamilton to his Philadelphia home. The meeting signaled both the president's certainty that deploying troops was inevitable and his conviction that the American people would soon have firm evidence that the insurgents did not want peace. Washington wanted a frank intelligence report from his two cabinet members. How many additional troops might be needed? When should the public in the states supplying troops be informed of the mobilization? What were the details of troop placement and rendezvous points? The questions reflected Washington's long career as a military man before he took the reins of government.

When Hamilton reported that 1,500 additional men were needed, it was decided to draw them not from Pennsylvania but from three neighboring states. Other decisions were made, too: the New Jersey militia would gather at Carlisle; the Pennsylvania militias at Carlisle and Chambersburgh; Maryland at Williamsport; and Virginia at Winchester. They would all unite at Bedford and Cumberland by October 1. Yet Washington's natural caution led him to a final choice. Although the governors of Maryland and New Jersey had announced their orders for mobilization in mid-August, the president asked the governor of his home state of Virginia to wait until September 2 to make his mobilization order public. There was no need to give the anti-administration party of Jefferson, so strong in that state, too much time to protest.[87]

On August 28, the promised meeting of the insurgents' executive body, the Committee of Sixty, took place. The federal commissioners allowed themselves the small hope that this committee would agree to set in motion the general population's oath of obedience to the law. This hope was dashed, however, when a sizeable number of radicals on the executive committee demurred, accusing their own negotiators of accepting bribes from the government and refusing to ask the people of their communities to comply with the law. Although the committee ultimately voted 34 to 23 to agree to the commissioners' demands, the size of the opposition created a problem for the federal government. Most westerners would interpret the close vote as a rejection of the government's terms while the general American public was likely to see it as a decision to submit. This would allow the resistance to continue while the public would judge a military expedition unnecessary.

On August 29, a new committee of rebel negotiators, calling itself the Committee of Conference, submitted a request to delay compliance with the law. It wanted until October 11 so that it could "take the sense of the people." The commissioners' reply came swiftly: no. They saw no reason why, suddenly, the rebel leaders had to go back to the people for instructions. "You represented the people; you were their voice; now you want to ask them to say yea or nay?" To temporize in this fashion, the commissioners argued, was dishonorable. The September 1 deadline would stand. The leadership had until the end of the day to declare its readiness to support a submission to the laws of the United States.[88]

By this time, most state officials in the western counties were urging compliance with the commissioners' terms. Even Judge Alexander Addison, who had, from the beginning, sympathized with his fellow westerners' complaints and had downplayed the violence they had committed, now exhorted the rebels to relent. In his charge to the grand jury of Allegheny County on September 1, Addison spoke emotionally about the choice before the rebels. "If we accept the terms we shall have peace. If we reject them we shall have war." The stakes, he declared, were too high for the president to back down now. His choice was stark: "The whole force of the United States must be exerted to support its authority now, or the government of the United States must cease to exist." Alexander Hamilton could not have said it better.[89]

Like Addison, the members of the rebel committee knew this was the only option. On September 2, they declared their conviction that it was in the interest and duty of the people to submit. They were now ready to work with the commissioners to fix the time, place, and manner of securing the loyalty of the people. An agreement soon followed, its terms unequivocal and surely humiliating: All citizens eighteen years and older must assemble in their township on Thursday, September 11, between noon and 7 p.m. Under the direction of two or more members of the Parkinson Ferry leadership, or a justice of the peace, they were to publicly answer these questions: "Do you now engage to submit to the laws of the United States, and that you will not hereafter, directly or indirectly oppose the execution of the revenue acts? Will you support the civil authority in protecting all revenue officers and other citizens? Answer yea or nay." The yeas and nays were to be immediately counted, and all who answered yea were to sign a written declaration to henceforth "submit to the laws of the United States." These declarations were to be signed in the presence of the Parkinson Ferry committee members or the justice of the peace. On September 13, these officials would report the results and give their opinion whether the community's submission was general enough to allow an office of inspection to be immediately established in the county. The final reports were to be transmitted to the commissioners, waiting at Uniontown, on or before September 16.[90]

If all these conditions were met, the commissioners made three new promises in return. There would be no prosecutions for treason or any other indictable offense committed against the United States if those who committed these offenses had given the assurances required. On July 10, 1795, a general pardon would be granted and oblivion given for all offenses except those committed by men who had answered nay to the required pledge of compliance. Positive arrangements would be made for adjusting existing tax and registration delinquencies and for resolving existing prosecutions for penalties. The two Pennsylvania state commissioners followed the lead of the federal commissioners, declaring that Pennsylvania, too, would grant a general pardon if assurances to obey state laws were made and kept. No one could deny that the terms being offered to the rebels were generous. Whether they would be accepted was the question.

11
"An amicable accommodation [is] so very doubtful."
—Henry Knox, September 1794

IT DID NOT take long for the hope that the rebellion was over to fade. By September 5, notes of despair began to creep into the correspondence of the officials on the scene in western Pennsylvania. General Wilkins now confided to Clement Biddle his certainty that soon "we shall be involved in all the horrors of a civil war." Only a few days later, Henry Knox told Mifflin that all the intelligence he had received left "an amicable accommodation so very doubtful."[91]

Perhaps just as disturbing, resistance to the revenue laws continued to crop up elsewhere. On September 6, Alexander Hamilton told the governor of Maryland that the president had learned of riots taking place in upper parts of Baltimore County. Washington believed it was necessary for Governor Thomas Sim Lee to act immediately to "check the progress of an evil, which radically threatens the order, peace and tranquility of the Country." Hamilton added his own advice that "an early display of energy" was essential. It was clear that the secretary of the treasury believed these riots were an outgrowth of the rebellion in Pennsylvania. He was not alone in this conviction. In a letter of September 1 to General John Davidson, Lieutenant John Lynn described the influence of the Pennsylvania insurgents in Maryland. The resistance in his town of Fort Cumberland was not strong enough to accomplish "their infernal designs," but this did not prevent them from insulting law-abiding citizens or boasting that they would erect a liberty pole. The local volunteer company, Lynn assured Davidson, stood ready to put a stop to it. Later that month, Colonel Thomas Sprigg reported to Governor Lee that troublemakers in Hagerstown threatened to raise a liberty pole and to steal arms from the local magazine. When Hagerstown militiamen disobeyed the orders of their officers and put up a liberty pole, officials had it removed. The militiamen were unfazed; they put up another pole and threatened reprisals against anyone who disturbed it. Reports like these gave credence to Hamilton's fears: flagrant disregard for the federal government and its laws was spreading like a cancer over the land.[92]

On September 13, the commissioners received the results of the polling in the western counties. The news was not good. From Washington County, the rebel leader David Bradford and twenty-seven other county delegates to the Parkinson's Ferry congress reported that "we . . . do find ourselves under great embarrassment to express our sentiments and opinions that we cannot guarantee submission of the people." They hastened to guarantee, however, that "no opposition shall arise from us, the undersigned." As leaders of the rebellion, they knew they needed amnesty. They added their strong conviction that a large majority of the inhabitants of the county townships would also comply—but admitted they could not promise it.[93]

The report from Westmoreland was even more distressing. Some residents had given "only general assurances of their submission and disposition for peace" but had not individually signed a pledge to do so. And, as "ill-disposed lawless persons could suddenly assemble and offer violence," the men submitting this report did not think the government should attempt to establish an office of inspection in Westmoreland in the near future.[94]

The Fayette County results came in on September 16. According to Albert Gallatin and six others, the people in county election districts 1 through 3 met as instructed, but no justice of the peace or member of the Committee of Sixty presided in districts 4 or 5. They were able, therefore, to certify only that 560 of 721 men did declare their determination to submit. The 721 who were polled, however, represented less than a third of the male citizens in the first three districts. Despite this poor showing, Gallatin and his colleagues assured the commissioners that the great majority was disposed to behave peaceably.[95]

Although (or perhaps because) they were excluded from the commissioners' terms, Ohio County, Virginia, rebels issued an adamant rejection of compliance. In a set of ten resolves, a delegation of two men from each militia company in the county made clear their determination to continue to oppose the whiskey tax "at the risk of our lives and property."[96]

Though not happy with the results, Hamilton was not surprised by them. Writing to Rufus King on September 22, he reported that "the most influential men & a respectable body of others" had cast their votes in favor of compliance, but a great number of men of violent disposition remained defiant. This meant there would be "no assurance of submission to the laws without the application of Force." Hamilton's enemies would later suggest that he was pleased with the outcome. Given the circumstances, all the assigned militia were heading to western Pennsylvania as rapidly as the terrain and provisioning allowed. In an earlier note to King, Hamilton had expressed his relief that all of Virginia except the mountain counties were dedicated patriots. New Jersey too was full of positive support for the military action, and in much of Maryland, including Baltimore, "a pretty good temper prevails." The most positive sign, however, was that an "excellent & productive zeal" was evident in Philadelphia among both Federalists and their political opponents.[97]

Hamilton took considerable satisfaction in the fact that Governor Mifflin was finally exerting himself in earnest. Once he received a direct order from the federal government to call out his militia, further resistance was risky. With the imminent arrival of thousands of troops from other states, he had decided a show of loyalty was his best option. Thus, since the beginning of September, Mifflin had taken a number of steps to prove his unconditional support for military suppression of the rebellion. He had addressed the state's assembly and senate, referring as so many Federalists and Republicans did to "the deluded inhabitants" of western Pennsylvania and the need to prevent the disgrace that came with noncompliance. Mifflin's only remaining problem was the refusal of many militia officers to report for duty. He had warned the president that Pennsylvanians would be reluctant to take up arms against their fellow citizens; now his prediction was proving true. Hoping to raise the spirit of patriotism among Philadelphia's men, the governor had addressed the city's reluctant militia in stirring terms, calling on them to unite against the rebellion, "for the honor of the militia, for the sake of our laws, and for the preservation of the Republican principles." As a further spur to patriotic behavior, he had made the surprising decision to ride at the head of the Pennsylvania militia forces.[98]

Hamilton's impatience with any delay in mounting the military attack was palpable. He was aware that the citizens of Pittsburgh had barely fended off an invasion by the rebel army that summer, and he had received reports in August that some men, including Presley Neville, General John Gibson, and Major Abraham Kirkpatrick, had been driven from the city, exiled by order of David Bradford and his fellow rebel leaders. The federal garrison at Pittsburgh's Fort Fayette had been threatened, and its commanding officer, Major Thomas Butler, warned that he and his men must leave or the fort would be burned down. Believing that it was "extremely important to afford speedy protection to the well disposed," Hamilton urged Governor Lee of Maryland to press his militia forces forward as rapidly as possible. Hamilton also confided to Lee his belief that the situation in Pennsylvania was proof of the dangers of leniency. The failure to quickly punish insurgents was "perhaps the principal cause of the misfortune which now afflicts itself and through it the United States."[99]

Washington, too, felt a sense of responsibility toward the law-abiding citizens of the western counties, but unlike Hamilton he also wanted to make sure that the vote by the Committee of Sixty did not give the public the false impression that the rebels had surrendered. Thus on September 25 he issued a new and deftly argued proclamation. He sketched the government's view of the situation in the West: a small but violent minority had rejected all overtures of forgiveness, and thus there would be no voluntary end to the attacks on revenue officials. Under these circumstances, the government could not—must not—allow "a small portion of the United States [to] dictate to the whole union" or permit the outrages of citizens upon their own government to sully the reputation of the United States. To enforce respect for the law and to protect the men willing to obey it, the president had set in motion a military expedition. The proclamation ended with the stern warning that no one was to "abet aid or comfort the Insurgents." With this public statement on the Whiskey Rebellion and the government's response to it, the Washington administration had crossed its own Rubicon; there would be no turning back.[100]

12
"To arms once more."
Poem, 1794

NO ONE WAS more pleased than Hamilton to see mobilization begin in earnest. Although he continued to send letters of instruction to the superintendent of military stores for the army and to officers leading the militia units, he was not content to direct the military expedition from the comforts of Philadelphia. On September 19, he had sent a brief note to the president on a subject that rarely occupied his thoughts: public opinion. "In a government like ours," he wrote, "it cannot but have a good effect for the person who is understood to be the advisor or proposer of a measure, which involves danger to his fellow citizens, to partake in that danger." In other words, Hamilton wanted to ride with Washington against the whiskey rebels. Whether Hamilton had other, less political motives is unknown. Perhaps years of office work had made him long for the excitement of battle and the camaraderie of military life. Perhaps he felt he had been cheated of his share of military glory because Washington had called him from the battlefront to serve as one of his aides-de-camp in 1777. Whatever had inspired Hamilton's request, Washington could not deny his former military assistant the chance to don a uniform once again. By early October, the president and his secretary of the treasury were at the army camp at Carlisle, Pennsylvania.[101]

There would be little opportunity for Hamilton to prove himself this time on the battlefield, however. His own instructions to Henry "Light Horse Harry" Lee, the Virginia governor chosen to head the expedition, made it clear that all-out war with the whiskey rebels was not the army's mission. The president's goals were straightforward: the restoration of public safety and order, and compliance with the revenue act. Lee was authorized to use his troops to force any hostile armed resisters to surrender, but the only men to be taken prisoner were the leaders of the rebellion. Their followers should be disarmed and sent home, unless they had been guilty of particularly violent acts. Once law and order was reestablished, civilian rules of due process would apply. The judge and attorney who accompanied the army would issue the legal papers required in the cases of arrests, forfeitures of delinquent distillers, and seizures of stills and whiskey. And before Lee withdrew his army, he was to issue a general pardon in the name of the president to all who had not been arrested.

It is telling that neither the president nor any member of his cabinet considered calling for mass arrests. This was due, in large part, to their assumption that a small group of demagogues, joined by a band of naturally violent men, was responsible for the "phrenzy" that grew into the Whiskey Rebellion. They shared with elite men of all political stripes the assumption that the general population was susceptible to manipulation by charismatic yet irresponsible individuals. And, like Mifflin and Addison, they believed the people could easily fall victim to their passions. The remedy, however, was not mass execution or imprisonment; as Hamilton was so fond of saying, the antidote to rebellion was to act quickly and firmly to punish the demagogues and restore the sanity of the gullible ordinary citizens who had followed them. This patronizing view of ordinary men made it easier for federal officials to pardon the rebellion followers, but it denied the rebels any claim that their response to the excise was rational or justified.[102]

Hamilton had ended his instructions to Lee with a warning: preserve discipline among your troops and respect the rights of persons and property. In a few cases, however, the discipline Hamilton called for failed. On October 10, he had to send a letter to Jared Ingersoll, the attorney general of Pennsylvania, about a homicide. The man accused of the murder was a member of the New Jersey contingent at Carlisle, Pennsylvania. Although the death may have been accidental, Hamilton ordered the matter brought to the courts. He then immediately sent off a second letter, this time to Governor Mifflin, expressing Washington's regrets regarding this event and a second homicide attributed to the New Jersey army as well. "It is a very precious & important idea," Hamilton declared, "that those who are called out in support & defence of the Laws, should not give occasion, or even pretext to impute to them infractions of the law." It was a lesson the revolutionary generation had grasped as witnesses to the abuses of the British army during the war for independence.[103]

On October 9, two men closely associated with the rebellion entered the camp at Carlisle. William Findley and David Redick ostensibly came as representatives of the rebel Committee of Safety, entrusted with a set of resolutions addressed to the president. But it became clear that they were there as much to distance themselves from the rebellion as to act as its messengers. Washington recorded his meeting with these two men in his diary. Findley, Washington wrote, gave assurances that the people in the towns and countryside that he knew best "had seen their folly" and were ready to submit to the law. Civil authority, he said, was beginning to reestablish itself. Yet his characterization of the people of the region who had looked to him for leadership was far from flattering: "Ignorance, & general want of information among the people far exceeded any thing he had any conception of." It was not only the excise law that they opposed, but "all law, & Government."[104]

Redick's report was no less damning of the rebellion. He regaled the president with a tale of terrified government supporters who had slept with their weapons by their bedside when the "frenzy was at its height." After the riots began, men so distrusted one another that "even friends were affraid [sic] to communicate their sentiments to each other." The people, he said, had mistakenly believed that opposition to the excise law was universal across the country and that no troops would be willing to march against them. Until recently they had dismissed all accounts that an army was coming as "fabricated tales of governmental men." Now, however, they were alarmed, and many were planning to sell their land and leave the country, probably for British-held Detroit. The remaining rebels, Redick assured Washington, would not oppose the army, and, even if they wished to, "there was not three rounds of ammunition for them in all the Western Country."[105]

ON THE DAY after this meeting with Findley and Redick, Washington set the troops in motion. William Macpherson's Pennsylvania battalion, known as "Macpherson's Blues," along with a Jersey regiment and a second Philadelphia unit began their march to the rebellious counties. The following day, cavalrymen followed. Washington would soon learn whether Redick's prediction that they would meet with no resistance was correct. In the meantime, he headed back to Philadelphia. With the militia army in the able hands of Governors Henry Lee, Thomas Mifflin, and Richard Howell of New Jersey as well as Major General Daniel Morgan of Virginia, the president felt confident that he could return to his duties as president. Hamilton, however, would remain in the field, traveling with one wing of the army and continuing his supervision and direction of the supply chain for the troops.

Light Horse Harry Lee believed Redick's prediction was correct. "The insurgents," he wrote in his notes, "tremble to each extreme. They now see the rod of their offended country shaken over them with a powerful hand and shrink from it, with a degree of pusillanimity, that is equaled only by their former audacity." Yet Lee was cautious about disbanding the military expedition too precipitously. He responded with skepticism to the Parkinson's Ferry resolutions that had pledged the leaders' support for civil authority and to their assurances that those who failed to take the oath would comply. Nor was he convinced that law and order would prevail once the army departed. He thought it prudent, therefore, to "hold the army in this country until daily practice shall convince all that the sovereignty of the constitution and laws is unalterably established."[106]

The reality of an army eager to suppress the insurrection had, in fact, sent several western townships, and a number of prominent leaders of the rebellion, scurrying to express their support for the laws of the federal government. Towns like Tioga and Greensburgh sent resolutions supporting the government, and men who had served on rebel committees hurried to portray themselves and their friends as moderates who had labored to prevent rather than foment acts of violence. In a deposition before Judge Richard Peters of the US district court, Alexander Addison admitted to being present at the Redstone meeting when the rebel negotiators reported on their conference with the commissioners. According to Addison, Albert Gallatin and Hugh Henry Brackenridge, far from being rabble-rousers, had urged compliance with the law in the face of rebel leader David Bradford's call for continued resistance. Brackenridge, eager once again to show his loyalty to the government, forwarded a set of resolutions drawn up by several Washington County townships, pledging support to civil authorities. Even Bradford insisted in a letter to Mifflin that his conduct was "greatly misrepresented or entirely misunderstood." He confessed that he had always disliked the excise law, but he had never intended to go further than nonviolent opposition. None of the leadership, it seemed, had advocated armed rebellion; they had simply been unable to prevent it.[107]

13
"We are very strong & the Insurgents are all submissive."
—Alexander Hamilton to Elizabeth
Hamilton, October 1794

AS NOVEMBER 1794 began, General Daniel Morgan was eager to start arresting the rebellion's ringleaders, but his orders were to wait until civil authorities completed preliminary investigations of those alleged to be guilty. As Lee had reminded Governor Mifflin, there could be no seizures, even of "the deluded," until the civil authorities had completed their duties. But as the investigations dragged on, Hamilton urged the president to allow the army to bypass these bureaucratic procedures. The troops were growing impatient, he told Washington, and the approach of winter threatened to make military action difficult if not impossible. Even the local district attorney, William Rawle, agreed that the military should act as quickly as possible.

Hamilton was especially eager to begin the arrests, for he feared that the most notorious ringleaders would seize the opportunity to flee to safety farther west. He was also concerned that some of the guilty might escape full prosecution by claiming they had aided the commissioners. He was particularly concerned that the man he considered "the worst of all scoundrels," Hugh Henry Brackenridge, would escape justice. Brackenridge, for his part, feared that the military might act in a more summary—and lethal—way in dealing with him. In an effort to protect himself, the novelist published an open letter addressed to the military. In it he reminded the troops that they, as much as the rebels, must obey the law. Although they might consider him a criminal for his role in the rebellion, they must acknowledge that a man was presumed innocent until proven otherwise. To strengthen his claim of innocence, he announced dramatically that he would not flee the country. "I stand firm," he declared, "and will surrender myself to the closest examination of the Judges."[108]

On November 9, General Lee gave the instructions to proceed in a summary manner "against those who have notoriously committed treasonable acts." Lee provided his lieutenants with two lists: the first, of those who were exempt from arrest and punishment; the second, of men understood to have committed acts of treason. Two days later, Hamilton informed the president that both arrests and the seizure of a number of stills were imminent. Hamilton wanted to make public examples of a few carefully chosen men whose punishment would demonstrate the high price of resistance of federal law. "I hope," he wrote Washington, "there will be found characters fit for examples & who can be made so."[109]

In the same letter, Hamilton took time to acknowledge the attacks aimed at him by Benjamin Bache, the editor of Philadelphia's most partisan Republican newspaper, the *Aurora or General Advertiser*. Bache, the grandson of Benjamin Franklin, regularly hurled accusations of corruption and abuse of power at the administration, sparing neither the president nor his secretary of the treasury. He had charged that Hamilton had no business being involved in a military expedition. "I observe what Mr. Bache is about. But I am more indifferent to it as the experience has proved to me . . . that my presence in this quarter was in several respects not useless." He added, in characteristic fashion, "And it is long since I have learnt to hold popular opinion of no value. I hope to derive from the esteem of the discerning and in internal consciousness of zealous endeavours for the public good the reward of those endeavours."[110]

Hamilton considered the arrest of rebel leaders to be one of his major "endeavours for the public good." On November 15, he reported with satisfaction that arrests had at last been made. Twenty men were being held in the town of Washington, and additional prisoners were soon to arrive. Several of these men appeared "fit subjects for examples," as the evidence collected on them was enough to promise a conviction. The likely candidates included the local Baptist minister John Corbly, the sheriff of Washington County, Colonel William Crawford, John Hamilton, and three additional Washington County residents, David Lock, Thomas Sedgwick, and John Munn. The selected group included one rebel leader from Ohio County, Virginia, a man named John Laughery. A warrant had also been issued for the arrest of Thomas Gaddis of Fayette County, but Hamilton feared Gaddis was one of the culprits who had escaped.

On November 17, Hamilton sent William Rawle a list of ten additional men to be denied amnesty. The names of three of the suspected ringleaders, Albert Gallatin, Hugh Henry Brackenridge, and William Findley, were not among them. Hamilton had personally interrogated Brackenridge over the course of two days but found no evidence that he had planned to overthrow the government. When Brackenridge later published a history of the Whiskey Rebellion, he recounted Hamilton saying, "My impressions were unfavorable to you, you may have observed it. I now think it my duty to inform you that not a single one remains. Had we listened to some people, I know not what we might have done. Your conduct has been horribly misrepresented. . . . You are in no personal danger, and will not be troubled even with a simple inquisition by the judge." Whether Hamilton was, in fact, so effusive in his apology is unknown.[111]

William Findley painted a very different picture of Hamilton's interrogation technique in his own history of the Whiskey Rebellion. He insisted that Hamilton had terrorized both Brackenridge and a man named Powers who Hamilton was hoping would incriminate Albert Gallatin. He described his own interrogation as "an inquisition held on my character" that was designed to prove he was "a bad man, as well as a criminal." The Irish-born Findley also claimed that Hamilton expressed surprise that the whiskey rebels had placed their confidence in foreigners like him and the Swiss immigrant Albert Gallatin. Findley said he found the comment astonishing because it was widely known that Hamilton was a native of the West Indies.[112]

Although Findley, Brackenridge, and Gallatin avoided charges, rebellion leaders David Bradford, Edward Cook, Thomas Spiers, and Benjamin Parkinson were not so lucky. Yet to Governor Lee's great consternation, Bradford, the most notorious ringleader, eluded capture. On November 15, one Captain Francis D'Hebecourt reported that he had spotted Bradford going downriver in a canoe and sent four men to arrest him. But when they caught up with him, they found thirteen others "ready to protect Bradford, and massacre any who would undertake to take him away." Outnumbered, the soldiers retreated, and Bradford was free to "safely preach his doctrine, and spread the flame of a new insurrection."[113]

By the end of November 1794, the militias had returned home. Daniel Morgan was left in charge of the small force that would remain through the winter months. Only the legal processes— recognizances, depositions, trials—along with a few more daring escapes occupied federal officials. Satisfied, Hamilton began his journey back to Philadelphia on November 19. On the 29th General Lee issued his proclamation of sweeping pardon to "all persons residing within the counties of Washington, Allegheny, Westmoreland, and Fayette, in the State of Pennsylvania, and in the county of Ohio, in the State of Virginia, guilty of treason or misprision of treason against the United States, or otherwise directly or indirectly engaged in the wicked and unhappy tumults and disturbances lately existing in these counties." Exempted from this general pardon were those charged and in custody or held by recognizance to appear in court, those who had avoided fair trial by abandoning their homes, and thirty-three men listed by name in the proclamation. Yet, by the summer of 1795, charges had been dropped against a number of the men Lee had exempted. The Whiskey Rebellion was over.[114]

14

"The spirit inimical to all order."
—George Washington, 1794

IN THE REBELLION'S aftermath, who to blame for its start remained a point of contentious dispute. In their histories of the rebellion, written largely to vindicate their own role in the uprising, both William Findley and Hugh Henry Brackenridge painted Alexander Hamilton as the story's villain. They pointed out that it was Hamilton who initiated the hated excise tax and Hamilton who urged the use of the military to suppress the protest in the four western counties. Both of these claims were, of course, true. But Findley's critique of Hamilton lacked substance. Findley argued that Hamilton had invented many of the violent episodes he reported and that he had "enumerate[d] the acts of opposition with the highest colouring they would possibly bear." He accused Hamilton of hoping for a rebellion so that the government would have an opportunity to prove its military strength. Findley repeated as true a rumor that Hamilton "expressed his sorrow that the town of Pittsburgh had not been burned by those who rendezvoused at Braddock's field," for this would have justified the government's immediate use of force. Although Brackenridge did not go so far as to accuse Hamilton of escalating the rebellion, he did accuse the treasury secretary of purposely failing to discriminate between peaceful remonstrances and allegedly "intemperate" resolutions. This, Brackenridge declared, proved that Hamilton would gladly take away the right of the people to petition or to legally resist oppression.[115]

To no one's surprise, the Republican editor Benjamin Bache joined the chorus of those accusing Hamilton of villainy. By his presence at the head of the army that invaded western Pennsylvania, Bache wrote, Hamilton was guilty of "meddling interference in a department totally irrelative to his official duties." Some, Bache noted, whispered that he was there without invitation, and many, he added, believed that Hamilton's conduct during the entire crisis was "a first

step towards a deep laid scheme—not for the promotion of his country's prosperity—but the advancement of his private interests and the
gratification of an ambition, laudable in itself, if pursued by proper
means."[116]

These accounts are clearly biased. Hamilton may have failed to
appreciate the difficulties faced by western farmers, and he may have
been impatient with their complaints. But his motive for passing the
excise tax had been to collect revenue, not to foment a rebellion. He
had been given the task of setting the finances of the nation aright,
and this required finding new revenue sources. To avoid a tax on
property that would arouse near-universal condemnation, he turned
to an excise tax. It is certainly true that he was invested in the success of his own economic system, but Bache was mistaken in his
claim that Hamilton intended it as a vehicle for his own personal
gain or as a monument to his personal ambitions. The ambition that
burned in Alexander Hamilton was grander than this; it was not personal glory but national glory that drove him.

Despite Brackenridge's claim, the militia had not marched
against men guilty only of "peaceful remonstrances" and "intemperate resolutions." The whiskey rebels were guilty of insurrection.
They had flouted the law; they had resorted to violence against the
agents of the federal government; they had threatened citizens who
opposed their cause. There is no doubt that Hamilton had preferred
to assert the government's readiness to enforce its laws at the first
sign of insurgency. He believed that the need to preserve order and
enforce law, essential for all governments, was especially critical for
the survival of a republic, especially one as young and untested as
the United States. Whether the suppression of the rebellion in its in-
fancy would have been wise cannot be known, because Washington
chose a more cautious and deliberate policy that allowed the government to claim all legal and diplomatic methods had been exhausted.
If Hamilton's approach appeared too abruptly punitive, Washington's
meant that the government faced a larger, better-organized rebellion.
It was Washington's good fortune that this march of one part of the
people against another had ended without bloodshed.

For Hamilton, there had been more at stake than the reputation
of the federal government or its sovereignty. The president may have
sent the militia army into western Pennsylvania to restore law and

order, but implicit in his success was a victory for the Hamiltonian system. If the president had not been willing to risk his government's reputation, that system might have unraveled. Certainly, successful resistance to the excise would have encouraged anti-administration forces to continue their efforts to dismantle all that Hamilton had created.

When President Washington pondered the cause of the rebellion, he did not look to the economic burden of the whiskey tax on distillers or what they saw as the inconvenience of its regulations or the character of the men appointed for its collection. He found the cause in the demagoguery of a few men who had tapped into the "spirit inimical to all order" among the rebels. In his sixth annual message to Congress, he located the source of the rebellion in men "who labored for an ascendancy over the will of others, by the guidance of their passions." Among the chief guilty parties, Washington declared, were certain "self created societies," known as Democratic Societies, that regularly condemned the government. The violence that resulted, he declared, "was not pointed merely to a particular law"; it arose from the strains of anarchy within these frontier communities. Fearing that those strains had not died with the defeat of the whiskey rebels, he recommended that Congress enact legislation that would allow the federal government to call out a "well regulated militia" to execute the laws of the Union, suppress insurrections, and repel invasions.[117]

In pointing a finger at "self created societies," the president had publicly acknowledged the party strife that he believed was the greatest domestic threat to the Republic. His insistence that organizations calling themselves Democratic Societies were the serpent in Eden prompted Thomas Jefferson to condemn this "extraordinary act of boldness . . . from the faction of Monocrats." Washington's message also roused the ire of the Republican forces in Congress. The result was an acrimonious debate over the rights of free association versus the maintenance of law and order. Federalist members echoed their president's concern, condemning the societies as dangerous to the Republic and labeling them extralegal pressure groups, guilty of spreading lies about the government's policies, slandering members of the administration, and spurring rebellion. House Republicans, however, opposed any attempt to censor these societies, preferring, they said, to let the public decide whether to support, ignore, or oppose the views they espoused. Four years later, a similar, and far more consequential, argument would take place over the regulation of newspapers. But, for the moment, the House, now dominated by Republicans, chose to skirt the issue of extragovernmental political organizations and their role in the insurrection. In its reply to the president, the House expressed only a general regret that "individuals or combinations of men" might have misrepresented the government and its proceedings to "foment the flagrant outrage which has been committed on the laws." This careful language was enough to make Washington realize he had been rebuffed. The Federalist-dominated Senate, however, roundly condemned the Democratic Societies, declaring their mission was "calculated, if not intended, to disorganize our government." Party loyalties had determined both points of view.[118]

In August 1795, Washington issued a proclamation pardoning all persons found guilty of treason or failure to report treason in the Whiskey Rebellion. Immediately afterward, Governor Mifflin did the same. Meanwhile, two landmark events in 1794 and 1795 greatly eased the anxieties of the western Pennsylvania communities and relieved their economic distress. General Anthony Wayne's August 1794 victory over the Indians of the Western Confederacy in the Battle of Fallen Timbers led to a peace treaty that alleviated fears of attack within the western Pennsylvania communities. And in October 1795, the United States and Spain negotiated the Treaty of San Lorenzo, giving Americans the right to free navigation of the Mississippi River and duty-free transport through the port of New Orleans. Half a decade later, in 1801, President Thomas Jefferson's government repealed the whiskey tax. It is not without irony that the man who oversaw that repeal was a former whiskey rebel, Secretary of the Treasury Albert Gallatin.

Epilogue

DESPITE FINDLEY AND Brackenridge, despite Bache and the anti-administration members of Congress, the American people applauded Washington's handling of the Whiskey Rebellion. Over the months that followed, legislative bodies in Pennsylvania and its adjoining states expressed their gratitude and affection for the president, Governor Mifflin, and the brave soldiers of the militia army. They applauded the preservation of the federal government and the blessings of American liberty. Towns and churches sent resolutions of support and appreciation. It was the general view that the federal government had demonstrated to its citizens, and to the world, that it could withstand domestic rebellion without resorting to tyrannical measures. In their resolutions, Washington's admirers and supporters expressed their appreciation for a president who had shown patience in his attempt to restore law and order through legal and judicial means and had not resorted to force until all other avenues had been traveled. And they applauded the government's decision to show both resolve and leniency.

There was little recognition, or consideration, of the fact that Washington's strategy of delay might have ended in disaster. He had pursued a policy of restraint not from any knowledge that the rebels' response would be compliance but because he wished to protect the reputation of his administration and the public's image of its president. In a circumstance where the commitment to resistance and the goals of an insurgency were unknown and unpredictable, Hamilton's approach—to act quickly, before the rebellion was well organized and its membership large—had merit. But Hamilton thought like a soldier while Washington thought like a politician. The burdens of office on these two men were different: Hamilton was responsible for fiscal policy; Washington, for securing the loyalty of the people to a national government.

To a great extent, the public response to the handling of the Whiskey Rebellion revealed how critical the charisma of George Washington remained for the survival of the federal government. The affection and respect for George Washington was still the major source of the affection for the government he headed. The man, not the institution, still mattered most. Yet, by 1794, there were clear signs that a transfer of loyalty to the Constitution and to the federal government had begun. The Whiskey Rebellion had drawn people's attention to that government and to the role it could play in maintaining law and order. Fears of the government's potential for tyranny were calmed, and attention to its capacity for justice had emerged. The cooperation of several states in putting down the rebellion had promoted nationalism rather than the provincialism so prominent in the Antifederalist battle against ratification. And, ironically, the fact that a Republican opposition could arise and that its battles were waged within Congress rather than on the streets suggests that acceptance of the legitimacy of the Constitution and its government was growing.

Part II

THE GENET AFFAIR

IN 1793, IN the midst of the Whiskey Rebellion's growing challenge to the authority of the federal government, a young and brash Frenchman named Edmond Charles Genet arrived in America as the revolutionary government's minister to the United States. Citizen Genet, as he called himself, would pose a foreign challenge to America's federal government as disturbing as the domestic rebellion in western Pennsylvania. His primary mission was to press Washington's government to accept the French interpretation of the treaties signed by the two countries in 1778. This would allow France to establish a base of operations on American soil and in American territorial waters. France would then use the United States as a launching pad for privateers who would prey on British ships and recruit an army of American citizens for an invasion of Spanish-held Louisiana and Florida. Genet had also been instructed to demand a single full payment of the loans France had made to America during the Revolution. Genet was confident that he could achieve all these goals. He was certain that Americans were grateful to the French for their assistance in the war for independence, and that they were

eager to stand by their sister republic in the war it was waging with
Europe's monarchies to expand "the empire of liberty."

From the moment of his arrival, Edmond Genet challenged the
president's major foreign policy decision: American neutrality in the
European war. The English, of course, challenged that neutrality
too, but they confined themselves to manipulating American trade,
while Genet brought French manipulation directly into the cabinet,
the ports of Philadelphia, New York, and Charleston, and the countryside of Kentucky. In his brief tenure, he insulted the sovereignty
of America, exacerbated the tensions between Republican supporters
of France and Federalist supporters of Great Britain, and ignored
every protocol of diplomacy foreign ministers were expected to obey.
Perhaps his greatest insult was to the authority of the president himself. When Washington took steps to curtail Genet's activities, the
Frenchman threatened to go over the head of the president and appeal directly to the people to support his demands. The challenge for
Washington and his cabinet was to end the Genet crisis in a manner
that upheld the president's prerogatives in diplomacy and assured
the American people of their government's autonomy in navigating
America's place in world affairs.

The prevailing interpretation is that Genet was a diplomatic
failure of epic proportions. He was ignorant of American political
structures and refused the tutelage and advice of his only ally in the
administration, Thomas Jefferson. He underestimated Washington's
popularity and the respect citizens had for their president while he
fatally overestimated the readiness of Americans to join the French
fight with Great Britain and its allies. Although this judgment by historians is harsh, it is nevertheless correct.

Yet, despite the problems Genet posed, his impact has largely
been measured by his role in the contest for power between Federalists and Republicans. In this framework, Genet is important only
as a catalyst for political divisions between the parties within the
Washington administration. But, looked at in a different light, Genet's behavior and his attitude toward the federal government exposes
the pervasive sense of the fragility of American sovereignty in the
1790s. Public and private documents in 1793 and early 1794 reveal
an almost palpable anxiety in both Federalists and Republicans about
whether the more powerful and established European nations would

respect America as a sovereign nation; whether they were and would continue to be contemptuous of its independence; and whether they would attempt to direct American economic, fiscal, and military destiny as if this country were merely a satellite of a stronger empire. If Federalists and Republicans differed on who the European enemy of American sovereignty was, their fear of domination was the same. The correspondence between Genet and Jefferson, the records of cabinet meetings, the policy statements of Washington's administration, the congressional debates, and the instructions from the French government Genet labored so zealously to fulfill—all these bear witness to the crisis of sovereignty the French minister heightened when he arrived on American shores. It is this story that we must understand if we hope to grasp how a small, constitutionally limited federal government managed to not only hold the nation together but bind Americans more firmly to the idea of the nation itself.

1

"France is on the high-road to despotism."
—Gouverneur Morris, 1792

ON APRIL 1, 1789, the first session of the House of Representatives finally achieved a quorum and the business of the First Federal Congress began. Five days later, the Senate opened its session by electing its officers. With that, the era of a new representative government had started. A month later, across the Atlantic Ocean in France, King Louis XVI found himself forced to convene his own nation's long-dormant assembly in order to raise much-needed taxes. That summer, while congressmen debated James Madison's proposed Bill of Rights, a Paris mob stormed Paris's notorious Bastille prison. It was the start of a revolution. Over the course of the next four years, most Americans watched with amazement and delight as a second republic rose from the ashes of monarchy with a cry of "Liberty, Equality, Fraternity"—far more dramatic than their own rallying cry of "No Taxation Without Representation."

America's positive response to the revolution in France was no surprise. Most Americans felt gratitude toward the nation that had supported them in their struggle against British rule. There was a

general consensus that monarchy, as a form of government, was inevitably abusive and a general wish that the world would someday see
the wisdom of a republic based on the sovereignty of the people. But,
above all, America's enthusiasm arose from a realization that the system of representative government it had embraced had found a new
and powerful champion. The idea of a republic based on a constitution
could no longer be dismissed as a quixotic and doomed experiment,
for a major European nation had given it legitimacy. In this sense, the
French Revolution was a vindication of America's own Revolution;
Americans realized that the United States was no longer alone.

Few Americans demurred from the celebration of events in France.
Indeed, Alexander Hamilton was almost alone in 1790 in predict-
ing that the revolution would lead to anarchy and greater bloodshed
rather than to the creation of a stable republic. By 1792, however, the
escalating violence of the revolutionaries persuaded other Americans
that Hamilton was right. The US ambassador to France, Gouverneur
Morris, did not mince words in his condemnation of the revolution's
direction. "France is on the high-road to despotism," he wrote to his
friend William Carmichael on May 14, 1792, adding, "They have
made the common mistake that to enjoy liberty it is necessary only to
demolish authority." His conviction grew when the Marquis de Lafayette, hero of the American Revolution, was forced to flee France for
Austria, and it hardened when he learned of the massacre that August
of more than a thousand Royalists being held in the Parisian pris-
ons. Writing to Thomas Jefferson, a staunch supporter of the French
Revolution, Morris recounted the execution of two to three hundred
clergy and the beheading and disemboweling of a noblewoman whose
"head and entrails [were] paraded on pikes through the street." When
news reached America that the king had been executed in January
1793, a number of other leading Federalists—including John Adams
and his family, and George Washington himself—concluded that the
trajectories of their own revolution and that of France had dramatically and irrevocably diverged.[1]

In the United States, the effect of the increasing radicalism of
the French Revolution was an increasing partisanship. Federalists
began to take pains to distinguish their own country's revolutionary
past from the violence committed in the name of liberty and equality
across the Atlantic. As Thomas Boylston Adams wrote to his father

on April 7, 1793, "Since the Execution of the King . . . nothing can be thought too mad or extravagant for the National Convention to commit." The younger Adams questioned whether France could be called a republic, for no laws existed there and there was no power to enforce new laws if they were passed. France had become living proof that "nothing would be easier than to create a Republic in any Country, for they have only to destroy the existing Government." The Secretary of the Senate Samuel Allyne Otis agreed with these sentiments. Writing to John Adams on April 17, he conceded that his friend had been correct when he predicted "Egaulite [*sic*] would be so bloody."[2]

Federalists may have abandoned support for the new French regime, but the Republican coalition led by Thomas Jefferson and James Madison refused to turn its back on the Revolution. In the same month that the young Adams wrote his blistering commentary, James Madison sent a thank-you note to the French government for honoring him with the title "French Citizen." The act that conferred this honor, Madison declared, spoke of "the magnanimity of the French Nation." The Virginian expressed his personal wish that the French people achieve "all the prosperity & glory . . . which can accrue from an example corresponding with the dignified maxims they have established, and compleating the triumphs of Liberty." Jefferson's support for the Revolution did not waver. Despite Gouverneur Morris's vivid descriptions of beheadings of nobles and royalty, Jefferson still maintained, as he had in 1787, that "the tree of liberty must be refreshed from time to time with the blood of patriots & tyrants." By 1793, the disagreement over the promise of the French Revolution had become a distinguishing feature of the rivalry between Federalists and Republicans.[3]

The Federalist conviction that the two revolutions had taken different paths intensified as French leaders exported theirs. The Girondin faction, who held the reins of power in France by early 1792, had little political experience but unlimited revolutionary fervor. They were proselytizers, men with a utopian vision of spreading their revolution across Europe, even if this meant an invading army would carry the banner of "Liberty, Equality, Fraternity" into neighboring countries. The Girondins would not let existing treaties with other European nations nor the pressing needs of their own citizens stand in the way of their sacred mission to expand the "empire de la liberté." Confident that the oppressed subjects of kings and tyrants would greet their troops as liberators, they ignored the warnings of Jacobin leader Maximillian Robespierre that "no one loves armed missionaries." By April 1792 they had declared war on Austria, and, by February of the following year, they had extended the war to Britain, Russia, Prussia, Portugal, and Spain. These nations, along with Austria, quickly formed an alliance to halt the expansion of the so-called empire of liberty.[4]

Americans watched these events unfold, assuming that their country would remain out of the fray, cheering France or condemning it but never becoming active participants. John Adams was among the Federalist leaders who quickly embraced "a Neutrality, absolute total Neutrality" as the only option for the United States. The problem was that the Girondins would not tolerate neutrality. They expected Americans to support their efforts to spread republican ideology and republican institutions to the monarchies of the world, if not on the battlefield then through the provision of money, supplies, and a safe haven for French ships in France's emerging naval contest with Britain. Their reading of the 1778 treaties signed between America and France made them confident of their right to demand American support. Some members of the Girondin leadership knew that a pro-British faction existed in the United States and that it wielded considerable influence within Washington's administration, but they did not consider this problem insurmountable. Anglophiles might delay the desired alliance between the two republics, but they could not prevent it. France, after all, had come to the aid of the Americans in their hour of need; it was unthinkable that America would not reciprocate.[5]

2
"I find him to be a great treasure to sustain and employ."
—Count de Segur to Count de
Montmorin, 1788

IN NOVEMBER 1792, the Girondins appointed their new minister to the United States. The instructions they drafted for Edmond

Genet left no doubt about his mission: he was to see that the federal government did everything in its power, short of sending troops
to the battlefields of Europe, to assist in the victory of liberty over
tyranny. He was to negotiate a new commercial treaty that would
marry the economies of the two nations. Among other things, the
envisioned treaty would provide France with a favored nation status when it came to US charges on foreign ships and goods. He was
also to assert the right of France to use US ports as provisioning and
repair stations and as points of embarkation for attacks on British
ships. The French government's interpretation of the treaties of 1778
granted it an exclusive right to sell captured enemy goods to American buyers and to transform captured merchant marine vessels into
warships in American ports. Although the treaties made no mention
of recruiting Americans to serve in the French navy or of Americans
turning their own vessels into French privateers, the minister was not
to ignore those possibilities. In fact, he would be provided with blank
government licenses, known as letters of marque, to be delivered to
Frenchmen and Americans willing to arm privateers. He was also to
make clear that the British must not enjoy any of these advantages.

It was also crucial that the French minister secure an arrangement for full liquidation of the US debt to France rather than its
gradual payment. France intended to pay for its purchases from
American suppliers with this money. The funds would also be
used to finance the Girondin government's land and naval operations against the Spanish and British territories in North America.
These invasions—or, as the French government thought of them,
liberations—would originate in the United States. The leaders of the
French government fully intended to turn the United States into a
base of operations for campaigns to liberate Canada and Louisiana
from the grip of British and Spanish monarchies. To pave the way for
these invasions, they were prepared to deploy spies and secret agents
to these enemy territories and to provoke French inhabitants there
to join in armed rebellion. And they were eager to recruit American
citizens from border areas like Kentucky to do the fighting. In the
army to expand the empire of liberty, all men could be considered
French soldiers.

In return for American compliance with these demands, France
offered to lift all restrictions on American goods and ships in French

ports. This was a gesture less generous than selfish, for the French desperately needed the supplies that America could provide. And, finally, as evidence of his nation's affection for its revolutionary brothers-in-arms, the minister was to pledge French protection of America's borders—even if it meant stationing French forces on American soil. This assurance cavalierly ignored American sovereignty over its own territory, just as the proposed recruitment of Americans for the invasion of Spanish territories ignored its sovereignty over its own citizens. That France appeared oblivious of this insult to American sovereignty was telling: the British flag no longer flew over its former colonies, but, in the minds of America's powerful transatlantic neighbors, the United States remained a dependent of Europe.[6]

Despite the fact that his sisters were attendants of the queen, the new minister, Edmond Genet, was an enthusiastic supporter of the Revolution. He had made this clear while serving in the diplomatic corps in Russia in 1791. His open—and very vocal—approval of the new French constitution and the extreme limitation on the king's authority led the Russian empress Catherine, who had once been charmed by Genet, to declare him "an insane demagogue . . . and a crazy little fool." No friend to republics or constitutions, the empress expelled Genet from her country. He returned to France, proud of his daring show of patriotism in the face of unrestrained tyrannical power. He preferred to think of his actions not as impolitic but heroic. The French government appeared to agree. It rewarded him first with an appointment as minister to Holland and then with the appointment as minister to the United States.[7]

Genet did seem the perfect choice in many ways. He had grown up in a family devoted to government service. From his father, a career diplomat, Edmond had inherited elegance and charm as well as a talent for languages. The young Genet spoke English by the age of five and, soon afterward, began to learn Greek. At twelve, he was awarded a medal from the king of Sweden for his translation into French of a work of Swedish history. In 1792 at twenty-nine, he was fluent in German as well. His linguistic skills had allowed him to take over as head of the Bureau of Interpretation in the Ministry of Foreign Affairs when his father died. Soon afterward, Edmond began his promising career as a diplomat. One of his patrons described him in glowing terms. He is "a very distinguished young man . . . in all respects suitable. He unites agreeable talents with profound knowledge. He is erudite without pedantry, bright without pretension; his logic is just, his zeal indefatigable, his wit is ornate, his manner of thinking noble and attractive." Above all, the young Citizen Genet radiated boundless energy, enthusiasm, and optimism.[8]

Genet was not without his critics, however. Some who knew him well conceded that he had an excellent mind but also a lazy one. Genet, they said, was content with only a general knowledge of a subject rather than its mastery. Some considered him overimpulsive—a trait his behavior in Russia might suggest. Perhaps his supporters in the French government worried about that too, for as he headed to America he was explicitly warned to "scrupulously observe the forms established for official communications between the government and foreign agents and never engage in any move or proposals which might offend free Americans concerning their constitution which differs in many respects from the principles established in France." It is unlikely that Genet thought these warnings necessary for, like his superiors, he was confident that Americans would be eager to assist France in any and every way possible.[9]

Genet came to his assignment with two serious disadvantages, neither of which he was aware of until it was too late. First, he did not read the political situation in France as clearly as he should have, failing to consider that the men who had appointed him might not remain in power. Second, he had not thoroughly studied—if he studied at all—the political context in America. He did not understand the distribution of power and authority among the branches of the federal government. Rather, he assumed that the American legislature, like the legislature in revolutionary France, was the sole representative of the will of the people. He also assumed that the fundamental political division between the emerging Republican Party and the Federalists was based upon their respective loyalties to France or Britain; he did not appreciate that it was primarily the struggle over the nature of the American Republic itself that pitted the Federalist priorities of law, order, and stability against the growing Republican emphasis on liberty and equality.

Genet paid little attention to the problems that the European war was causing America. Despite the thousands of miles of ocean that separated the United States from that war, most Americans realized that the cords of commerce connected their country to the belligerents in Europe. America's economic recovery and its fiscal stability depended upon foreign trade, and that trade, in turn, depended on the goodwill of its key trading partners, Britain and France. Any obstacles these two great powers imposed on US imports or exports could be disastrous. In fact, in the wake of the French Revolution, both had begun to pass legislation or establish policies that restricted US trade with their territorial possessions. As open war between Britain and France loomed, each began to target US trade with the enemy. American merchant ships were vulnerable to attack and seizure on the high seas, for, in 1793, the United States had no navy to protect them from pirates or the British and French navies that controlled the Atlantic. The American public might be willing to sing the "Marseillaise," but, once France declared war against Britain, both Francophiles and Anglophiles in Washington's cabinet recognized they would need to cautiously navigate between the two European rivals. In this situation, the French minister's agenda was likely to create a crisis. One thing was certain: it would find a fierce and powerful opponent in Secretary of the Treasury Alexander Hamilton.

That Hamilton would reject Genet's demands was foreshadowed by a simple fact: the nation's primary trading partner was Great Britain. Any decision that alienated Britain meant an interruption, if not a cessation, of this vital revenue flow. Hamilton's position on America's existing treaties with France, on Genet himself, and on Genet's mission would not stem from a personal hatred of France, as many of his own opponents would argue; it would arise from his desire to protect the system he had constructed.

But there were men in Washington's cabinet who saw a different source of equally dire developments on the horizon. Like many of the revolutionary generation, Thomas Jefferson nurtured an intense Anglophobia. In his eyes, the rapid growth of commerce and industry in Britain had spawned greed and political corruption. He was certain that Hamilton's system cultivated this same moral degeneracy in the American Republic. Indeed, in Jefferson's view, all of Hamilton's programs privileged commerce over agriculture, the manipulation of money over the cultivation of the soil, and the emergence of an elite minority devoted to profit rather to public service. Jefferson was convinced that the assumption of state debts, the funding of the combined debts, the honoring of government-issued certificates at face value, and the establishment of the Bank of the United States were designed to destroy the agrarian bedrock on which the Republic stood. He also maintained an unshakeable conviction that Hamilton's ultimate goal was the establishment of an American monarchy. In the face of what he saw as a betrayal of the American Revolution, Jefferson had begun to organize a political movement to contain and ultimately to overturn Hamilton's fiscal and economic system. The survival of the French Republic was critical to his efforts, for he believed the French example would keep the love of liberty alive in the hearts of Americans until Hamilton's system could be undone.

The cabinet was thus rapidly becoming an intellectual and political battleground, with Hamilton and Secretary of War Henry Knox on one side and Jefferson and in most instances Attorney General Edmund Randolph on the other. Washington sought advice from both camps, and, though he may have longed for unanimity, he accepted that compromise was the only triumph possible.

3

"FREEMEN, WE ARE YOUR BROTHERS AND FRIENDS."
—Embuscade *banner, 1793*

ALTHOUGH GENET WAS appointed in November 1792, he had not yet reached American shores by March 1793. Nevertheless, Jefferson was anxious for the president to decide how the minister of a revolutionary government should be received. Washington sought Hamilton's advice. Hamilton opposed any steps that would link America's future too closely to France, but he reluctantly conceded there were no grounds to totally reject the credentials of a minister appointed by the revolutionary government. Hamilton did advocate some restrictions, however. His caution resonated with Washington, whose own alienation from the French cause had been steadily growing. Busy with preparations for a visit to Mount Vernon, the president told Jefferson it was probably best to receive the credentials of the man they all erroneously called "mister Genest" but it should be done without "too much warmth or cordiality."[10]

The new French minister did not set sail for America until February 1793, and he did not arrive until April. His winter crossing of the Atlantic had not gone well, for bad weather forced his ship, the forty-gun *Embuscade,* off course. When the *Embuscade* finally docked in the United States on April 8, Genet found himself in Charleston, South Carolina, rather than Philadelphia. His arrival was theatrical; his reception was exuberant.

Genet wanted Americans to know that the French considered them brothers-in-arms, and he conveyed the message—in unsubtle fashion—through the *Embuscade* itself. The ship's figurehead was a liberty cap, and a second liberty cap was carved on its stern. The foremast had been converted into a liberty pole, one of the favorite symbols of American radicals before independence was declared, a symbol soon to be revived by the whiskey rebels. Around the mizzen top a message blazed: "FREEMEN, WE ARE YOUR BROTHERS AND FRIENDS." The foretop carried a warning to tyrants: "Enemies of Equality, relinquish your principles or tremble!" A delighted Charleston embraced the minister, the ship captain, and the crew. Genet was swept up in a whirl of fetes, dinners, balls, and receptions, and the many French merchants in residence in the city vied with one another in offers to prepare warships at their own expense for the fight against Great Britain.[11]

The local enthusiasm for the French cause prompted Genet to abandon all thoughts of following protocol. Rather than making his way immediately to Philadelphia to present his credentials to the secretary of state and the president, he decided to begin his mission. He had arrived armed with some two hundred letters of marque that authorized a privateer to attack and capture enemy vessels and bring them before an admiralty court for condemnation and sale. With these licenses, he quickly commissioned four privateer vessels and enlisted American sailors to man them. He then blithely bypassed the American judicial system by instructing the local French consul to exercise exclusive admiralty jurisdiction over any prizes these privateers brought into port. Thus he established French law in the port of Charleston. Genet also began to recruit American volunteers for an attack on Spanish East Florida.

Genet encountered no interference from South Carolina's Republican governor William Moultrie. Moultrie conveniently overlooked the authority of the federal government to rule on admiralty matters and did nothing to hinder Genet's recruitment of American citizens to serve under a foreign flag. He allowed the French minister to use the port of Charleston to arm and man vessels to prey on British ships, and he also suggested the names of men who might be interested in financing or joining Genet's military operations in East Florida.

Moultrie's actions—and inaction—roused some criticism from the small number of South Carolina Federalists. But no one was likely to be surprised by Moultrie's support for Genet. Local Federalists and Republicans alike knew the governor felt a deep affection for France, as evidenced by his close friendship with Michel Ange Bernard Mangourit, the French consul at Charleston. It was also known that Moultrie's first and second wives were members of a religious group, the Huguenots, who had been persecuted by French kings and the Catholic Church. But Moultrie may have had other reasons than friendship and marital loyalties for undermining the authority of the federal government. One was personal. Only a year earlier, in 1792, President Washington had rejected his application to command the US Army, a decision that stung Moultrie deeply. Another was political. The president had refused to mount a military campaign against the Creek Indians who posed a continuing threat to the state's western settlers. Yet another was financial. Moultrie had land claims that would benefit if the Spanish were removed from Florida. These slights and grievances surely inclined William Moultrie to a liberal reading of French rights under the treaties of 1778. Although he was careful not to officially endorse Genet's recruitment activities, the governor felt justified in giving the Frenchman free rein; after all, the federal government had not issued any explicit directives forbidding these actions by a sister republic.[12]

While Genet was busy recruiting Americans into the service of France, the United States received official word that his government had declared war on Great Britain and Holland. This news brought Washington hurrying back to Philadelphia from Mount Vernon. He arrived in the capital on April 17, 1793, and called for a cabinet meeting on the 19th. At Hamilton's urging, Washington sent every member of his cabinet thirteen questions about how the president should respond not only to Genet but to what, in effect, was now a full-scale war between America's two major trading partners. Behind these questions was another: How could the United States avoid being drawn into the conflict?

Washington's questions all appeared to hinge on the extent of America's obligations to France under the treaties of amity and commerce and mutual defense signed in 1778 after the American victory at Saratoga. Should the United States even consider those treaties applicable to the present situation, or could they be held in suspension until the current government of France was, as Hamilton put it, firmly established? Was France engaged in an offensive or defensive war? If it was offensive to any degree, did the promise of mutual *defense* contained in the treaties apply? Did any article in either of the treaties prevent the warships of France's enemies from coming into American ports as convoys protecting merchant marine vessels? If the French regent—who, with the king dead, was the current representative of the old regime—also sent a minister to America, should he be received as well?

Washington also wanted advice on what immediate action he should take. Should he call the recessed Congress into early session to debate America's position on the European war? Should he issue a proclamation to put a stop to US citizens participating on either side in that war? Collectively, the answers given to all these questions at the cabinet meeting would amount to the first instance of American foreign policy.[13]

The hand of Hamilton was evident in the formulation of the thirteen questions. He had, in fact, raised many of them—and provided his own answers—in a letter to his Federalist friend, John Jay, on April 9. The reception of Genet must be reconsidered, he explained. "The King has been decapitated. Out of this will arise a Regent, acknowledged and supported by the Powers of Europe almost universally . . . and who may himself send an Ambassador to the United States." To receive Genet and refuse the regent's emissary would effectively destroy any semblance of neutrality. Similarly, the concession to French treaty demands was likely to destroy all hope of avoiding war with Britain. There was only one solution: the United States must insist that France did not yet have a government "competent to demand from us the performance of existing treaties." Until then, he argued, "the *applicability* of the Treaties is suspended."[14]

The cabinet meeting on April 19 was contentious, and few of the issues raised were resolved. An official reception of Genet was confirmed, although there was intense disagreement over whether it should be unqualified or qualified. A qualified reception signaled that the United States did not consider itself bound by the treaties of 1778. As this was a critical question—and as Hamilton and Jefferson were certain to offer opposing views—the president thought it best to ask for written opinions. The two men were given until May 6 to submit their arguments.[15]

In the meantime, there was one matter on which the entire cabinet did agree: the president should issue a proclamation prohibiting the interference of US citizens in the war. Yet the language in the proposed proclamation produced another heated exchange between Hamilton and Jefferson. Both knew that France had a desperate need for American supplies, and, because of this, strict American neutrality would favor Great Britain. Thus, Hamilton urged a firm declaration of neutrality while Jefferson, hoping to keep the option of some preferential treatment for France alive, vigorously opposed the use of the word "neutrality." The secretary of state insisted that an official policy of neutrality would be unconstitutional because the power to decide "there should be no war" fell to the legislative, not the executive, branch. Such a declaration from the president would be, in effect, a major expansion of the office's role in foreign affairs. But Jefferson's argument was weak; although Congress did have the power to *declare* war, it was doubtful that a declaration *to stay out of war* was an instance of presidential overreach. To bolster his case, Jefferson made the suggestion that there might be benefits to presenting the American position as uncertain. It could, he argued, give the United States an opportunity to wring concessions out of the major powers as a price for American neutrality. Hamilton bristled at the idea; American neutrality, he declared, was not a negotiable commodity. Jefferson's proposal appears naïve, at best. Because both England and France had the power to disrupt American shipping, close valuable ports to American trade, and, if necessary, bring the war to the United States, the recognition of American neutrality would be their gift to the United States, not something they would have to bargain for. There was little point in the beggar at the table pretending to negotiate from strength.

The question was settled at the next cabinet meeting, on April 22. The often cautious Washington agreed not to include the word "neutrality" in the otherwise strongly worded proclamation he issued that day. Although he had fought hard for this victory, Jefferson knew there was little to celebrate in this small concession. He viewed any step that diminished American support of the French as tantamount to a defeat. In fact, it proved no real victory for him at all, for, despite this effort at finesse, the press and the public—not to mention Jefferson himself—would immediately refer to the document as the Proclamation of Neutrality.[16]

Drafted by Attorney General Edmund Randolph, the proclamation was essentially a warning to individuals or groups of Americans who might follow the pied piper Edmond Genet. It forbade the active participation of American citizens in warfare on the high seas or in hostile land actions against nations at peace with the United States. It warned American shippers and ship captains not to carry any articles deemed contraband to either of the belligerents. But missing from the proclamation were any concrete guidelines on the use of American ports by the navies of the belligerent nations. Nor did the proclamation spell out America's policy on the sale of the cargoes of captured vessels or the arming of those vessels by their captors. It did not delineate who, the states or the federal government, would be responsible for enforcing its restrictions or for establishing the punishment for infractions. As spring ended, American foreign policy remained a product of trial and error, of reaction to circumstances as they arose, and of the difficulty of finding common ground within a deeply divided administration.

Both Hamilton and Jefferson submitted their written opinions on Genet's reception before the deadline set by the president. Each took the opportunity to present arguments on other unresolved questions, and each anticipated the arguments of the other. Hamilton stressed the domestic instability of the current French government and the uncertainty of its success in the war it was waging. Under these circumstances, he believed the United States would be wise to consider the treaties with France temporarily and provisionally suspended. He was not even sure, he added, that the treaties were still valid. They had been signed with King Louis XVI, not with the revolutionary government that had deposed and executed him. Perhaps, he suggested, the treaties had died with the king. If the president did decide to honor them, Hamilton urged Washington to remember that the demands they laid upon the United States were limited: they bound the United States only to *defend* France if it were attacked; they did not commit the United States to support France in an *offensive* war. Hamilton ended on a Machiavellian note: supporting a losing cause might have dire consequences for us. If Britain won the war, the defeated revolutionary government would be unseated, replaced perhaps by a restoration of royalty. If that happened, "What would be our situation with the future Government of that Country?" But Hamilton reserved his most compelling argument for last: to receive Genet without qualifications would be read by the English as an open declaration of war.[17]

Jefferson took several equally shrewd positions in his arguments against suspension of the treaties. He denied that the United States was facing an all-or-nothing situation. We could, he argued, postpone decisions on certain troubling treaty issues without resorting to suspending them completely. He advised not to adopt a policy that defended against possible problems in the future, like a French defeat or a minister sent by the regent. He countered Hamilton's warning of war with England by suggesting that France would consider treaty suspension a hostile act. He did not believe the treaty obligations would place the United States in direct conflict with the English. Article XI of the Treaty of Alliance, for example, pledged mutual protection of each other's possession. But would a nation without a navy actually be called upon to defend the French West Indies? Article XXII of the Treaty of Amity and Commerce stipulated that the enemies of France could not equip privateers or sell prizes in US ports, but they contained no stipulation that the United States must grant France these privileges. Jefferson dismissed the idea that the treaties were now invalid because they had been signed with the late king. Treaties, he rightly pointed out, were made with nations, not particular governments. Finally, Jefferson warned of the domestic damage to America's reputation if the government appeared more ready to make alliance with a monarch than a sister republic.[18]

Ultimately, Jefferson's arguments, if not his underlying motives, carried the day. Washington refused to renounce or suspend the treaties; in his judgment they were valid, even if the two nations involved did not agree on the interpretation of certain key clauses. Thus, when Citizen Edmond Genet at last presented his credentials in Philadelphia, he would be received without qualifications.

Despite their disagreement on fundamental matters, Hamilton and Jefferson both acknowledged that America was too weak and too vulnerable to openly engage in the European war on either side. Both understood the risks inherent in any policy decision that was too blatantly partisan—and both realized that America could not control how the belligerents interpreted the administration's actions. But if these men agreed that a policy of neutrality was best, this did not prevent each of them from engaging in personal acts of partisanship. Both rationalized these actions as efforts to prevent American involvement in the war. To assuage any anger or concern on the part of Great Britain, Hamilton would provide British minister George Hammond with privileged information and inflated assurances of his personal control over the administration's policies. For his part, Jefferson would labor to modify Genet's expectations and his behavior, hoping to persuade the Frenchman that patience and cooperation would net far better results than insults and demands. He would persuade his fellow Virginian Edmund Randolph to support him in cabinet meetings against Hamilton and Knox, and he would pressure fellow Republicans to mobilize public support for France. Washington's cabinet may have publicly supported a policy of neutrality, but in fleshing out that neutrality Jefferson and Randolph rallied to the tricolored flag, Hamilton and Knox to the banner of John Bull.[19]

4

**"The Republics of France and America: may they
be forever united in the cause of liberty."**
—*Genet banquet toast, May 1793*

ON THE SAME day Washington issued the Proclamation of Neutrality, he wrote to a friend in England. "I believe it is the sincere wish of United America to have nothing to do with the political intrigues, or the squabbles of European nations." But the question remained: Would France and England respect American neutrality? The answer, it turned out, was no. France and England were engaged in a war whose stakes were even greater than those of the Great War for Empire that ended in 1763. Neither could afford to play fair, and both hoped to use America to their own advantage. Their competing policies were designed to make the United States a dependency rather than an independent entity in transatlantic affairs. The only choice they seemed to leave to the American government was which master the United States preferred.[20]

Shortly after France declared war on England, Britain's prime minister made clear his nation's position on American shipping. Writing to George Hammond, the British minister to the United States, Lord William Grenville dismissed any notion of American neutrality on the high seas. He asserted England's firm rejection of the principle of "free Ships making free Goods." The British navy would not hesitate to capture American ships carrying any supplies to French ports that would, in his words, "enable the Enemies of this Country to carry on the War against Us." There was even less hope that France would accept American neutrality. Genet's actions in South Carolina had shown that he believed the treaties of 1778 gave him a wide berth in seeking both American naval and military support for the French cause. Although South Carolina governor William Moultrie reconsidered his collaboration with Genet after Washington's proclamation of neutrality, the French minister was undeterred by news of the government's policy. It did not alter his agenda; it only angered him.[21]

Genet learned of the proclamation as he made his way to Philadelphia to belatedly present his credentials to the president. Rather than sail to the capital, Genet chose to send the *Embuscade* ahead and make the journey by land. Thus, while the cabinet was debating how to receive the French minister, Genet was basking in the affection shown to him by supporters along the route from South Carolina to Pennsylvania. Not everyone was charmed by him, of course. Writing to Alexander Hamilton, North Carolina congressman John Steele conceded that Genet had "a good person, fine ruddy complection, quite active and seems always in a bustle, more like a busy man than a man of business." But Steele was not taken in by Genet's conviviality. He had seen another side of the young Frenchman when Genet responded angrily to an insult to a countryman. "For a moment," Steele wrote, Genet "deviated from his system which is I think, to laugh us into the war if he can." Steele then summed up the American dilemma perfectly: "The best informed men in this State . . . continue uneasey [sic], from an apprehension that our political connection with France, and our commercial intercourse with England will place the United States in a delicate, if not a dangerous situation during the war."[22]

Steele may have resisted Genet, but hundreds of Philadelphians were eager to succumb to him. Their feverish enthusiasm offended Hamilton. "If we feel kind dispositions towards France for the assistance afforded us, in our revolution," he wrote in an unfinished article intended for newspaper publication, "it will not do us honor to forget that Louis the XVI was then the sovereign of the Country—that the succour afforded depended on his pleasure." The execution of that friend to America by the revolutionary government, Hamilton added, made "any extraordinary honors to the representatives of those who consigned him to so affecting a doom . . . as little consonant with decorum and humanity, as with true policy."[23]

The first director of the US Mint, the celebrated astronomer, inventor, and mathematician David Rittenhouse, disagreed with the treasury secretary. Rittenhouse was one of seven distinguished Republicans who greeted Genet and escorted him to his lodgings when he arrived in Philadelphia on May 16. There, as a large, cheering crowd gathered in the streets, Rittenhouse read a welcoming address. Genet responded, in his perfect English, with uncharacteristic modesty: "I am no orator and I should not at any time affect the language of eloquence. . . . I cannot tell you, gentlemen, how penetrated I am by the language of the address to which I have listened, nor how deeply gratified my fellow-citizens will be in reading so noble an avowal of the principles of the Revolution of France, and on learning that so cordial an esteem for her citizens exists in a country for which they have shed their blood and disbursed their treasures." He then artfully combined assurance that France did not expect America to become a party to the war with a reminder that France "has already combated for your liberties."[24]

The speech, calculated to win the hearts of the crowd, drew loud shouts of support and even tears from Genet's audience. Over the following week, delegations of admirers came to his hotel, and dinners were given in his honor. A banquet was held for officers of the

Embuscade, and Americans and Frenchmen alike joined in the singing of the "Marseillaise." The ship's captain, Jean Baptiste Francois Bompard, invited a group of leading Philadelphians aboard, and the boatswain gave a speech, noting that many of the crew had "risked life and shed blood" for American independence—and were ready to do so again. At a banquet for Genet attended by two hundred people, toasts were made to "the people and the law," "the people of France," and "the Republics of France and America: may they be forever united in the cause of liberty."[25]

A very different celebration in Philadelphia that same week, honoring King George III's birthday, paled by comparison. The toasts offered here were not to one but three Georges—George III, George Washington, and the evening's host, George Hammond. Glasses were also raised to this lengthy toast to Washington's foreign policy: "The Proclamation of neutrality: may the heart that dictated and the head that proposed it live long to enjoy the blessings of all true friends to humanity." That head was understood to belong to Alexander Hamilton.[26]

The response by Philadelphians to his arrival further persuaded Genet that the American public, if not its government, had cast its lot with France. A more seasoned diplomat might not have moved so quickly and surely to this conclusion, given the absence of most of the city's influential merchants in the adoring crowds. A more cautious diplomat might have suspended his judgment until he met with the president and key cabinet members. A more thoughtful diplomat might have asked himself, Would the enthusiasm translate into compliance with the French agenda? But Genet's boundless confidence in himself and in his mission skewed his perception of what was a far more fraught situation than he imagined it to be.

Indeed, the Washington administration was already attempting to deal with British complaints about France's apparent disregard for American neutrality or sovereignty. George Hammond reported that the French consul at Charleston had passed judgment on the legality of the sale of a captured British ship. He also alerted the administration that the French had fitted out a privateer at Charleston, manned it with several American citizens, and, when it captured a British vessel, had taken the prize back to Charleston. These complaints prompted Jefferson to send a long letter to the outgoing

French minister, Jean Baptiste Ternant. In it, he reminded Ternant that he had already written protesting the capture of the British ship *Grange* by Genet's own frigate, *Embuscade,* on the Delaware River. The government had ruled this a clear violation of neutrality and expected "the crew be liberated and the vessel and cargo restored to their former owners." Although it is unlikely Jefferson doubted the truth of Hammond's charges, he took pains to qualify the administration's acceptance of them, declaring that the United States "have not full evidence" that the consul was guilty of overstepping his authority nor "perfect" information on the outfitting of a privateer at Charleston. And he assured Ternant that the US government did not believe "the French nation could be wanting in respect or friendship to us, on any occasion." Still, he appealed to Ternant to prevent any such affronts to American authority in the future. It was a request that would have little impact. Ternant was headed home, and the man chosen to replace him was on his way to Philadelphia. The retiring minister simply passed the letter along to his successor. Genet would do nothing to allay the administration's concern.[27]

Naturally, Hamilton took a far sterner view of France's alleged infractions. In a memorandum to the president of May 15, he accepted the British minister's information as completely reliable and insisted that the United States must comply with the demand for restitution of all prizes taken by privateers recruited on American soil. Genet's actions in Charleston might be forgiven as they occurred before the proclamation was issued, but the case reported on May 8 by William Vans Murray of Maryland could not. Murray told Hamilton that a second prize vessel had been taken into custody as it sailed up the Choptank River on its way to be sold. The captain taking the ship upriver was an American with a French commission. By actions like these, Hamilton declared, France not only made the United States "an instrument of hostilities against Great Britain" but also gave serious insult to American sovereignty. "The jurisdiction of every *Independent* Nation within its own territories," he wrote, "naturally excludes all exercise of authority, by any other Government, within those Territories." How could French actions be excused or overlooked when "the equipping manning and commissioning of Vessels of War, the enlisting, levying or raising of men for military service, whether by land or Sea . . . [were] among the highest and most important exercises of sovereignty"? Citing the legal opinion of Emer de Vattel, the noted Swiss expert in international law, that "no person is to enlist soldiers in a foreign country without the permission of the sovereign," Hamilton repeatedly characterized Genet's actions as an injury, an affront, and an insult to the American government. If France were allowed to continue this behavior, Hamilton predicted it would soon feel free to commission American troops to invade Spanish and English territories. Anyone privy to Genet's instructions would know Hamilton was right.[28]

On May 16, amid the festivities welcoming him to Philadelphia, Citizen Genet sent his credentials to Jefferson. His brief cover letter was the first of at least eighty letters and memorials—many of them long and heated—that remain of his lengthy correspondence with the secretary of state. Two days later, Genet sent the French text of his credentials to George Washington. It is likely that he also presented Washington with two letters from the French government. The first, from the National Convention, announced the creation of the French Republic, justified the abolition of monarchy, and labeled the support for the American Revolution shown by king and court as deceitful and self-interested. It went on to declare the French Republic's solidarity with America in the fight for liberty and linked the recent successes of the French army with America's triumphs at Saratoga, Trenton, and Yorktown. After thanking the United States for its aid to beleaguered French colonies in the Caribbean, the letter expressed France's eagerness to strengthen the commercial and political ties between the two countries. The second letter, dated January 13, came from the Provisional Executive Council. It assured the president that Genet had the authority to negotiate any agreement that would strengthen the "ties of friendship and commerce." Genet's success, the council added with less-than-subtle flattery, depended on the "virtuous and talented President" who had shown himself a friend to France.[29]

Hamilton's response to this correspondence was unambiguous. In a letter to an unidentified friend, he dismissed the comparison of France to America during its revolution. "Would to heaven that we could discern in the Mirror of French affairs, the same humanity, the same decorum the same gravity, the same order, the same dignity, the same solemnity, which distinguished the course of the

American Revolution." Hamilton saw instead "horrid and systematic massacres," prompted by Marat and Robespierre, men who now held powerful positions in the French government. He compared them unfavorably to an idealized King Louis XVI, whom Hamilton lauded as benevolent and no enemy to liberty. The treasury secretary could see nothing to admire in the men who now wielded the "sword of fanaticism" to subdue citizens of other countries and confiscated religious treasures from their own nation's churches. Passion, tumult, and violence defined their revolution, Hamilton wrote with obvious disgust, and the difference between the two revolutions was as great as the difference between "Liberty & Licentiousness."[30]

Jefferson, by contrast, was excited about Genet's arrival. "It is impossible for any thing to be more affectionate, more magnanimous than the purport of his mission," he wrote James Madison on May 19. Genet had pledged that France would not call on the United States to help defend the French islands in the Caribbean. He had gone further, assuring Americans that the French "wish you to do nothing but what is for your own good, and we will do all in our power to promote it." Jefferson was delighted to learn that Genet believed Americans "the only persons on earth who can love us sincerely & merit to be so loved." In Jefferson, these words produced profound optimism. In his view, Genet was offering the United States everything and asking nothing in return except a deeper commitment to liberty. Jefferson would soon have reason to regret that the charming Citizen Genet had been made the spokesman for his country's cause.[31]

Jefferson was not without worry, however. He surely regretted his failure to prevent a proclamation of neutrality, for he now realized the policy must be enforced. If it were not, American control over its foreign relationships would not be taken seriously. And, by its very nature, the neutrality policy meant little if its reach were not extended. It was not enough to forbid American citizens from engaging in the European war; the administration also had to make an unequivocal statement on the outfitting of privateers and the disposition of prizes brought into American ports. This proved to be the agenda for the next cabinet meeting, probably held on May 20.[32]

Before the meeting, Jefferson had been confident that Genet's actions in Charleston could be considered only a "slight offense." His notes from the cabinet meeting reflected his belief that French citizens residing in America had the right to buy, arm, and man privateer vessels with their own money. He believed the United States should impose only one condition on these French patriots: they must not commit acts of hostility within the limits of the United States. Jefferson ended these notes with a musing on motives and conspiracies. Who would profit from a sharp reprimand of the French minister? For Jefferson, the answer was obvious: England. And this led him to other, darker questions: Are we the dupes of England? Is England prodding us into reprimands of Genet that will force France to attack us? These questions reflected a realization, perhaps dimly recognized, that the United States was not the master of its own fate.[33]

Hamilton and Knox saw the issue of enforcement far differently. According to Jefferson's notes, they insisted that France must either give up a prize taken by a privateer, or the privateer and the prize must leave the United States immediately. In this instance, Edmund Randolph broke ranks with Jefferson and urged that the privateer be sent away. The crucial opinion was Washington's, and the president agreed with his attorney general. In fact, Washington was ready to go further. Soon after the cabinet meeting, Jefferson had the duty of reporting the president's decision to Genet: all French privateers commissioned in the United States must be withdrawn from American ports in order to preserve American neutrality. Once again, the secretary of state had found himself conveying a policy he personally opposed.[34]

5
"Our common enemies are trying to dampen American zeal for liberty."
—Edmond Genet, May 1793

ON MAY 22, Edmond Genet began what became a steady flow of correspondence to Jefferson that revealed French determination to shape American foreign policy. In this opening salvo, Genet proposed a redirection of American trade and a major change in the management of American debt. The French government, he wrote, had decided to bolster American trade revenue by drawing "the greatest part of the subsistence and stores necessary for the armies, fleets and colonies of the French republic from the US." This was, of course, a transparent attempt to portray French need as French generosity. The funds for these purchases, however, were to come from the money America owed to France. Genet was demanding a change in the payment arrangement: America must fully liquidate its Revolutionary War debt rather than continue to make fixed annual payments. As Genet saw it, this proposed change operated more to the benefit of the United States than to France: it would enrich American citizens, raise the value of their products and their land, and break what he characterized as England's stranglehold on the American economy. These proposals were couched in a rhetoric that would become painfully familiar to Jefferson. "It is time, Sir," Genet told the secretary of state, "that this commercial revolution, which I consider as the completion of your immortal political revolution, should accomplish itself in a solid manner; and France appears to me to be the only power which can operate this incalculable good."[35]

If Genet expected instant compliance, he was destined to be disappointed. Clearly impatient, he followed this letter with another rhetorically rich missive on May 23, in which he explained the urgency and the righteousness of his request. France, he wrote, stood alone "against innumerable hordes of tyrants and slaves who menace her rising liberty." In such a dire situation, the French nation had the right to claim the obligations to assist France imposed on the United States by the treaties of 1778. France, he reminded Jefferson, had cemented those treaties with its blood. "But at a time when our common enemies are trying to dampen American zeal for liberty," his own country sought to increase American prosperity and add to the happiness of the American people. Although the "perfidious ministers of despotism"—that is, England—have tried to stop the progress of commerce between France and America, they have failed. Instead, the French Republic has opened all her ports in Europe and in the Caribbean to American vessels, granting them all the favors French citizens enjoy. Echoing his earlier speeches to cheering Philadelphia crowds, Genet declared his mission was to establish "a true family compact" between the two nations.[36]

Genet's radical demands and his claims to shared revolutionary goals were likely to increase the tensions between Federalists and the Republican opposition. But his rhetorical excess was not the Republicans' only problem; far more serious was the fact that the attacks on the president in the partisan press were increasing Washington's hostility to the Republican camp. Washington had little experience with this sort of criticism. It is true that, during the Revolution, his military abilities had been called into question by some generals and by members of Congress, but his personal and his political integrity had always been widely admired and praised. Now, however, he suffered not only criticism but wild accusations.

In late May, Washington unleashed his anger on the partisan press—and, by implication, the Republican Party—in a tense meeting with Jefferson. The president, who normally kept his temper under tight control, was clearly livid at the claims in Republican newspapers that a monarchical plot was afoot within his administration. Jefferson's notes on the meeting left little doubt of the president's mounting anger. The charge, Washington declared, was absurd. If anybody actually wanted to turn the US government into a monarchy, he was certain it was only a few individuals. More to the point, no man in the United States would set himself against it more strongly than he. The rise of an American monarchy was not his worry, Washington told his secretary of state; he was far more concerned about the social and political anarchy that could result from the constant criticism of the administration in newspapers like Philip Freneau's *National Gazette.*

The conversation was particularly uncomfortable for Jefferson. For Washington knew Jefferson had put Freneau on the State Department payroll as a translator. That this was a sinecure for the poet-turned-propagandist was obvious: Freneau knew no foreign language other than French, a language Jefferson needed no help with at all. It was not hard to guess that Washington wanted Freneau fired, but Jefferson would not comply. Without the government salary, Freneau could not afford to continue as the editor of the *Gazette.* "I will not do it," Jefferson wrote in his notes, for Freneau's paper "has saved our constitution which was galloping fast into monarchy." The president, Jefferson concluded, was simply not aware that the Monocrats, as the Republicans called Federalist leaders like Hamilton, *were* plotting to take over or he would realize the public service the *Gazette* provided. Although the paper had allowed "some bad things" to appear, the good it had served far outweighed them.

Nothing Jefferson could say, however, would persuade the president that Hamilton and other staunch Federalists were wrong in believing that the greatest danger to the Republic came from the president's critics and opponents here at home.[37]

As unsettling as the conversation with the president had been, Jefferson needed to turn his attention to the foreign problem who called himself Citizen Genet. On May 27, the French minister wrote a long and rather remarkable response to the complaints and concerns Jefferson had outlined in his May 15 letter to Ternant. He dismissed several out of hand but devoted considerable time to the question of America's treaty obligations to France. His reading of the terms of the Treaty of Commerce of 1778 left America no legitimate right to regulate the traffic of French war vessels and their prizes into and out of American ports. That treaty, he declared, "authorizes exclusively all the vessels of war French or American, armed by the two states or by individuals, to conduct freely, wherever they please the prizes they shall have made of their enemies." It was the "wherever they please" part that the Washington administration did not accept. Genet then elaborated on the privileges he believed the treaty extended to France when its ships brought a prize into an American port. They were free to enter "without being subjected either to admiralty or any other duties . . . or . . . stopped or seized, or the officers of the places being permitted to take cognizance of the validity of said prizes." With that, Genet swept away the authority of American customs collectors and the jurisdiction of American admiralty courts.

Genet was not finished. The privileges he described in this letter were exclusive to France; no other nation enjoyed them. "We alone," he declared, "have at present the right of bringing our prizes into the American ports, and of there doing with them as we please." In effect, Genet was setting himself up as the arbiter of American foreign policy.

Never inclined to restraint and often ready to boast, Genet went on to report the success of the privateers he had commissioned at Charleston. These ships, he noted, have "condemned to inaction, by the terrour which they have spread among the English, all the sailors and vessels, of that nation, which were in the ports of the United States."

Had the granting of these commissions in Charleston encroached on American sovereignty? Genet was confident they had not. The vessels armed and commissioned at Charleston belonged to French citizens. They were commanded and manned by Frenchmen or by Americans who, at the time, were subject to no restrictions by the Washington administration. The Proclamation of Neutrality had come too late to challenge what occurred in Charleston that April, he declared—and, anyway, Washington's policy of neutrality had no real authority to prevent such things from happening again, as it did not supersede or abrogate the 1778 treaties.

Genet ended his letter with assurances that the French, "collectively and individually . . . will seize every occasion of showing to the sovereign people of the United States their respect for their laws." And with that, Genet was finally done.[38]

6

"No one has a right to shackle our operations."
—Edmond Genet to Thomas Jefferson,
June 8, 1793

IN HIS SPIRITED defense of French rights, Genet had almost casually mentioned that the crews of the privateers in question had included American seamen. One of these Americans was a sailor named Gideon Henfield, who at the time of Genet's writing was being held by Pennsylvania authorities. In a brief note, written on the same day, Genet demanded that Jefferson use his good offices to have Henfield released immediately. Then, on June 1, before Jefferson could respond to either of the May 27 letters, Genet sent a second request for the release of Henfield. This time he mentioned a second American, John Singletary, as a victim of injustice, but Singletary would soon disappear from Philadelphia and thus escape any legal proceedings. In language that suggested he was highly agitated, Genet described the charge against these men as a "crime which my mind cannot conceive, and which my pen almost refuses to state . . . the serving of France, and defending with her children the common and glorious cause of liberty."[39]

Who was Gideon Henfield—and how had he come to serve as a French officer? The Massachusetts-born seaman had signed aboard the aptly named *Citoyen Genet,* one of the privateers commissioned by the French minister in Charleston. He had participated in the capture on the Delaware River of the *William,* a Scottish merchant vessel, and, when he arrived in Philadelphia as the ship's prize master, he was arrested by local authorities. Henfield's actions were a direct challenge to the president's neutrality policy regarding the participation of individual American citizens in the war. But the case raised a diplomatic as well as a domestic issue for the United States: France had defied American neutrality by attacking and capturing a British ship in American waters.

Jefferson informed Genet that he had forwarded all correspondence on the Henfield matter to the president. He had also asked Attorney General Randolph for his legal opinion, which he enclosed. Jefferson then summarized the situation: as Henfield was in the custody of the civil magistrate, the matter was outside the jurisdiction of the executive branch. The law would take its due course: "The act with which he is charged will be examined by a Jury of his Countrymen, in the presence of Judges of learning and integrity, and if it is not contrary to the laws of the land, no doubt need be entertained that his case will issue accordingly." Put another way, autonomous American legal procedures could not be violated.[40]

On June 5, Jefferson turned to the larger diplomatic issue raised by the Henfield case. His letter to Genet that day was carefully worded and had been read and revised by Randolph and Hamilton. Jefferson began by reminding Genet that the president had determined that "the arming and equipping of vessels in the Ports of the United States to cruise against nations with whom we are at peace, was incompatible with the territorial sovereignty of the United States." The president had therefore ordered the departure of such vessels from American ports; in his words, their exit would prove a "proper reparation to the Sovereignty of the Country." Genet had challenged this decision in his lengthy letter of May 27, but his argument had not persuaded the president or his cabinet. "After fully weighing again however all the principles and circumstances of the case, the result appears still to be that it is the *right* of every nation to prohibit acts of sovereignty from being exercised by any other within its limits; and the *duty* of a neutral nation to prohibit such as would injure one of the warring powers." Jefferson then wrote as plainly and as definitively as possible: "The granting military commissions within the United States by any other authority than their own is an infringement on their Sovereignty, and particularly so when granted to their own citizens, to lead them to commit acts contrary to the duties they owe their own country."[41]

Yet Jefferson may as well have been shouting into the wind. Genet's startling response arrived on June 8. It began with an upbraiding of the president, who, in Genet's words, "persists in thinking that a nation at war had not the right of giving commissions of war to those of its vessels which may be in the ports of a neutral nation." Such thinking, Genet insisted, was simply wrong. But Washington was more than wrong. Genet declared the president had overstepped his authority by attempting to enforce his erroneous interpretation of French rights in America. That authority, Genet insisted, belonged to Congress alone. Unless Congress prohibited these actions by France, "no one has a right to shackle our operations." Nevertheless, in the interest of maintaining "good harmony" between the United States and France, Genet had instructed his consuls in the port cities to grant letters of marque only to the captains of these ships. These captains would give oaths to protect the territory of the United States "and the political opinions of their President, until the representatives of the sovereign shall have confirmed or rejected them." With this, Genet had pronounced Congress the only branch of government entitled to express the people's sovereign will and had reduced the president's proclamation and his decisions regarding the arming of ships in American ports to a "political opinion" rather than a legitimate state policy.

Genet ended his letter with a standard Girondin flourish. "Every obstruction by the government of the United States, to the arming of French vessels, must be an attempt on the rights of man, upon which repose the independence and laws of the United States." He wished that the federal government shared the people's sentiments and that it would give the world an example of true neutrality, "which does not consist in the cowardly abandonment of their friends in the moment when danger menaces them."[42]

Hamilton wasted no time in informing George Hammond of Genet's defiance of American neutrality. In reporting the news to his superiors, Hammond characterized Genet's language as "offensive and intemperate" and accused the Frenchman of making "some direct menaces." The British minister was eager to learn how Washington would respond to Genet's "singular performance" and to discover what measures the president intended to pursue in response. But Genet's rudeness was not Hamilton's main concern. Instead, he wanted to assure Hammond that the United States would not give in to the request that the Treasury pay the full debt owed to France rather than continue its payment in annual installments. Nor would the Treasury convey upcoming installments earlier than they were due. Genet needed these funds badly to purchase supplies from American sources and had tried to pressure Hamilton into complying by refusing to pay the outstanding bills from American suppliers. The French minister hoped that this would embarrass the administration into acceding to his demands. Washington, however, refused to be intimidated. Instead, Hamilton later told Hammond, the merchants holding the bills would have to wait.[43]

Genet's demands had only deepened Hamilton's hostility both to him and to the government of France. But Genet would not be subjected to Hamilton's anger, for it was the secretary of state's duty to give him the bad news. On June 11, Jefferson wrote to the French minister, explaining that full payment would far exceed the ordinary resources of the United States. To buttress his point, Jefferson enclosed the recent Treasury report. Jefferson assured Genet that America's fiscal policies were designed to enable the United States to pay its debts "with punctuality and good faith." Making this defense of the Hamiltonian system must have been painful for Jefferson, who had opposed every element in it. The news was equally painful to Genet, who had applied most of his available funds to his various projects—including arming privateers and attempting to mount expeditions against Spanish territories—and was now desperate to complete the purchases of American produce needed in France.[44]

By early June, Jefferson seemed exhausted, as much by the tensions within the cabinet as by the demands of his office. Writing to the American minister in France, Gouverneur Morris, on June 13, he lamented the impact of the European war on the administration. "Questions respecting chiefly France and England," he observed, "fill the Executive with business, equally delicate, difficult and disagreeable." The course of strict neutrality dissatisfied both Republicans and Federalists, he added, but the president remained adamant that this policy must be enforced.[45]

Washington, too, was weary, worn down by criticisms of his neutrality policy. A long letter from Henry Lee, written on June 14, must have raised his spirits, however. Despite the newspaper attacks on neutrality, Lee was convinced that nine-tenths of Americans applauded the policy and felt increasing gratitude and love for their president. As for Washington's critics, Lee allowed that only a stranger could assume widespread opposition and only if he gathered his information in taverns where "wicked & abandoned" men assembled to drink and gamble the night away. Lee described his own encounter with Edmond Genet. He had done his best to convince the Frenchman of the benefits that would accrue to France from American neutrality. Given the superiority of the British fleet, he had argued, neutrality was the only way America could ensure the delivery of provisions to France. Lee had also assured Genet that the president preferred the interests of France to those of all other parties, a claim that was now far from true. But, with no fleet, no army, and no money to authorize participation in the war, he explained that Washington was limited in the assistance he could provide. Genet's response was to warn that if royal government were reestablished in France, the kings of Europe would combine to destroy American liberty. Genet's message was clear: America's destiny was linked to the destiny of the French Republic.[46]

The most immediate danger to those linked destinies was Genet himself. He had already insulted Washington, a man highly sensitive to criticism and attacks on his integrity. Then, on June 14, Genet sent two blustering letters to Jefferson that did not improve his relationship with anyone in the administration. The first was a response to the news that the debt to his country would not be paid in full. It began abruptly: "It is the character of elevated minds, of freemen, not to expose themselves twice to a refusal." He had made clear the needs of his country; without sufficient produce from America, both the million Frenchmen in arms and the people of the French colonies would suffer "the horrours of famine." By its decision, the United States would assist the king of England and his fellow monarchs in destroying the French nation by starvation. Because the president had refused Genet's every proposal regarding payment of the debt, the French minister now asked that the secretary of the treasury be ordered to immediately recalculate the total amount of the American debt to France. The letter ended with a vague threat: he would have no recourse but to put in motion an "expedient . . . onerous to the French nation."[47]

The second letter returned to the issue of the treaties and the right they gave France—as Genet interpreted them—to sell prize ships and to arm and send out privateers from American ports. He reported that, in Philadelphia, civil and judiciary officers of the United States had stopped the sale of vessels and, in New York, they had prevented the sailing of a vessel commissioned by the Executive Council of the Republic of France. Jefferson, he declared, should inform the president that these officials had committed the infractions against the laws and treaties in his name. The president, he insisted, must intercede to defend "the interests, the rights and the dignity of the French nation" against the pro-English faction within his government.[48]

Genet's conviction that a pro-English faction was "labouring secretly" against France and its minister resonated with Jefferson's own belief in a conspiracy by members of the "Anglomancy" to establish a monarchy in America. Genet made the mistake, however, of assuming that the two men were natural and firm allies and that their political agendas must be complementary, if not identical. But the danger Jefferson saw was domestic; it was not the downfall of France but the destruction of the American Republic by men like Hamilton that he hoped to prevent. Although Jefferson was ready to assist France, he was not prepared to lead the United States into a disastrous war with Great Britain. Later, when at last Genet realized that Jefferson would not advocate unequivocal support for the French cause, he would conclude bitterly that the secretary of state had pretended friendship but all along had intended betrayal.[49]

On June 17, 1793, Washington called his cabinet together to discuss the question of French privateers. A letter from British minister George Hammond lent the meeting an air of urgency, for Hammond pointedly asked whether two privateers were going to be allowed to return to a US port or send their prizes to American ports for sale. Hammond complained that one of the ships, the *Sans Culottes,* still remained at Baltimore, watching for any movement of a British ship that was also there. The cabinet reassured Hammond that these vessels had been ordered to return to French territory and that the government expected their speedy departure.[50]

Jefferson turned to the task of explaining to Genet the differences between vessels armed for defense against the aggression of an enemy and those armed, equipped, and manned in the United States "for the purpose of committing hostilities on nations at peace with the United States." It was this latter practice that prompted the administration to issue orders to all the states and ports to ban the arming of privateers. He reminded Genet that he had addressed this matter in an earlier letter of June 5, in which he had clearly stated the opinion of the president. Washington's opinion, Jefferson added, was not, as Genet continued to insist, contrary to the principles of natural law, the usage of nations, the engagements which unite the two people, nor the president's own Proclamation of Neutrality.[51]

The following day, Genet returned to the topic of money—and the hardships caused by the administration's refusal to pay the debt in full. Because the United States had not met his demands, his only option was to refuse to pay his American creditors. The US government would have to do so. This time, Hamilton drafted the curt reply for Jefferson: pay your debts. When Genet refused, the cabinet took it upon itself to do the only thing it could to remedy the situation: it approved Hamilton's proposal that the federal Treasury pay all the suspended bills out of the September 1793 installment on the debt due to France. Hamilton had stared down Genet—and won.[52]

7

"[Genet] has threatened to appeal from The
President of The United States to the People."
—Alexander Dallas reporting to Thomas Mifflin,
July 6, 1793

GENET WAS CONVINCED that the president was intentionally thwarting his mission, and he did not have to look far to discover Washington's motive: jealousy. Writing to Paris on June 19, he complained that "the old man Washington, who differs greatly from the one whose name history has recorded, does not forgive my success and the enthusiasm with which the whole city precipitated itself after me." Consumed with envy, Washington had determined to "hinder my business in a thousand ways and forces me secretly to urge the assembly of Congress."[53]

But the French minister was undaunted. Three days after Jefferson had essentially warned him to abandon his course of retaliatory action, Genet once again expressed his disappointment and anger over the behavior of the American government in the matter of two of the detained privateers. "Let us explain ourselves as republicans," he urged Jefferson. "Let us not lower ourselves as ancient politicks by diplomatic subtleties." In his mind, the secretary had resorted to sophistry in the interpretation of French rights in the treaties of 1778. Jefferson's reasoning was "extremely ingenious" but unacceptable, because arguments based on what he insisted on calling "the private or publick opinions of the President of the United States," or the opinions of such experts on international law as the Swiss philosopher Emer de Vattel, were no excuse for ignoring the obligations set by those treaties. The Washington administration showed no gratitude for France's generosity and no respect for its own Constitution. Washington had not waited until Congress—the branch of government that expressed the people's sovereign will—could make its decision on the nature of Franco-American relations. As Genet saw it, Washington and his cabinet had done little but present him with "multiplied difficulties and embarrassments" at every turn. Was this what the American people desired? Genet was certain it was not. Jefferson chose not to respond to Genet's tirade with yet another defense of American neutrality.[54]

IT WAS AS clear to the French and the British ministers as it was to the beleaguered secretary of state that America simply did not have the ability to enforce its rules. Although France was the greater offender, Britain too continued to capture enemy vessels in American territorial waters and fit them out as privateers in American ports. Sometimes this was done surreptitiously, sometimes it was done in open defiance of American policy. Sometimes ships belonging to both countries escaped seizure by the US authorities by sailing away before action could be taken. Thus, despite the repeated declarations to Hammond and Genet that the US government did not allow the commissioning, equipping, or manning of vessels in American ports to cruise against any of the belligerents in the European war the practice continued. It was proving easier for the American government to establish rules than to enforce them when the bureaucracy was cumbersome, the personnel inadequate, and the belligerents sneaky.

Matters came to a head in early July. On April 17, a British merchant ship, the *Little Sarah,* had been captured in American waters by Genet's old flagship, the *Embuscade,* and brought into port at Philadelphia. Despite clear warnings against arming a privateer in an American port, the French minister allowed the *Little Sarah* to be transformed into the *Petite Democrate,* arming it so that it could accompany the *Embuscade* to New Orleans as naval support for Genet's planned offensive against the Spanish territory of Louisiana. The administration had not learned of the *Little Sarah* affair until late June. On June 22, Governor Thomas Mifflin forwarded to the president a report by the port's master warden, who suspected the ship was being outfitted as a French privateer. At Washington's behest, Henry Knox asked Mifflin to inform the president promptly of any armaments being added to the vessel. But Mifflin, who was often loath to cooperate with the Federalist president and his administration, soon reported that nothing at all suspicious was occurring. At the time, the president was at Mount Vernon, and no one in the administration replied to the governor. Hearing nothing, Mifflin was content to let the matter drop. But, on July 5, Alexander Hamilton informed Jefferson and Knox that the outfitting of the *Little Sarah* was, in fact, well advanced. Faced with Hamilton's implicit criticism, Mifflin decided not to deny this was true. Instead, he asked whether he should detain the vessel.[55]

Before the cabinet had time to reply, the situation took on crisis proportions. On the evening of July 6, Alexander Dallas, a loyal supporter of the Republican opposition and secretary of the state of Pennsylvania, learned that the *Little Sarah* was preparing to sail the next morning. Mifflin decided to call out a militia detachment to prevent the ship's departure, even at the risk of hostilities between the ship's crew and the militiamen. Dallas persuaded the governor to wait until he met with Genet; perhaps he could persuade the French minister to keep the ship in port until the president had time to rule on whether American neutrality had been violated.

The late-night meeting between Dallas and Genet went badly. From the beginning, Genet was combative and uncooperative. He defended his right to transform the *Little Sarah* into a privateer and refused to delay its sailing. He denounced the federal government's hostility toward the French Republic and swore to meet force with force if the militia tried to prevent the ship's departure. And, in a dramatic escalation of his defiance, Genet announced he would vindicate his actions by appealing directly to the American people over the head of the president. Dallas reported the conversation to Mifflin. The governor was, of course, no friend to Washington or the Federalists, but he was not willing to aid a foreigner in breaking federal law. He sent out the call to a unit of the militia. He then conveyed an urgent message to Jefferson and Knox, explaining the situation and asking for their guidance.[56]

Haunted by the vision of a violent confrontation on the docks of Philadelphia, Jefferson decided to meet with Genet himself. On July 7, the two men talked, and Jefferson walked away believing that Genet had pledged the ship would not sail until the president returned to Philadelphia and considered the case. No doubt relieved, Mifflin disbanded the militia unit. But the incident persuaded Jefferson of the futility of establishing or sustaining a reasonable relationship with Citizen Genet. On the same day as his meeting with the Frenchman, he vented his anger—and frank amazement—at Genet's behavior. "Never in my opinion," he wrote to James Madison, "was so calamitous an appointment made, as that of the present minister of F. here. Hotheaded, all imagination, no judgment, passionate, disrespectful & even indecent towards the P. in his written as well as verbal communications, talking of appeals from him to Congress, from them to the people, urging the most unreasonable & groundless propositions, & in the most dictatorial style." He added that Genet "renders my position immensely difficult."[57]

Washington did not return to the capital until July 11, but Knox, Hamilton, and Jefferson considered it necessary to meet on July 8. In preparation for this rump cabinet meeting, Hamilton and Knox had composed a long memorandum on the *Little Sarah* crisis. It was, in effect, an indictment of Edmond Genet, laid out in thirteen sections.

The president, they noted, had made it clear that the fitting out of privateers in US ports was not permitted. Thus, the French representatives in America who defied the president's policy had committed a "gross outrage upon and an undisguised contempt of the Government of the US." They saw Genet's continued noncompliance as a tactic to force the United States into the war and as a concerted effort to control the American government itself. They were appalled by Genet's memorial of June 22, calling it "the most offensive paper, perhaps, that ever was offered by a foreign Minister to a friendly power with which he resided." They resented his imputation that the president harbored ill will toward France and was "under the instigation of foreign influence." They were insulted by his suggestion that the president had gone beyond his authority. And they were shocked by Genet's audacity in threatening to appeal to Congress, if not to the people themselves. He had, they now knew, declared this as his intent in his meeting with Alexander Dallas. Genet's refusal to firmly assure that the *Little Sarah/Petite Democrate* would not sail until the president had made his determination was, in their view, "an additional high-handed contempt of the Government."

In this memorandum, Hamilton and Knox insisted that the government must act immediately. Indecision would sacrifice the dignity and the essential interests of the nation, but more than this it would "destroy, both at home and abroad, a due respect for the government . . . and ultimately . . . put the country in the condition of being dictated to by that foreign Agent." Would there be repercussions from France if the US government acted decisively to enforce its policy? The two cabinet members insisted that France could not reasonably complain about an action that was "merely a vindication of our own sovereignty." The greater risk was that inaction would make the United States *"an instrument of the hostilities of France"* and thus an enemy of Britain.[58]

Hamilton made clear he would not hesitate to use military force to sustain the federal government's authority and sovereignty in the face of French contempt. At the cabinet meeting, he pressed for the creation of a battery on Mud Island, which sits on the Delaware River below Philadelphia. The battery was to be manned by militia who would be under orders to arrest and prevent the *Little Sarah* from departing American territorial waters. When Secretary of War Henry

Knox quickly concurred with Hamilton, the decision was made. The time for firm action had arrived.[59]

Jefferson demurred, however. In a minority opinion written that day, he explained his opposition to the creation of the Mud Island battery. He remained convinced that Genet would keep the ship in harbor until the president returned to the capital. But if construction of the battery began, the French minister might change his mind. And if the crew of the vessel found guns ready to fire on it, it was "morally certain that bloody consequences would follow." This would be catastrophic, especially because twenty French warships, along with more than one hundred privateers, were expected to arrive momentarily in New York harbor. Better to allow the ship to leave port than to risk war with France.

Jefferson's reasoned argument could not mask his fierce opposition to any action that would aid Britain, which he still saw as a more serious threat to American sovereignty. He offered the standard Republican argument: the English, he argued, have armed their ships with far more of our guns than the two cannon allegedly added to the *Little Sarah*. If the rumor was true that fifteen to twenty Americans have joined the crew of this privateer "with their own consent," it was also true, he contended, that the English had forcibly taken ten times that number from American merchant ships at sea. He described the situation in broad terms: "It is inconsistent, for a nation which has been patiently bearing for ten years the grossest insults and injuries from their late enemies, to rise at a feather against their friends and benefactors." He would not—could not—agree to "gratify the combination of kings with the spectacle of the two only republics on earth destroying each other for two cannon." France could commit no abuse of neutrality great enough to justify American support for England. The United States must not "turn the scale of contest, and let it be from our hands that the hopes of man receive their last stab."[60]

Two days later, Jefferson reconstructed the conversation he had with Genet on the evening of July 7. In edited form, this account was ultimately sent to the president. In it he reported Genet's outbursts to Dallas and to him but stopped short of reporting any threat by Genet to go directly to the people with his complaints. He had taken the opportunity to patiently explain the structure of the federal government to Genet. The executive branch conducted all diplomacy, and although Congress was sovereign in making laws, the executive was sovereign in the execution of those laws. When Genet insisted that Congress was responsible for seeing that treaties were observed, Jefferson had corrected him. This was the president's responsibility and the Constitution made the president the court of final appeal. Genet was astonished. He said he had "never before . . . had such an idea." Jefferson had continued with his lesson in sovereignty—and diplomacy. Each party to a treaty had the right, he told Genet, to interpret the terms of that treaty as it saw fit. If Genet disagreed with America's interpretation, his only recourse was to raise the issue with his own government. In the meantime, he must acquiesce in the administration's decisions. Finally, Jefferson had warned Genet that it would be a serious offense if the vessel in question departed before the president's return. Genet appeared to understand, Jefferson told the president, and agreed to keep the ship in port.[61]

8

"Is the Minister of the French Republic to set the Acts of this Government at defiance—*with impunity?*"
—George Washington to Thomas Jefferson,
July 11, 1793

JEFFERSON'S EFFORTS TO educate Genet were in vain. On July 9, the French minister sent the secretary of state a brief note on the *Little Sarah*. He made no effort to deny arming the vessel, nor did he attempt to justify the decision to do so. The ship was solidly built; it was a "swift sailer"; it would be an advantageous addition to the French naval force. Therefore, he had ordered it repaired, completed its armament with cannon he claimed to have found on board four French vessels, manned it with French sailors—and readied a commission for it. There were no grounds for further discussion, Genet added, for "when treaties speak, the agents of nations have but to obey."[62]

A second letter followed on the same day. Ignoring the possibility that an aggressive stance might not aid his cause—or simply blind to the consequences—Genet went on the offensive. The consul at

Philadelphia, he informed Jefferson, had requested that the governor of Pennsylvania order out of port a British ship, the *Jane,* on the grounds that it had shown no signs of distress to justify its docking there. The governor, however, replied that he could take no action during the president's absence from the city. Genet disagreed. Citing article XXII of the Treaty of Amity, he insisted that it was not necessary to await a decision of the president. The American people, he declared, consider these treaties "as the most sacred laws." He was therefore requesting that Jefferson order the governor to perform the duties "our treaties impose on him."[63]

On Washington's return to Philadelphia two days later, he learned that the cabinet decision to build a battery was moot. Genet had ordered the *Little Sarah* relocated south of the capital, out of range of Mud Island. Washington read the correspondence forwarded to him, including reports from others that Genet had threatened to appeal over the president's head to the people. Washington's response was to fire off an angry note to his secretary of state. "What," the president demanded, "is to be done in the case of the *Little Sarah,* now at Chester? Is the Minister of the French Republic to set the Acts of this Government at defiance—*with impunity?* And then threaten the Executive with an appeal to the People. What must the world think of such conduct, and of the Government of the U. States in submitting to it?" Washington's anger and frustration were directed as much at Jefferson as at Genet. He demanded Jefferson's opinion on how to proceed before the next day.[64]

Genet was not the only minister registering complaints. Hammond had written, reporting French infractions regarding the outfitting of privateers. Faced with a variety of charges and countercharges from the ministers of France and England, the president and his cabinet decided to seek the opinion of the judiciary. Until the justices tendered their opinion, Washington expected both Genet and Hammond to refrain from sending any of the ships in dispute out to sea. The *Little Sarah,* the *Jane* and the *William,* the *Citoyen Genet* and its two prizes, the *Lovely Lass* and *Prince William Henry,* along with the brig *Fanny* were to remain in port until "persons learned in the law" had advised the president.[65]

Jefferson had little expectation that this moratorium would hold. As he told James Madison in a letter of July 14, "I am excessively afraid that an open rupture will take place between the Fr. min. & us. I think there has been something to blame on both sides, but much more on his." Jefferson knew the Federalists had already begun to take political advantage of Genet's outrageous behavior by issuing newspaper appeals to the people to stand by the president. "They know too well that the whole game is played into their hands, & that there is right enough on both sides to marshal each nation with its own agents, and consequently against one another." The only winners, Jefferson feared, would be the American monarchists and their beloved Great Britain. Madison could do little but sympathize. Genet "must be brought right if possible," he wrote on July 18. "His folly will otherwise do mischief which no wisdom can repair."[66]

Jefferson at last vented his frustrations at Genet in a long letter addressed to the Frenchman, written on July 16. He dismissed the claim that French consuls had jurisdiction over prizes brought into American ports. Every nation, he wrote, has a natural right to exclusive jurisdiction over the territory it occupies, and every nation has a right to preserve peace, to punish acts that breach that peace, and to restore property taken by force within its own limits. He declared Genet's assertion that the president should not have made several decisions without congressional approval both presumptuous and incorrect. The executive "is the sole organ of our communications with foreign governments," and agents of those governments "are not authorized to judge what cases are to be decided by this or that department." Genet's claim that the will of the people differed from the will of the president was equally wrong. The French minister may have come to this conclusion by listening to men neither qualified to speak nor authorized to pronounce on the subject. Better to look closely at the Constitution, Jefferson said, for here you will find that the people freely give the president the power to execute his office as he thinks wisest and best. For Jefferson, this was an unrestrained tirade; having written it, he chose, probably wisely, not to send it to Genet.[67]

The cabinet met once again on July 23—and it was here that Genet's fate began to be decided. Although the meeting was ostensibly to discuss money matters raised in several of Genet's letters to Jefferson, the president had something else on his mind: what to do about Citizen Genet himself. The Supreme Court justices had declined to rule on the administration's neutrality policy, so the cabinet alone would need to resolve the problems of enforcement. Washington made clear his own preferred course of action: send the entire correspondence with the French minister to Gouverneur Morris, the American minister in France, and instruct Morris to request Genet's recall. Washington thought that the request should be cushioned by declarations of friendship to the French nation and assurances that the American government distinguished between Genet and his nation.

Hamilton, according to Jefferson's notes on this meeting, did not want the request made with such sensitivity; in his view, the president should make a firm demand. Hamilton was well aware of the propaganda value in revealing Genet's insults to the public, and so he also urged Washington to lay the entire correspondence before the American people, who must be informed of the many crises Genet had generated. Otherwise, they might come under the sway of those "incendiaries" who hoped to see the federal government overthrown.[68]

Hamilton had already begun to warn the public about the danger the young nation faced. Writing as "Pacificus," he had published a series of essays in Federalist newspapers arguing that the objections to the president's right to issue the Proclamation of Neutrality were unfounded and had been put forward by American opponents of the Washington administration as well as by French officials. By July 31, he would begin another essay series, this one entitled "No Jacobin." In the opening sentence of the first essay, he exposed the rumor that Hamilton himself knew to be fact: Genet *"has threatened to appeal from The President of The United States to the People."*[69]

During the July 23 cabinet meeting, Knox concurred with all of Hamilton's suggestions. The secretary of war then attempted to stoke the president's ire with examples of incendiary talk among American citizens. He recounted the tale of a woman who had overheard Washington called a great tyrant who would soon need to be chased out of the city. But Washington did not need convincing. Only two days before the meeting, he had confided his concern about the critics of his administration to his friend Henry Lee. Every country had its discontented characters, he wrote, and some of these were motivated by a genuine belief that the government's policies are harmful. But others, he said, are "diabolical." Their intentions were not only to impede the Government but also to "destroy the confidence which it is necessary for the People to place . . . in their public Servants." As for the personal attacks, he insisted, "I care not." He knew that he had neither ambitious nor self-interested motives for his conduct in office. "The arrows of malevolence therefore, however barbed & well pointed, never can reach the most valuable part of me." Yet his close associates knew he did care deeply. Jefferson had seen how profoundly offended and angered Washington was by the criticism from the Republican press. His statement to Lee that "the publications in Freneau's and Beach's [Bache] Papers are outrages on common decency" was more revealing than his claims about his disregard of criticism.[70]

Despite Washington's intense feelings, he was not yet willing to see a public dissemination of Genet's correspondence. And although the president himself had raised the topic of Genet's recall, no final decision appears to have been made. In matters of diplomacy, just as in the handling of domestic disorder, Washington did not want the public to think he was acting precipitously. He had no doubt that Genet would continue his irritating, insulting behavior and that eventually, the people would support the French minister's recall.

9

"He will sink the republican interest if
they do not abandon him."
—Thomas Jefferson to James Madison,
August 3, 1793

THE PRESIDENT WAS disturbed by the criticism he received in the press and by the growing political divisiveness these newspaper attacks reflected. But his frustration also stemmed from the almost daily problem of enforcing a rather nebulous neutrality policy. It was the administration's hope that a test case in the courts would ease, if not solve, this dilemma. That case was brought against Gideon Henfield, the American sailor who, in May, had served as prize master for France on the captured British vessel the *William*. At issue were several questions: How was neutrality defined? How was it to be enforced? Under whose jurisdiction did that enforcement fall? On

July 22, 1793, the Henfield case came before a special session of
the US Circuit Court of Pennsylvania. On July 27, the seaman was
indicted by a grand jury. The indictment, drafted by Edmund Randolph and perhaps amended by Alexander Hamilton, charged Henfield with violating the law of nations and the peace and dignity of
the United States.

The US government was not on the firmest ground in prosecuting Gideon Henfield. There was no congressional act that expressly
forbade an American citizen from enlisting in a foreign service when
the United States was at peace. But Randolph had been adamant
from the beginning: Henfield was indictable under federal law for
serving on the privateer and for participating in the capture of the
William because these actions violated the American treaties guar-
anteeing peace with Britain as well as the Netherlands and Prussia.
These treaties, Randolph declared, were the supreme law of the land.
Henfield's actions were also indictable under common law because
they disturbed the peace in the United States.

When the government first raised the issue of Henfield's enlist-
ment in the French navy Genet had fiercely defended the American's
right to volunteer. Henfield, he told Jefferson, was guilty of nothing
more than "embracing the cause supported by the United States,"
and, for that reason, the Massachusetts sailor deserved the support
and protection of the French Republic. Genet had decided to provide
that support in the form of three skilled lawyers. Peter Stephen Du
Ponceau was a French philosopher and jurist who had immigrated
to the American colonies in 1777 and had served in the Continental
Army during the Revolutionary War. Jared Ingersoll was a signer of
the Constitution, a man with a reputation as a very able lawyer who
spoke well and understood his subject thoroughly. The third in this
impressive triumvirate was Jonathan Dickinson Sergeant, a New
Jersey political leader and attorney who had moved to Philadelphia
in 1777.

The prosecutor, District Attorney William Rawle, argued to the
jury that Henfield's actions threatened reprisals from the nations at
war with France and violated the federal government's exclusive right
to wage war. Henfield's attorneys conceded that he had committed
the acts he was accused of but argued that he had done so after
he renounced his American citizenship by entering French service.

Furthermore, they argued, his actions had taken place before the president's proclamation was issued, and the US treaty with France did not forbid an American citizen from enlisting in French service. In his charge to the jury, Supreme Court justice James Wilson upheld the prosecution's contentions, but the jury refused to convict. On July 29, Gideon Henfield was acquitted on all counts. The decision stunned and embarrassed members of the cabinet and the prosecution. Genet, of course, hailed the acquittal as a vindication of his right to enlist Americans in the service of his country.[71]

The acquittal of Henfield forced the cabinet to make a series of individual judgments on the various cases pending. It also prompted it to at last set down a clear set of rules that would identify what was—and what was not—allowed to belligerents whose ships came into US ports. By August 3, Hamilton, Knox, and Jefferson were ready to present the president with eight rules, several of which actually showed some bias in favor of France. Once Washington approved these rules, Knox included them in his circular letter to the state governors. Despite this, and despite a congressional act on the subject in June 1794, the problem of defining and enforcing neutrality would continue for two decades.[72]

Genet's vocal and financial support of Henfield was simply the last in a long list of diplomatic missteps by the French minister. Indeed, as August 1793 began, the cabinet seemed determined to see him removed from his post. Throughout the month, it met with the president to discuss Genet's conduct. Hamilton prepared a rough outline of the justification for demanding the minister's recall. He understood, perhaps better than the others, Genet's underlying problem: "If his constructions were right his course was wrong." Genet, in short, was his own worst enemy, alienating those he needed to negotiate with, persisting in practices that clearly offended the administration, and attacking the president's reputation and authority. Genet, so eager to carry out his instructions, was temperamentally and intellectually the wrong man for the job.[73]

Although all members of the cabinet agreed that Genet must be recalled, they still did not agree on the tone or the content of the letter Gouverneur Morris was to present to the French government. Nor did they agree on how confidential their actions should remain. As Jefferson later recalled, a number of proposals were made. The first was that Morris receive a full statement of Genet's conduct and that this letter, along with the French minister's correspondence, should be communicated by him to the Executive Council of France. The cabinet unanimously agreed to this. But then the question of phrasing arose. Here, agreement broke down. Once again Jefferson proposed the demand be expressed "with great delicacy," but Knox and Randolph now supported Hamilton's preference for preemptory terms. Knox went so far as to propose that Genet be sent off immediately, but no one supported this drastic step. The fourth proposal was to inform Genet of the decision to ask for his recall. Jefferson feared this might prompt more recklessness from Genet, but the president and the other three cabinet members approved this proposal. It was the fifth proposal—that the whole correspondence between Genet and Jefferson should be made public—that most starkly illuminated the divide between Republicans and Federalists in the administration. Hamilton made what Jefferson described as an inflammatory and declamatory "jury speech" in favor of the publishing of these documents. Randolph immediately opposed the idea. Jefferson remained silent on the issue until the following day, when, after Hamilton finished a second, long defense of the idea, the secretary of state voiced his opposition.

The president seemed to favor the publication of the correspondence. Once again, Henry Knox played the role of provocateur, hoping to stoke Washington's outrage at his critics by citing a broadside entitled "The Funeral Dirge of George Washington and James Wilson, King and Judge." The poem, said to be the work of the *National Gazette*'s Philip Freneau, described the execution of the president and the Supreme Court justice by the guillotine. Knox's efforts were rewarded with one of the president's rare tirades, which Jefferson described as "one of those passions when he cannot command himself." He was sick of the personal abuse heaped upon him, Washington said, and he defied any man on earth to produce evidence that he had ever acted out of any but the purest motives. "By god," Jefferson recalled him saying, he would "rather be in his grave than in his present situation . . . [or] on his farm than to be made *emperor of the world*." Yet here they were, claiming he wished to be a king. He was furious that Freneau sent him three copies of his paper every day, as if he expected the president to distribute them. This was nothing more than "an impudent design to insult him." When Washington finished, there was a brief and uncomfortable silence in the room. Then, the discussion began again. The president, now calm, declared that he saw no reason to immediately decide whether to publish Genet's letters. He hoped events would make such an appeal to the people unnecessary.[74]

Jefferson now fully understood the threat that continued support of Genet posed to the Republicans. The tide of public opinion, already showing signs of shifting, was certain to turn dramatically if Genet's correspondence were made public. Only a few days earlier, Charles Adams had lamented to his brother, John Quincy, that anyone who ventured to disapprove of a single measure of the French was excoriated as an "Aristocrat." But now Jefferson considered it necessary to advise his fellow Republicans to abandon Genet or "*he will sink the republican interest.*" Jefferson was appalled that the Frenchman had loudly defended his "unfounded pretensions" on the treaty without any knowledge of the opinion of leading legal authorities like Vattel. "His ignorance of everything written on the subject is astonishing," Jefferson told Madison. "I think he has never read a book of any sort in that branch of science." To Jefferson, there were few more damning critiques one could make of a man.[75]

A few days later, Jefferson set about to assuage Washington's fears that Genet and partisans like Freneau were producing a crisis of public confidence in the executive branch and an irreparable political division within American society. He assured the president that Congress would take no radical or irresponsible action when it reconvened in December and that the Republicans in the legislature would abandon Genet the moment they learned of his conduct. The president responded with assurances of his own. He believed, he told his secretary of state, that the motives of the Republicans were "perfectly pure" and that they arose from a sincere belief that a faction existed that was determined to create a monarchy. But, he continued, Jefferson must realize that the president would never support such a plan. Jefferson hurriedly replied that "no rational man in the US suspects you of any other disposition." However, he insisted that not a week passed without declarations from the monarchical party that the federal government was good for nothing, that it was "a milk and water thing that cannot support itself," and that it must be knocked down and replaced with something more energetic. Though apparently certain of the existence of a monarchical plot, Jefferson offered no specific examples to back up this claim.[76]

10
"We stand united and firm."
Gazette of the United States,
August 14, 1793

IT FELL TO Jefferson as secretary of state to draft the letter to Gouverneur Morris for presentation to the French Executive Council. On August 15, Jefferson presented a rough draft to the cabinet meeting. At the August 20 meeting, the letter was read and amended, paragraph by paragraph, before it was finally approved. Hamilton was then instructed to obtain a ship to carry the cover letter and the request for Genet's recall to Morris. On August 23, the letter received the president's final approval, but it would not reach Morris until October 5.[77]

And what was Genet doing while, unknown to him, his fate hung in the balance? Naturally, he was busy pursuing his grand plans to invade Spanish and British American territories. Writing to the French minister of foreign affairs on August 2, Genet outlined his plan of conquest. He would first send the French fleet, which had just arrived in New York, to Canada, where crews of Frenchmen and American volunteers would destroy the British fisheries off the Canadian coast and burn Halifax. Then he would send the ships to capture New Orleans and, with the help of American land forces, liberate the entire Louisiana Territory.[78]

From the beginning, Genet planned to find his American army largely among Kentucky settlers. It was no secret that Kentuckians were angry that Washington's government had failed to negotiate a treaty with Spain to open shipping on the Mississippi River. Indeed, the Whiskey Rebellion, which at that time was growing more threatening, was the best evidence of frontier discontent with the federal government. Genet was certain he could harness this growing unrest for his own ends. He had already acquired a famous volunteer to lead the American troops: the Revolutionary War hero George Rogers Clark.

The tall, red-haired Clark, acclaimed by Americans as the "Conqueror of the Old Northwest" and known as "Long Knife" among the Indian tribes, had, in fact, volunteered his services to Genet earlier in 1793. Writing to Genet on February 5, he praised the French war against the despots of Europe as "the most awful, interesting and solemn . . . that has ever arisen in the world." The wish to join the struggle, he added, was "strong and vivid in my bosom." Clark, however, was no longer the bold warrior of the 1770s. He had fallen on hard times after the war, due in large part to debts incurred when he personally signed for materials needed by his troops. After the war, neither his home state of Virginia nor the federal government proved willing to settle those debts. Angry at being abandoned by these governments and weary of being pursued by creditors, Clark began to drink heavily. By 1793, he was a desperate, almost broken man. Nevertheless, Genet gave Clark the rank of major general in his invasion army.[79]

Jefferson had actually known of Genet's designs since early July. On July 5, the French minister had paid him a personal visit, confiding in him as a private citizen rather than as the secretary of state that he intended to mount a multipronged campaign against Spanish-held territory. He also shared with Jefferson the instructions he had drafted for Andre Michaux, a botanist willing to serve as Genet's recruiting agent in Kentucky. It would fall to Michaux to stir up the French in Louisiana and to link up with discontented Kentuckians willing to join in a march on New Orleans. Even before this meeting, Genet had inquired about the possibility of Jefferson making Michaux a consul to Kentucky, but Jefferson denied the request, explaining that consuls were not permitted in the interior of the country. Jefferson had been happy, however, to write a strong letter of introduction for Michaux to Kentucky governor Isaac Shelby.

Genet's later account of this meeting differed greatly from Jefferson's. Jefferson warned him, he reported in a dispatch to France, that America could not officially participate in the invasion of Louisiana because the government was engaged in negotiations with Spain over use of the Mississippi. But "he gave me to understand that he thought a little spontaneous irruption of the inhabitants of Kentucky into New Orleans could advance matters." Jefferson then gave the French minister the name of a contact in Kentucky who would assist Genet in local recruitment. In Jefferson's account, however, he claimed to have sternly warned Genet that "enticing officers & souldiers [sic] from Kentucky to go against Spain, was really putting a halter about their necks, for that they would assuredly be hung if they commd. hostilities agst. a nation at peace with the U.S." Yet he admitted he had also told the French minister he did not care whether insurrections were incited in Louisiana.[80]

At the end of July, Genet learned that the French fleet had reached New York. As these ships figured prominently in Genet's invasion plans, he was eager to take command of them. He was certain, he wrote in one of his dispatches home, that "the whole city will come to meet me." He was wrong. There was a cheering crowd when he arrived on August 7, and church bells heralded his arrival, but his welcome was eclipsed by a pro-administration rally organized by Federalists. According to Hamilton's friend Robert Troup, the rally was "the most respectable meeting for numbers—character—& property—ever assembled in this City." Federalists, Troup declared, were no longer afraid to show their support for the proclamation and for peace. The beleaguered president must have been heartened by the report that appeared in Philadelphia's *Gazette of the United States* on August 14. "Citizens of all parties, and every class were present," the article noted, adding, "Their unexampled unanimity it is hoped will discourage the few, the very few, turbulent men among us, and cannot fail to instruct foreigners, that however we may disagree in our local politics, we stand united and firm, in our decision to maintain our neutrality, and to support and defend the President of the United States."[81]

While Genet was busy with his grand plans of conquest, Jefferson found his anxiety increasing about the impact of the French minister's impetuous and ill-considered behavior on his Republican Party. He had come to realize the impossibility of rescuing Genet from himself, and now the news of the pro-administration rally in New York confirmed Jefferson's worst fears. He had learned from private sources that Genet's New York welcoming committee was made up of "boys & negroes" and that nine out of ten New Yorkers appeared to be in favor of the proclamation and opposed to the French minister. The people of Philadelphia, once so enthusiastic about Genet, were also turning their backs on him. Given this dramatic change in opinion, Jefferson again warned his fellow Republicans to be wary. He told Madison it was essential for members of the party to approve a policy of neutrality when Congress met once again—and they must "abandon G. entirely." This, Jefferson told his fellow Virginian, is exactly what he had done. "I adhered to him as long as I could have a hope of getting him right," he declared, but "finding at length that the man was absolutely incorrigible, I saw the necessity of quitting a wreck which could not but sink all who should cling to it."[82]

Even Genet was beginning to perceive the shift in public sentiment. On August 12, New York Federalist leaders John Jay and Rufus King published a signed letter in a New York newspaper attesting to the truth of "a report having reached this City from Philadelphia, that Mr. Genet, the French Minister had said he would Appeal to the People from certain decisions of the President." The two had received this information from Hamilton, who had himself received it from Thomas Mifflin. Although Mifflin was a critic of the administration, he had been decidedly upset by Dallas's report of the meeting with Genet about the *Little Sarah*.[83]

On the day the Jay-King testimonial appeared in the New York press, Genet sent a long letter to the president, denying he had ever threatened Washington that he would bring his case to the American people. He knew, however, that "certain persons" had descended to personal abuse in hopes of turning public opinion against him. "It is become necessary, Sir, to dissipate these dark calumnies by truth, and publicity." Toward this end, he proposed that the president make an explicit public declaration that Genet had never intimated to him any intention of appealing to the people. Genet's phrasing was both clever and careful: it was true that he had never directly threatened Washington with an appeal to the people, but if Dallas's account of his meeting with Genet was accurate, the French minister *had* made the threat to someone else.[84]

The president did not reply to Genet's request. Instead, Jefferson sent Genet a brief and formal note, pointing out that "it is not the established course for the diplomatic characters residing here to have any direct correspondence with [the president]. Furthermore, the President did not think it his duty to bear witness against a declaration, whether made to him or to others." A wiser man would have accepted this pointed rebuff. But Genet was not that man. Instead, he gave his letter to the president and Jefferson's reply to a local news-paper, the New York *Diary,* which obliged him by publishing them both on August 21.[85]

Throughout the rest of the month, Hamilton received the wel-come news that, as William Loughton Smith would put it, an "anti-Gallican spirit . . . has lately burst forth." A letter to Jefferson from Robert Gamble of Virginia confirmed that people in that state were alarmed by Genet's insults to the American government. Gamble predicted, "The flame will Spread." Jefferson himself admitted to Madison that support for the president and opposition to Genet was "universal." It was particularly galling to Jefferson to see that the Fed-eralists in his home state had organized several pro-administration public meetings. Virginia Republicans were simply slow to respond, and they were also at a distinct disadvantage when they at last mo-bilized. They could not support Genet or attack the president; they could not criticize the neutrality proclamation. In the end, men like Madison and Monroe drafted resolutions that focused on solidarity with the republicanism of France. They had some success with this approach. In Caroline County local Republicans even managed to pass a resolution that criticized Jay and King as well as Genet. But this was little consolation.[86]

11

"He is abandoned even by his votaries."
—James Madison to James Monroe,
September 15, 1793

IN JULY, GENET had assured his superiors in Paris that the inva-sion of Spanish and British territories would succeed. He had also assured them that the American people supported those invasions "in spite of their stupid government." Yet, by the end of August, that support was vanishing, and Genet's plans were falling apart. The commanders of the French fleet proved uninterested in mounting an attack against Spanish or British territory in America. They preferred to go home. By November the ships were on their way to France rather than Canada or New Orleans. The recruitment of troops in Kentucky had produced few results, in part because Genet's deputy,

Andre Michaux, had never reached the region and in part because Genet's funds had dried up. The French consul in New York, Alexandre Maurice Blanc de Lanautte, Comte d'Hauterive, now dismissed the invasion as a foolish and undiplomatic scheme. Writing in his journal, d'Hauterive privately condemned Genet's military preparations in New York as a blatant insult to American sovereignty. "We have here," he wrote, "supplies of stores, a military hospital, an arsenal, sentinels going and coming, rifles on their shoulders: it is as Mr. Jefferson says, a sovereignty within a sovereignty."[87]

The collapse of his invasion plans and public support were not Genet's biggest problems, however. He did not yet know it, but there had been a regime change in France. The Girondins had been ousted in early June, although the news did not reach the United States until August. In the place of the Girondin leader Jacques Pierre Brissot and his fellow idealists, Maximillian Robespierre's Jacobins now held power. Robespierre believed in the need for a heavy hand in governance. "If the spring of popular government in time of peace is virtue," he declared, "the springs of popular government in revolution are at once *virtue and terror:* virtue, without which terror is fatal; terror, without which virtue is powerless." This philosophy would lead, by September, to the start of massacres in which more than 16,000 French men and women were guillotined and some 25,000 more killed by summary execution.[88]

For two months Genet's dispatches had been going to men decidedly less sympathetic to his efforts in America than were those who had appointed him. While the Girondins had looked outward, eager to wage a war of liberation for all the oppressed of Europe, the Jacobins preferred to stabilize the Revolution within France and to defend their nation from the allied European monarchies. They had no interest in forging a closer brotherhood with the United States; they simply wanted the provisions for their army and their civilian citizens that America could offer. Given this practical agenda, it is not surprising that they frowned on Genet's crusading.

Once the Jacobins began drafting them, government dispatches to Genet took on an unfriendly tone. In his report to the home government on July 31, Genet had blamed his failures on Washington and his cabinet, yet a July 30 dispatch to him from the new minister of foreign affairs, Francois Louis Michel Chemin Deforgues, offered a quite different explanation. Deforgues, who had read both of Genet's earlier reports, insisted that the minister's impulsive behavior and obvious egotism led to his failures. Deforgues was cruelly blunt. He told Genet that his popularity led him to believe "that it depended on you to direct the political operations of this people and to engage them to make common cause with us in spite of their government." The Executive Council of France never authorized him to "exercise proconsular powers in a friendly and allied nation, to undertake a line of conduct without the positive consent of the government and before being recognized by its leaders." Deforgues insisted that Genet's instructions were "directly contrary to this strange interpretation; you are directed to treat with the *government* and not with a *portion of the people,* to be to Congress the organ of the French Republic and not the chief of an American party, to conform scrupulously to the established forms for communication between foreign ministers and the government." But Deforgues was rewriting history, for Genet's instructions had indeed demanded the ends, if not the means, that the French minister had so zealously but unsuccessfully pursued.

Deforgues ended his upbraiding by sweeping away Genet's last excuse for failure. "You say that Washington does not forgive your success and that he impedes your business in a thousand ways. . . . Dazzled by a false popularity you have alienated from you the only man who should be for us the organ of the American people, and if you find your business impeded, you have only yourself to blame." Neither Washington nor Hamilton nor even Jefferson could have put it better.[89]

More criticism followed. In September, a report by the French Committee of Public Safety did not spare Genet: "The giddiness of this minister is the more surprising in that he should have known that only the government, and not the portion of the people that played on his vanity, could procure him the advantages he was charged to solicit." Genet mounted the only defense he could. On October 7, he would write to Deforgues, "Seeing myself abandoned by [Jefferson] on whom we had to count the most . . . seeing that all the decisions of the federal government were opposed to us . . . I took the only course there was left to take. I surrounded myself with the most pronounced republicans, and in the local governments, the

special tribunals of the states, the popular juries, the democratic societies which have formed themselves from north to south in imita-
tion of ours, in the anti-federal gazettes, in all good citizens, in all
men more attached to the social weal of America than to the mer-
cantile interest, in the entire body of the militia, I have found the
most energetic support." It was to no avail; the Jacobins were not
moved to change their opinion.[90]

Deforgues's dispatches did not reach Genet until later in the
fall. However, the French minister's efforts to defend himself suggest he realized the new government would be critical of his failures. What he may not have fully realized was how dramatically the
Jacobin agenda diverged from the one the Girondins laid out in his
instructions. Robespierre and his colleagues did not dream of lib-
erating the French residents of Louisiana. They did not envision a
combined force of Americans and Frenchmen battling the British on
the oceans and making use of the safe harbors of the United States
to arm and repair their ships. They did not want to shame the American government into providing aid and succor, nor did they have any
interest in meddling in the domestic politics of the United States.
Deforgues and his superiors did not want to test the revolutionary
fervor of the American people; they simply wanted a beneficial trade
relationship with Washington's government. In short, much of the
mission Genet had been given by the Girondins had become irrele-
vant. Genet was in the unenviable position of defending his lack of
success in achieving goals no one in power desired.[91]

Genet did attempt to personally play a more cautious hand in
the wake of the Jacobin ascendance. But he allowed his consuls who
served as French representatives in America's major port cities to
serve as his surrogates in aggravating the Washington administration and insulting the sovereignty of the American nation. American
officials responded firmly, upholding the president's directives. In
Boston, the consul, Antoine Charbonnet Duplaine, arrived at the
dock with an armed force and repossessed a vessel taken by the local courts. In something of an understatement, Jefferson told the
US district attorney in Massachusetts, Christopher Gore, that this
was a "daring violation of the laws." As Duplaine had no diplomatic
immunity, Jefferson told Gore that the president wished the consul
arrested. And, in Maryland, the local consul protested a threatened

seizure of French prizes, arguing, as Genet had so often done, that such an action violated French treaties with the United States. He closed his protest by demanding reparations. Governor Thomas Lee replied twice, both times noting that the action taken by his state conformed to instructions from the federal government "in which the interpretation of treaties is exclusively invested." These incidents had unexpected and important benefits for the administration: they encouraged state authorities to support federal policies just as Genet's attacks on the president encouraged American citizens to confirm the authority of their new federal government.[92]

The consuls' total disregard of American sovereignty gave British minister George Hammond an opportunity to assume the role of the innocent and injured party. The contrast between Hammond's and Genet's diplomatic styles became clear in the exchange of letters between the secretary of state and the British minister that September. Hammond expressed concern about the enemy's continuing seizure of British ships in American waters. In a September 4 memorial to Jefferson, he explained that he had, "to this moment," preserved the strictest silence on this matter. Now, however, he conceived it his duty to ask "whether the existence of [these circumstances] has come to the knowledge of the executive government of the United States." Jefferson assured Hammond that the United States was using "*all the means in our power*" to protect and defend the vessels of the three belligerent nations, Sweden, Prussia and France, with whom the United States had treaties. "Though we have no similar Treaty with Great Britain," he added, "it was the opinion of the President that we should use towards that nation the same Rule which . . . was to govern us with the other nations; and even to extend it to captures made *on the high Seas* and brought into our ports, if done by vessels which had been armed within them." Although Hammond surely doubted the efficacy of American enforcement, he chose to send a gracious reply. Should any further captures occur, he wrote, he would see that the evidence needed to substantiate his nation's complaints was obtained. "In the meantime, Sir, I esteem it an act of justice on my part, to offer my testimony to the scrupulous fidelity and vigilance, with which the collectors of the Customs have discharged the duty imposed on them by the President's directions." Without pointing a finger of accusation at the federal government, without any resort to rhetoric, Hammond could be confident he had gotten his point across.[93]

The following day Hammond did, in fact, submit a memorial with supporting evidence of French privateering in American waters. A brigantine had been captured half a mile from the shore of the American coast, but the French consul had prevented the marshal of New York from taking the ship into custody. Hammond smoothly inserted what he characterized as his concern for the American government in the face of repeated assaults on its sovereignty by France. "It would certainly be improper," he wrote, "for the undersigned to offer any observations on the various aggressions on the sovereignty of the United States, which a review of this single case presents—in the particulars of the capture itself—in the extent of the powers arrogated by the pretended tribunal of the French Consul—and in the nature of the threats thrown out by the person representing, in this country, the ruling party of France." Having voiced his solicitude, he closed with a direct challenge, posed artfully as a question: "Whether it be the intention of the executive government of the United States to grant to the French ships of war the permission of an *indefinite* continuance within its ports."[94]

Unlike Hammond, Genet was wholly lacking in this ability to blend, in one letter, a purported concern for America with a demand for action on the government's part. When New York governor George Clinton informed the French minister that the brigantine mentioned in Hammond's memorial must remain in harbor until the president decided its fate, Genet responded with obvious frustration. He had defended—"as long as I was able"—his country's incontestable right to fit out armed vessels in US ports, based on the treaties of 1778. In the face of the president's resistance to that right, he had conformed "as much as was in my power" to Washington's wishes. He could do no more. "It now belongs to my country to direct me what course I am finally to pursue. It belongs to the French nation [to] determine whether, to the sacrifices they have already made to you[r] country, they ought to add that of renouncing a right, the Exerc[ise] of which alarms the Politics of your government." Here was a hint that Genet recognized the change in regime might mean a change in his instructions, but here too was his predictable imputation that Washington and his cabinet acted dishonorably because they were pro-British. The charge had become a regular part of Genet's repertoire. It emerged in private conversation as well as official communications, with Genet declaring to Connecticut Federalist Noah Webster that the president was "under the influence of British Gold" and warning that the administration planned to make Americans slaves of Great Britain.[95]

12

"The people began to speak out."
—Henry Lee to George Washington,
September 17, 1793

GENET'S EARLY SEPTEMBER correspondence revealed fully his dislike of Washington and his cabinet members. Yet Washington endured Genet's barbs with greater equanimity than he had earlier in the summer. He knew that popular opinion was now firmly behind him, for new outpourings of support were arriving regularly. Yet although most of the memorials and town resolutions Washington received focused on Genet's insults to American sovereignty, the president's staunchest supporters read the situation differently. For men like Governor Henry Lee of Virginia, the French minister was only a pawn in a dangerous game being played by the Republicans. In a letter to Washington, Lee laid the blame for Genet's "mad conduct" on "the insidious & malignant councils of some perverse ambitious Americans," including the members of Philadelphia's Democratic Society. They had initially met with success in their attacks on the president, Lee conceded, but they had underestimated the American people. Soon enough their plan was finally understood and "consequently detested." This interpretation reinforced Washington's own belief that the more immediate danger came from domestic opposition; it was the opposition party and its extralegal organizations known as the Democratic Societies, not Genet's arrogance or ignorance, that threatened the federal government. Lee would soon have more reason to be convinced of this domestic danger, as the excise tax uprising in western Pennsylvania grew more serious. In that case, too, he would see the Democratic Societies as a motivating force behind the dissent.[96]

As the month continued, Genet's personal vendetta against the president only intensified. He had finally learned that his recall had been requested. Jefferson had composed a letter to Genet on September 7 informing the minister of the president's decision, but he had delayed its delivery for several days. The tone of the letter was harsh and its message clear: because Genet had operated in opposition to the laws of the United States, the president found it necessary to demand a replacement who would respect both those laws and the authorities who enforced them. The secretary specifically mentioned Genet's failure to restrain the consuls' actions, pointing out that the president had found it necessary to do this himself by revoking the diplomatic privileges of the French consul at Boston. The president, Jefferson added, would allow Genet to continue his functions until a new minister arrived—providing Genet obeyed the law and behaved appropriately.[97]

Genet's response was explosive. Indignant and feeling betrayed by Jefferson, Genet vented his anger in a long, accusatory letter to the secretary of state. With an abrupt salutation of "Sir," Genet lectured Jefferson on the constitutional powers of the United States executive and legislative branches as well as the source of those powers. He insisted once again that Congress alone represented the sovereign people and thus they alone had the right to decide issues relating to treaties. The president, in short, had overstepped his powers.

Because America's "aristocrats, partisans of monarchy, partisans of England, of her constitution" were now laboring to ruin him in his own country, Genet intended to speak out. He had no doubt that they were acting out of jealousy at his popularity with the American people and alarm at his "unshaken and incorruptible attachment to the severe maxims of democracy." He then launched into a review of the allegations made against him, followed by a vigorous denial that he had exercised "a *sovereign* influence over the American people" or attempted to make them take part in the war. He cited his responses to the many addresses made to him by citizens to prove that his only goal was to obtain a "true family compact" between the two republics. He was confident, he declared, that an inquiry by the next Congress into the motives of the president for demanding his recall would vindicate him entirely. He then informed Jefferson that he intended to publish all their correspondence as well as the instructions the French government had issued to him and to the consuls. This would allow the American people to see the falsity of the accusations against him.

Genet might have stopped there, but his indignation led him to press on with a litany of accusations against the president. These ran the gamut from Washington's failure to utter a personal greeting when the two men first met, to the president's continuing display of medallions of the former king, to the alleged persecution and arrest of Americans who had volunteered to serve the French cause and infringements of French rights under the treaties of 1778. But the president's greatest crime was his refusal to immediately call a session of Congress "to take the true sentiments of the people." Against all these insults to France and to its representatives, Genet declared, "It was indispensable that my resistance should be equal to the oppression."[98]

The September 18 letter amounted to a declaration of innocence, a vindication of behavior, and a condemnation of Washington and his administration. Its impact was muted by the fact that Jefferson, along with most of the government, had fled the Yellow Fever epidemic then raging in Philadelphia and did not return until the end of November. By the time the secretary of state read the letter on December 2, the Jacobin government had already determined to replace Genet with four commissioners.

On October 18, as the epidemic at last showed signs of ending, Gouverneur Morris sent two important dispatches to the president. The first reported that the request for Genet's recall had been delivered to the French government. But Morris devoted the bulk of this letter to the political situation in France. The Jacobin government, he said, was despotic in principle and in practice. They were arresting former allies and imprisoning many men on mere suspicion. The "emphatical Phrase in Fashion among the Patriots," he continued, is that *Terror is the order of the Day.*" The queen had been executed a few days earlier, and this act, Morris believed, would silence the opposition to the regime. He predicted that France "must soon be governd [sic] by a single Despot." Only a day later, Morris wrote once again, this time to report details of the French government's plan for the replacement of Genet. They will probably send over three or four commissioners, he told Washington, and these men will ask the president to assist them in securing the "person and Papers" of

Genet. The implication was that Genet would be another victim of the Terror. Morris hoped Genet would indeed be arrested. The seizure of Genet and his papers, he believed, would make his successors afraid to insult the US government lest they meet a similar fate. Morris's dispatches did not arrive in Philadelphia until January 1794. By that time, the new chief minister, Joseph Fauchet, and his commissioner colleagues were on board the frigate *La Charente,* bound for America.[99]

13
"It is with extreme concern I have to inform you . . ."
—George Washington to the Senate and
House of Representatives,
December 2, 1793

BY DECEMBER 1793, Genet was no longer the instigator of diplomatic crises; he was merely a pest. Yet even his pestering could occasionally create problems for the administration. Eager to remove one of the most serious blemishes on his record, Genet decided to charge Rufus King and John Jay with libel. He demanded that the attorney general prosecute the two men. Edmund Randolph asked Jefferson for guidance on the matter. Perhaps inadvertently—or perhaps to drive a wedge between Washington and two influential New York Federalists, Jefferson poured oil on the fire, telling Randolph that the president recommended considering Genet's request. In the end, Randolph rejected Genet's demand, but he attempted to soften the blow by suggesting the minister could find lawyers in private practice willing to pursue the suit. A thwarted Genet decided on a more dramatic alternative: he would publish his exchange of letters with the attorney general in the local press. A furious Rufus King wrote to the president, criticizing the administration for encouraging Genet's attack on his veracity. King demanded that Jefferson turn over his memo of July 10 that would vindicate the two New Yorkers. Washington rejected this demand, concerned that King would publish a cabinet document in the newspapers. The resulting breach in the friendship of Washington and King was not healed until the spring of 1794, when the president agreed to give King a certificate containing the relevant section of Jefferson's memo and King pledged not to publish it unless "very imperious circumstances" made it necessary. Fortunately no imperious circumstances arose, for the arrival of the four French commissioners ended Genet's interest in a libel suit.[100]

When the First Session of the Third Congress opened on December 3, Washington took the final steps to effectively neutralize the French minister. The president began by laying out the circumstances that compelled him to "admonish our citizens of the consequences of a contraband trade, and of hostile Acts to any of the parties" mentioned in his Proclamation of Neutrality. It was now up to Congress, he declared, to "correct, improve, or enforce" the admonitions and penalties he had set down. He concluded with a somber warning that America must arm itself and be prepared to defend itself against assaults by European powers. "There is a rank due to the United States among nations which will be withheld, if not absolutely lost, by the reputation of weakness. If we desire to avoid insult, we must be able to repel it."[101]

Two days later, on December 5, the president sent a second message to Congress in which he formally announced the request for Genet's recall. He left no room for doubt that the request was justified. Genet's actions had involved America in a war abroad and created "discord and anarchy" at home. As supporting documents, Washington sent Congress the correspondence between Jefferson and Genet, sworn affidavits relating to seizures of ships, and French government documents relating to the United States.[102]

At the same time that Congress was validating Washington's decisions, officials in the West and the South were taking steps to ensure that Genet's Spanish expeditions were aborted. Arthur St. Clair, governor of the Northwest Territory, issued a proclamation enjoining all the inhabitants of the territory to "abstain from every Act of hostility against the Subjects and Settlements" of Spain. And in South Carolina, a report by an investigative committee of the state's House of Representatives named five men, along with "other Persons unknown to your Committee," who were guilty of receiving and accepting commissions from Genet to "raise, organize, train and Conduct Troops within the United States of America." The committee took pains to condemn Edmond Genet for masterminding this "daring and dangerous attempt by a Foreign Minister to intermeddle in the Affairs of the United States." Genet, they said, used the men's affection for the French Republic to draw them into this nefarious scheme. The committee recommended that the Americans guilty of succumbing to Genet's "insidious Arts" should be tried for high crimes and misdemeanors. The South Carolina legislature unanimously concurred. William Moultrie, the man who had informally assisted Genet in the initial stages of this recruitment, now formally transmitted the legislative resolves to the president. His own links to the plot appeared nowhere in the committee report. After receiving the South Carolina report, the president debated whether to immediately revoke Genet's credentials. The question proved moot when the American ship carrying official French assurances of Genet's recall arrived in port.[103]

As for Genet, he declared himself ready to go home. His plans for the future were uncertain, but he thought perhaps he would start a new career in the military. It quickly became clear, however, that a very different fate awaited him. On his arrival, the new minister, Jean Antoine Joseph Fauchet, immediately demanded that Washington turn Genet over as a prisoner of the French Republic. The Jacobins, who had executed many Girondins as treasonous plotters against the Revolution, had concluded that Genet shared their guilt. He was no longer the zealous patriot; he was a counterrevolutionary traitor.[104]

Despite all the difficulties Genet had caused the president, Washington was not ready to hand the young Frenchman over to his new masters. As long as the United States had been "in danger from his Intrigues," Washington told Rufus King, the administration was justified in wishing him ill; but, now that he was deprived of his position and fated for the guillotine, the president admitted he felt compassion for Edmond Genet. That compassion led him to grant Genet asylum in America.[105]

14

"I augur more good than evil."
—Alexander White to James Madison,
December 28, 1793

FEDERALISTS HAD MUCH to celebrate that winter. Congress had approved the policy of neutrality set down in President Washington's proclamation. The president's popularity had soared. Pro-French sentiment had ebbed. As Robert Troup would put it to Hamilton, "It is the general opinion of the friends of the government here that the President has never appeared to greater advantage than in his last Speech to Congress. . . . Genet is completely on his back & I cannot now hear of any person who attempts seriously to defend his conduct." On December 15, former New York senator Philip Schuyler told his son-in-law that he rejoiced that the president's December 5 message to Congress had been "so explicit relative to the french [sic] Anarchist." Most Federalists would have agreed with Schuyler that "Genets [sic] intemperance has served the federal interest, instead of Injuring it." Others stressed the equally positive result that the "madness of Genet" had "silenced the declamations of our Demagogues."[106]

The Adams family, who were unsparingly anti-French, parsed out the personal and diplomatic failings of Genet as well as the motives of the French government. In their various commentaries on Genet's character flaws or on French deceitfulness or the poor judgment and fickleness of the American public, the Adamses revealed the Federalists' often contradictory efforts to identify the lessons to be learned from their year with Edmond Genet. John Adams boasted to his wife, Abigail, that he had taken the measure of the young Genet long ago, while serving as an American commissioner to the peace treaty negotiations that ended the Revolution in 1783. Then, as now, Adams declared, "He appears a Youth totally destitute of all Experience in popular Governments popular Assemblies or Conventions of any kind; very little accustomed to reflect on his own or his fellow Creatures hearts; wholly ignorant of the Law of Nature & Nations, the civil Law, and even of the Dispatches of ancient Ambassadors with which his own Nation and Language abound. A declamatory Style, a flitting fluttering Imagination, an Ardour in his Temper, and a civil Deportment are all the Accomplishments or Qualifications I can find in him." Adams's son, John Quincy, considered Genet "the most implacable and dangerous enemy to the peace and happiness of my country," yet he insisted that, fundamentally, Genet was no different from other French ministers to the United States. They were all equally contemptuous of Americans. "They have interspersed numerous menacing insinuations amid their warmest pretences of friendship," he declared, adding that "the murderous fangs of the tiger, peep through the downy velvet of her paws, at the moment when she fawns the most." John Quincy's younger brother, Thomas Boylston Adams, viewed Genet more sympathetically. The young Frenchman was nothing more than the unlucky agent of the French government's imperialist ambitions. "The Minister of the French Republic," he wrote, "has litterally [sic] pursued the Instructions of his Masters, the Executive Council of France." Abigail Adams proved the most pessimistic of all. Despite the blow dealt to the pro-French party by Genet's recall, she recognized that partisanship in America remained strong. "Partizans are so high respecting English and French politicks," she told her husband, and men "argue so falsly and Reason so stupidly that one would suppose they could do no injury, but there are so many who read and hear without reflecting and judging for themselves . . . that if we are preserved from the Calamities of War it will be more oweing [sic] to the superintending Providence of God than the virtue and wisdom of Man."[107]

The mood in Republican circles was glum. Few Republicans challenged the president's decision to have Genet recalled, and fewer still were so foolish as to deny the many failings of the French minister. In Congress, they had followed Jefferson's advice and joined in the praise of Washington for his decision to issue the Proclamation of Neutrality. The question for Republicans was this: Had pro-French sentiment evaporated as a result of the revelations about Genet? Virginia Republican Alexander White thought not. The French government, he assured his friend Madison, had only to disavow Genet's conduct and the attachment to America's sister Republic would surely increase.[108]

White's optimism proved correct: pro-French sentiment still ran deep, especially within the Third Congress. In 1794, with Genet's outrageous frontal attack on American sovereignty out of the way, a House of Representatives dominated by Republicans turned its attention to the economic insults of America's other major trading partner, Great Britain. Thus, at the start of 1794, the House of Representatives began a long and heated discussion over foreign commerce.

For three months, from January 3, 1794, to March 25, the House debated the relative value of commerce with Britain and France and the relative guilt of each in ignoring American neutrality. On

March 25, 1794, the House at last sent to the Senate a resolution "that an embargo be laid on all ships and vessels in the ports of the United States bound to any foreign port or place for the term of thirty days. . . ." Federalists would have viewed this as a minor victory, despite the serious damage it would do to US revenue, because it avoided a direct and exclusive challenge to Britain. Then, on April 17, 1794, it was agreed to continue the embargo until May 25, but only with those countries who did not have an existing commercial treaty with the United States. This, of course, meant an embargo on Britain. Politics had triumphed: on April 21, the Republicans pushed through a resolution imposing non-intercourse with Britain by a vote of 58–38.[109]

The fear that such a policy would be approved had left the President and his Federalist supporters with only one option: Washington must send a special envoy to London to negotiate a treaty with Great Britain. The result was the controversial Jay Treaty of 1794 that ended the embargo on Anglo-American trade. But for the rest of the decade—and into the next century—Americans would wrestle with two questions: Who is their most dangerous enemy, and how could they best protect and assert their country's sovereignty? On the answers to these questions, Federalists and Republicans would never agree.

Epilogue

IN NOVEMBER 1794 Genet married Cornelia Clinton, daughter of the very New York governor who had once challenged Genet's right to sell captured British goods in his state. Soon afterward, the Jacobin government was replaced by a more moderate regime, and Genet was given the opportunity to return to his homeland. But the conditions he hoped to impose—including a new diplomatic appointment— were rejected. Genet thus settled into the life of a New York country gentleman, busying himself with schemes to construct canals and prevent epidemics. He would never again involve himself directly in politics, although a scathing attack on him in 1797 by Congressman William Giles of Virginia prompted him to publish a long letter defending his career as a French minister to the United States. In it

Genet placed the blame for his downfall on the former secretary of state. Jefferson had posed as his friend, Genet wrote, but had betrayed his trust; he had sabotaged Genet's use of popular support to achieve his mission. Yet neither that betrayal nor the attacks in Congress by former friends like Giles persuaded Genet to trade his new country for his old. In 1804, at the age of forty-one, Edmond Charles Genet became an American citizen. When he died in 1834, it is said that the state papers of New York lined their columns in black, bands on steamboats passing the Genet home played dirges, and long lines of carriages followed him to his tomb.[110]

The country gentleman Edmond Genet became bore little resemblance to the young and brash revolutionary with the convert's zeal for a new cause. As Citizen Genet he had embraced the Girondin mission to reshape the European world and liberate oppressed people on both sides of the Atlantic. But zeal could not achieve what finesse and skill and knowledge might have. Genet demanded when he should have suggested; he harangued when he should have bargained; he barged ahead when he should have shown patience. Genet could be many things—charming, handsome, and creative—but he could not be a diplomat.

The Genet affair exposed the difficulties a weak nation faced in attempting to regulate its relationship with far stronger nations. Neither France nor England was willing to honor Washington's policy of neutrality; in the midst of the epic battle raging between them, they saw the United States as a supplier of goods who could not dictate the terms of exchange. It was also true that the neutrality policy itself was too nebulous and Washington's administration was too often reactive rather than proactive in establishing its basic rules. Even when those rules were generated, the government bureaucracy was too small to enforce them. The recall of Edmond Genet did not solve these problems; American neutrality would be contested as long as the war in Europe continued.

The Genet affair did have positive effects, however. These could be found in the domestic realm. Just as the Whiskey Rebellion would do, Genet's attack on Washington's authority galvanized American support for the president. But in this case that support was as much for the office he held and the powers given it by the Constitution as for the man himself. The Genet affair also alerted the public to the important and far-reaching role the federal government had as the country's representative to the wider world. Foreign diplomacy had been placed in the hands of the federal government by the Constitution; now it was widely accepted that this, in fact, was where it belonged.

Federalists like Hamilton and Knox were justified in celebrating both the new support for the federal government and their success in withstanding France's frontal attack on American autonomy. But the Genet affair was only the first challenge their government would face from France in the 1790s. The next one was less intrusive, but it inflamed Americans even more.

Part III

THE XYZ AFFAIR

LIKE ALL NATIONAL histories, ours has provided memorable and inspiring slogans. "Give me liberty or give me death" and "Damn the torpedoes, full speed ahead" are exclamations that still have the power to evoke patriotic indignation and defiance. The slogan of the XYZ affair—"Millions for defense, not one cent for tribute"—has similar power. In the context of the 1790s, when the United States was young and eager for respect from the more established, and more powerful, nations of Europe, it is often seen as the nation's first diplomatic line in the sand. The slogan captured America's determination to assert its sovereignty and its refusal to bow to foreign demands. Like the Genet affair, the XYZ episode involved France, but this time the conflict was more dramatic.

Historians have had little difficulty reconstructing the long and ultimately unproductive negotiations between Elbridge Gerry, John Marshall, and Charles Cotesworth Pinckney and the wily French minister Charles Talleyrand. John Marshall's dispatches, Elbridge Gerry's written accounts, French government records, synopses of cabinet meetings, the personal correspondence of American political leaders, and the many pages of debate and discussion preserved in the *Annals of Congress* all allow us to tell the story of what came to be known as the XYZ affair. But interpreting the significance of the XYZ affair has proven more difficult.

Here, just as in the Whiskey Rebellion and the Genet affair, most historians of the era have located the importance of the XYZ affair in the domestic party politics of the final years of the decade. From this perspective, the heart of the story lies in the nation's repudiation of the Federalists and the triumph of the Republican Party. In the aftermath of the XYZ affair, a fatal combination of war preparedness without a declaration of war and a futile effort to silence criticism and opposition in the nation's newspapers left the Federalist Party divided and with dwindling popular support. Together, the policies of preparedness and suppression eroded the popularity that President John Adams had enjoyed immediately following the revelation of French insults to America and led to the Republican victory in 1801.

This charting of the rise and fall of the Federalists is broadly accurate. But perhaps too narrow a focus on the impact of the XYZ affair in party politics eclipses another, equally significant outcome: the emergence of loyalty to the federal government and the Constitution as the sine qua non of patriotism. The XYZ affair quickened the processes set in motion by the federal government's response to the Whiskey Rebellion and the Genet affair. Again, a Federalist administration faced a dire threat to the country's legitimacy and sovereignty. Again, the members of the administration worried that the American experiment in representative government might fail. And, again, despite partisan divisions, the nation's leaders managed to win the devotion of the people of the disparate states and bind them ever more to the vision of government they had ratified.

1
"The conduct of the French Government
is so much beyond calculation."
—George Washington, April 1797

GEORGE WASHINGTON WAS carried into the presidency by a unanimous vote, but his successor John Adams won his election in

1797 by the slimmest of margins: only three votes stood between the feisty, fussy Massachusetts revolutionary and his opponent, the Virginian Thomas Jefferson. Adams, however, probably considered the underwhelming support for his candidacy just another example of the failure of his fellow Americans to appreciate his contributions to the nation. He knew he lacked the charisma of the other members of the revolutionary cohort. He was short and stout, without the military bearing of a Washington or the grace and physical beauty of a Hamilton. He was neither a fiery orator like Patrick Henry nor a master of prose like Jefferson. He was argumentative, often suspicious, and lacked the easy amiability of an Edmund Randolph or the elegant manners of a Charles Cotesworth Pinckney. In a moment of brutal self-evaluation, he had ceded writing the Declaration of Independence to Jefferson, declaring himself too "obnoxious, suspected, and unpopular" for the task. Over the years, Adams had frequently bemoaned the fact that his position in the pantheon of revolutionary heroes was not secure. Despite all he had done—despite his early and fervent call for independence, despite his sacrifice of family and fortune during years of service as a diplomat and treaty negotiator, despite his intellectual contributions to republican political theory— John Adams remained unsung. Yet, in 1797, here he was, the second president of the United States, being asked to follow a man lauded as the father of his country.[1]

Even had Adams been widely admired and liked, the problems before him as he entered the presidency would have been daunting. When Washington left office, an opposition party that took shape in the wake of Hamilton's fiscal policies was steadily expanding its reach, aided by the Republican press and brilliantly guided by Adams's own vice president, Thomas Jefferson. The new president had also inherited the tensions arising from the lines of political fracture, North and South as well as East and West, that played out in bitter debates in Congress and, during the Whiskey Rebellion, in open resistance to federal laws. Indeed, the close vote that carried Adams into the Executive Office was testimony to the tensions between the centripetal and centrifugal forces simultaneously shaping the early Republic: Adams carried New England, New York, and New Jersey while Jefferson carried the southern states and the Whiskey Rebellion strongholds of Pennsylvania and Kentucky.

The Federalist Party was still powerful enough in 1797 to elect a president, but the man it had put in office did not control the party; if anyone did, it was Alexander Hamilton. The majority of Adams's cabinet, carried over from Washington's second administration, looked to the former secretary of the treasury for direction in both domestic and foreign affairs. This bred a resentment and frustration in the president that grew into a deep hatred for his rival, Hamilton. The sensible thing for Adams to do was dismiss the cabinet and begin anew, with men loyal to him. But Adams, who had legislative and diplomatic experience but was a novice administrator, seemed strangely blind to the value of assembling such a cabinet. Even worse, he seemed reluctant to use patronage to win the support of important Federalists for his policies. Even if he knew how to wield patronage, however, he would have hesitated, for Adams did not identify himself as the leader of a political party. Instead, he saw himself as that republican ideal, the disinterested, independent statesman, a leader above "faction" who served the best interests of the citizens. It was a romantic vision in an era when ideological differences were impossible to ignore.

Yet Adams's problems went far beyond how to develop a governing style that would bring the Federalist Party under his control. And, to be fair, the problems were not of his own making. He had inherited the resentment of western farmers and southern slave owners that had emerged during Hamilton's tenure as secretary of the treasury. And he had inherited the Gordian knot of American neutrality in a still-raging European war. Throughout the 1790s, and beyond, England and France simply continued to redefine American neutrality as they wished, ignoring explicit policy when it was convenient and applying steady pressure on the US government through their own policies. They would sometimes woo the United States with offers to lift trade restrictions or to provide trade advantages, but just as often they disrupted American trade or devised strategies to provoke the United States into war with their enemy. The French had been the most blatant manipulators. A long line of French ministers to the United States, from Genet to Pierre-August Adet, followed policies that showed contempt for American sovereignty. Yet Britain also insulted American sovereignty. Throughout the 1790s, and into the next century, Britain refused to accept that sailors born in England or its territories could ever transfer their citizenship to the United States. No matter how assertive Washington's proclamation and Congress's Neutrality Act appeared, in reality America's foreign policy remained in 1797 just as it had been in Washington's administration—largely reactive.

For Adams, as for Washington, France would prove a far more serious challenge than Britain. By mid-decade, the French government had emerged as Europe's bully, treating all neutral nations, not just the United States, with open contempt for their sovereignty. American diplomats reported that the French intervened in the domestic politics of other countries, openly supporting men and parties who would be more responsive to French demands and more amenable to French needs. As Alexander Hamilton would put it in "The Warning, No. I," a newspaper essay of 1797, "The complaints of France may be regarded principally as weapons furnished to her adherents to defend her cause notwithstanding the blows she inflicts. Her aim has been in every instance to seduce the people from their Government, and by dividing to conquer and oppress."[2]

John Adams was no stranger to this French strategy. The French minister Pierre-Auguste Adet had openly supported the Republicans in the 1796 election campaign, asserting, as Oliver Wolcott Jr. put it, that "the election of Mr. Jefferson was necessary to prevent a rupture with France." Among other things, Adet had published the blistering attack on the Washington administration and the Jay Treaty of 1794 that he had originally sent to Secretary of State Timothy Pickering. Wolcott had feared the impact of this written attack; he assured his father that "if Mr. Jefferson is elected it will be owing entirely to the influence of this paper." Hamilton did his best to counter Adet's propaganda, publishing an essay called "The Answer" that criticized what he called Adet's "menacing tone." The French goal was clear, Hamilton declared: it was "to influence timid minds to vote agreeable to their wishes in the election of president and vice-president." This meddling, Hamilton added, "is certainly a practice that must not be permitted." If it led, as it might, to other ministers campaigning openly for candidates, America was certain to suffer the same fate as Poland, that "melancholy example of the danger of foreign influence in the election of a chief magistrate." Adet's less-than-subtle—and ultimately unsuccessful—actions prompted his recall by the French government, but his undisguised partisanship and his close relationships with Jefferson, Pennsylvania governor Thomas Mifflin, and other leaders of the Republican Party suggested a continuation of the French tendency to see the United States as a useful, if reluctant, satellite.[3]

Franco-American relations had deteriorated significantly since the signing of the Jay Treaty between the United States and Britain in 1794. The French voiced strong opposition to the treaty. They claimed it negated many of the promises in the treaties of 1778, and they insisted that it revealed America's return to British domination. Washington had relied on the American minister to France James Monroe to defuse the situation, but, as a Republican, Monroe seemed unwilling to support a treaty that mended relations with the English. Monroe's failure to defend the Jay Treaty led Washington to recall him, and this, in turn, provided the French an opportunity to openly criticize US foreign policy.[4]

The attack on US policy came when Monroe gave his farewell address to the French government, the Directory, in 1796. Monroe spoke of France in friendly and even laudatory terms but the Directory president, Paul Barras, responded with an explicit insult to American sovereignty. Dismissing America as a mere tool of the English, Barras declared that France "would not abase herself by calculating the consequences of the condescension of the American government to the suggestions of her former tyrants." This could be read only as a warning that retaliatory measures would be taken now that America had allegedly submitted, with the Jay Treaty, to the will of its former masters.[5]

Monroe's reaction to the Barras attack on America was entirely personal—his anger was aimed at the president rather than at the French government. He was furious at his recall by Washington. Soon after returning home, Monroe composed a long and bitter accusation that his removal was a flagrantly partisan political decision.[6]

The situation only worsened as 1796 ended. On December 6, Washington's new American minister to France, Charles Cotesworth Pinckney, arrived in Paris, eager to restore good relations between the two nations. Pinckney was an affable though far from brilliant South Carolina planter, distinguished by his moderate approach in all matters political. His guiding principles were honor and duty; his manner was genteel and gracious. Yet he would have no opportunity to test his skills at diplomacy. When he presented his credentials to Charles-François Delacroix, the new minister of foreign affairs, they were flatly rejected. The French government, he was told, would receive no US minister until a number of unspecified US injuries to France were redressed. Delacroix then insulted Pinckney by ordering him to go to the minister of police to receive the necessary passport home—just as any private citizen was required to do. By February, a flustered Pinckney was in Amsterdam, awaiting instructions from president-elect John Adams. Although Pinckney rightly viewed his treatment as a slight against the United States, it was not unique; the Directory had sent off thirteen other foreign ministers in a similar fashion.[7]

News of developments across the Atlantic traveled slowly, however. Adams did not learn of the rebuff of Pinckney until he had taken over the presidency. Although Benjamin Bache, the partisan Republican editor of the *Aurora,* was quick to blame the French refusal to accept Pinckney on the South Carolinian's "haughtiness," President Adams considered Pinckney blameless. The fault, he told Henry Knox and Benjamin Lincoln, was rooted in the overblown sense of importance shared by all Frenchmen. "They consider nobody but themselves," Adams declared. "Their apparent Respect and real Contempt for all men and all nations but Frenchmen are proverbially among themselves . . . they have no other rule but to give reputation to their Fools and to destroy the reputation of all who will not be their Fools . . . to a Frenchman the most important man in the world is himself and the most important nation is France." Former president George Washington had his own criticism of French behavior. "The conduct of the French government," Washington told James McHenry, "is so much beyond calculation, and so unaccountable upon any principle of justice, or even to that sort of policy which is familiar to plain understanding, that I shall not now puzzle my brains in attempting to develope [sic] their motives to it." Washington was clearly relieved that the burden of French aggression now fell on John Adams rather than on him.[8]

Did the rejection of an American minister mean war? Benjamin Bache, at least, was convinced that war was not the goal of France but of the Federalists. The Anglophiles within that party, he

declared, did not care that war would spell the end of republicanism in the world and a punishing economic depression in America.
Bache's fellow contributors to the *Aurora* went on to describe this
economic disaster in dramatic terms. Produce, they wrote, would rot
on the wharves as the French market for American crops vanished,
the Mississippi River would be closed to American traffic, the public debt would soar, corruption would be rampant, and the executive branch would become more powerful. Predictably, the Federalist
press responded, countering this nightmare vision with reassuring
cynicism: France was not going to declare war on the United States
as long as it could plunder American commerce so profitably.[9]

Adams, however, was uncertain whether this insult to American
sovereignty, blatant though it was, actually required a military response. He consulted his cabinet. Was the refusal to receive Pinckney a circumstance of such "Indignity, insult & Hostility" that no
further negotiations could be considered? If, instead of war, a peace
mission were undertaken, what demands should be made and what
concessions offered? What terms in the treaty with Great Britain
could also be offered to France? What articles in the treaties of 1778
should we propose be abolished? What demands for reparations
should our negotiators make? Several of the reparation demands Adams listed as examples dealt with abuses going back to the era of Citizen Genet. In his own notes on the situation, Adams sketched out
several retaliatory actions the United States might take, including an
embargo and the approval of American privateers. But he also considered preparations for war, such as increasing the size of the army,
creating a navy, and constructing additional fortifications along the
nation's coast.[10]

Adams seemed to be planning for peace but preparing for war. In
a letter to William Heath on April 19, the president declared, "There
is Such a Thing as a just and necessary War," but, he quickly added,
"if we have a War it will be forced upon Us." He ended with a note
of bravado: "I know not that We need tremble before any Nation at
a thousand Leagues distance, in a just Cause." He had struck this
same note of confidence in a letter to his oldest son that March.
"America," he told John Quincy, "is not Scared."[11]

2
"I have it much at heart to Settle
all disputes with France."
—John Adams to Henry Knox,
March 1797

THE REJECTION OF Pinckney's credentials was not the only issue with France facing Adams in his first months in office. On
March 2, only two days before John Adams entered the presidency,
France struck a serious blow against American commerce. On that
day, the Directory issued a decree that ended France's commitment to
the principle of "free ships / free goods." The decree made American
vessels carrying goods to or from Britain vulnerable to capture and
confiscation by the French navy and by French privateers. The Directory justified the change in policy as a response to the Jay Treaty,
which they claimed forged a new alliance between Britain and the
United States. The American minister to Great Britain, Rufus King,
believed this was simply an excuse. The French, he said, had also demanded that Hamburg and Bremen suspend all commerce with England, and these powers "have made no late treaties with England."
John Quincy Adams, the American ambassador to the Netherlands
at the time, also pointed out that "the neutrality of every other nation is as little respected by the French Government as that of the
United States." French contempt for weaker nations, whether allies
or enemies, could be seen in the comment of Claude E. J. Pastoret, a
member of the French Council of Five Hundred. "Are we not the sov-
ereigns of the world?" he asked his fellow council members, adding,
"Our allies, are they not then our subjects?"[12]

France had not only insulted Americans' pride by rejecting their
ambassador, it had also struck a blow against American independence and its economic linchpin, neutrality. The president thus decided that the French crisis was serious enough to merit a special
session of Congress that May. His old friend Elbridge Gerry was
pleased that Adams intended to put the French problem before the
House as well as the Senate. It was always good policy, the former
congressman from Massachusetts said, "to consult the representatives of the people," for "they are the nerves of the body-politic."

Personally, however, Gerry was strongly against war with France. He feared that a successful war would plunge the nation into debt and stifle economic growth while an unsuccessful war would lead to the overthrow of the American government and the creation of a new one modeled on the French system, "& we should hereafter be meer [sic] French colonies." Never an optimist, Gerry could see no positive outcome to the dilemma facing John Adams and the nation. In his reply to Gerry, Adams did not deny that there were high costs to both victory and defeat. Yet Adams argued that his friend could not deny France's long history of abusing American sovereignty. "You know as well as any Man," he wrote, "that france under all Governments from the Year 1776 . . . down to this moment have invariably preserved a Course of Intrigue to gain an undue Influence in these states.—to make Us dependent upon her, and to keep up a quarrell [sic] with England." Perhaps war was the only way to end that abuse.[13]

On May 16, Adams delivered a message to this emergency session of Congress. He began with a description of the Directory's humiliation of Charles Cotesworth Pinckney. "The refusal to hear him, until we have acceded to their demands without discussion, and without further investigation," he told Congress, "is to treat us neither as allies, nor as friends, nor as a sovereign state." Adams turned next to the speech by Barras, which he believed expressed sentiments "more alarming than the refusal of a Minister." The speech, he declared, evinced once again a disposition to separate the American people from their government, a tactic that required a firm response. "Such attempts," Adams insisted, "ought to be repelled with a decision which shall convince France, and the world, that we are not a degraded people, humiliated under a colonial spirit of fear and sense of inferiority, fitted to be the miserable instruments of foreign influence; and regardless of national honor, character, and interest." The president then argued that France's depredations of American commerce, its injuries to American citizens, and "the general complexion of affairs" demanded appropriate measures for the defense of the country. He called for a naval establishment that would include armed frigates able to protect merchantmen at sea. He also called for the creation of a provisional army. Still, Adams left the door open for peace. He intended, he announced, to open negotiations with France once again if possible.[14]

THREE DAYS LATER, the president forwarded to the House a number of documents relating to Pinckney's rejection, including the speech by Barras and extracts of Pinckney's correspondence with the secretary of state. On Monday, May 22, the representatives began a debate over the appropriate response to the president, a debate that would last almost two weeks. Threaded through this long and often heated discussion was a shared sense that America's position as an independent and sovereign nation was at risk. Republicans and Federalists alike roundly denounced all "attempts to wound our rights as a sovereign state," but there the unity ended. Republicans did not think Pinckney's expulsion merited a declaration of war, and they opposed steps toward preparedness that might provoke such a declaration from France. Virginia Republican John Nicholas proposed that the House response to the president include a defense of those pro-French American voices Adams had described as immoderate. Federalists rejected this. The president's criticism of these overzealous partisans was deserved, said William Loughton Smith, and any acquiescence to French demands—especially the demand for the annulment of the Jay Treaty—would be "virtually and essentially to surrender our self-government and independence." Smith's fellow Federalist, the wealthy thirty-two-year-old Bostonian, Harrison Gray Otis, was even more emphatic. Americans, he declared, must not respond with a "spiritless expression of civility, but a new edition of the Declaration of Independence." When Nicholas's motion was defeated, the focus of debate turned to a long and predictably tendentious comparison of the relative evils of France and England, but few if any minds were changed despite the impressive and lengthy citations of import and export data.[15]

George Washington was eager to learn how the House would respond to the president's message. He believed the crisis facing the nation called for "an unequivocal expression of the public mind." But, in a letter to Oliver Wolcott Jr., Washington focused his criticism on the "internal disturbers" of the country's peace who had

collaborated with the French ministers rather than on the recent behavior of France. In the former president's view, these were the same
reckless and ambitious men who had encouraged the Whiskey Rebellion in the West and excused the excesses of Edmond Genet. The
danger they posed to America ought to be obvious, he said; Americans had only to look at the victims of collaboration with France in
Europe, "so bewildered & dark, so entangled & embarrassed, and
so obviously under the influence of intrigue" to realize the damage
that these irresponsible men could inflict upon their own country.
John Adams had a still darker view. He believed the American people
as a whole were responsible for their plight. For him, as for many
New England revolutionaries, the survival of a republic depended
upon the moral strength and commitment of its people. There might
be enemies of the Republic among them who hope to undermine
their country's government and weaken its independence, but the
real danger, he told fellow New Englander Elbridge Gerry, "is in the
Universal Avarice & ambition of the People."[16]

At last, on June 3, the House settled on sending the president a
general, and vague, pledge of its "zealous cooperation" in any measures he might decide were necessary for America's security or peace.
But it gave its hearty approval to the opening of new negotiations
with France.[17]

Adams had already drafted four questions concerning negotiators to be sent to France, but he was uncertain to whom he could
turn for their answers. There were few men he could trust for sage
political advice on the crisis facing the nation and fewer still for unconditional support. He could not rely on his cabinet. His secretary
of state Thomas Pickering ought to have been Adams's chief advisor
on foreign affairs and the man who ensured that the president's decisions were carried out. But Pickering saw himself as an independent
officer of the government. Not even Hamilton was able to exert control over this tall, austere, and bespectacled man in his fifties who
had a brittle ego and an unforgiving temperament. Pickering was
unwilling to forgive France for its insults to the nation, especially the
escalating attacks on American commerce. In fact, months before
John Adams delivered his views on the French situation to Congress,
Pickering had acted on his own, presenting to the legislature a full—
and damning—accounting of France's past and present persecution

of US commerce. In his report to Congress, Pickering pointed out that officially sanctioned French attacks on American shipping had actually begun months before the decree of March 2, 1797. In August 1796 the Directory had issued instructions to the Windward Islands to attack American vessels. By November 1796, officials in the Leeward Islands were ordering the capture of all American ships bound for British ports. The Jay Treaty, therefore, was not the cause of the decree legitimating these attacks. Instead, Pickering argued, there was only one motive for escalating seizure of American vessels: greed. And, in his judgment, the only appropriate response to France was war.[18]

Pickering was correct, of course, in his assessment of France's new trade policy. Despite all the French government's indignant rhetoric, that policy seemed to be motivated more by privateering profits than by disappointment at America's alleged betrayal. Britain, it was true, had often ignored American claims to neutrality; it had impressed American seamen and imposed a variety of barriers to American commerce. But it had never completely cut off neutral trade.

The question remained: Was war America's best response? The president seemed to face an impossible choice between ruinous peace or ruinous war. He chose to continue down his middle path of preparing for war but pursuing peace. Ironically, the man who most closely shared Adams's view that a peace commission was the wisest course was Alexander Hamilton. Although he had been quick to advocate the use of military force in the domestic uprising by whiskey rebels, Hamilton doubted America had the capacity to challenge Europe's dominant power. He approved of the president's course of action.[19]

When Adams made it known that he would appoint a three-man commission to negotiate a new treaty with France, Hamilton urged that one of these men be a leading Republican, preferably Madison or Jefferson. Such a choice, Hamilton argued, would prevent accusations of an administration conspiracy to force France to reject the olive branch and allow Adams to declare war. Pickering, whose political finesse was limited, saw no reason to send a Republican commissioner, but then, he didn't want to send any commissioners at all. However, French military successes against Britain and its allies that spring and summer forced him to change his mind. He understood it would be wise to heed the warning of Rufus King, American minister to Great Britain, who reported rumors that England would soon make peace with the enemy, leaving France dangerously free to crush the United States.[20]

In the end, both Jefferson and Madison declined to serve as an American envoy. As vice president, Jefferson could make a case that such an appointment was inappropriate. Adams agreed. He had, he told Elbridge Gerry, "made a great stretch in proposing it, to accommodate to the Feelings, Views and Prejudices of a Party," but "upon more mature reflection I am decidedly convinced of the Impropriety of it." To send such a high-ranking member of the government, Adams said, "would be a degradation of our Government in the eyes of our own people as well as of all Europe." Madison's motives for rejecting the appointment were not hard to fathom; like his fellow Republican James Monroe, he had no interest in helping to preserve the reputation or prestige of the Federalists at home or abroad.[21]

Adams's calm acceptance of rejection by the two Virginians showed political sophistication, but his decision to appoint two diplomatic novices to the commission can only be wondered at. Indeed, all three of the men chosen were problematic. The appointment—or reappointment—of Charles Cotesworth Pinckney ran the risk of appearing aggressive, or worse, insulting, to the French. Perhaps the president believed he owed this vote of confidence to the South Carolinian who had not only been humiliated but had endured an expensive journey from Paris to the safety of the Netherlands. But Pinckney's brief moment as the US minister hardly qualified him for the delicate negotiations that lay ahead. The president's second appointee, John Marshall, had even less diplomatic experience—which is to say, none. Marshall, tall, lanky, and handsome, with jet-black hair and fine features, was considered a potential leader of the Federalist Party. He was known for his exceptional intelligence, his affable manner, and his tendency to dress carelessly. His less-than-stylish attire would not favorably impress even the most ardent French revolutionaries. But his amiability would be an asset. The forty-two-year-old lawyer was well liked in his home state, although his cousin Thomas Jefferson was not among his admirers. Jefferson found what he called Marshall's "lax, lounging manners" infuriating. Marshall returned the animosity, labeling Jefferson untrustworthy.[22]

It was not Marshall's "lounging manners" that made French observers in America shake their heads at this appointment. Alexandre d'Hauterive, the French consul in New York, told his superiors in Paris that "Mr. Marshall is a man of very pronounced character who hides neither his support for the English cause nor his distance from anything that favors French interest." Yet d'Hauterive conceded that Marshall's frank political views were "supported by a high standard of conduct, by a certain knowledge of human nature and of business, and by many talents." As for Pinckney, d'Hauterive was willing only to acknowledge his good character. The consul was convinced, however, that Pinckney's bitterness at his treatment by Delacroix would hamper his effectiveness. As neither Pinckney nor Marshall had any genuine experience as a diplomat, it was difficult not to conclude that the president was sending American sheep to French wolves.[23]

Adams's choice for the third member of the commission was even more difficult to explain. His recommendation was none other than Elbridge Gerry, perhaps the most unpopular American political figure of the era. Yet the friendship between Gerry and Adams was long standing, and the president believed that Gerry was, like him, a political independent who eschewed party loyalties. It was closer to the truth, however, that Gerry's political loyalties were simply erratic. He had been a delegate to the Philadelphia convention but had refused to sign the Constitution. He had campaigned against ratification but ran for a seat in the House as soon as the new government was approved. Although he described himself as a lone watchdog for the peoples' liberties, others considered him a leader of the Antifederalist faction in the early sessions of the legislature. But to most of the men who had served in the House with Gerry, the question of his party affiliation was less important than his remarkable irascibility. Sharp-tongued, argumentative, and exhausting to deal with, Elbridge Gerry was a man whose mission in life often seemed to be alienating others. The president's wife, Abigail Adams, was not blind to Gerry's eccentricity. "Poor Gerry," she wrote, "always had a wrong kink in his head." Those less tolerant of him would have agreed with the observation that Elbridge Gerry objected to everything he did not propose himself.[24]

Adams's proposal to add Gerry to the commission met with fierce protest from his cabinet. Secretary of War James McHenry, a veteran of debates with Gerry, warned the president bluntly, "If,

Sir, it was a desirable thing to distract the mission, a fitter person could not, perhaps be found. It is ten to one against his agreeing with his colleagues." In the face of the protest and warnings, Adams reluctantly backed down. He turned instead to Francis Dana, a fifty-four-year-old Massachusetts jurist who had signed the Declaration of Independence and supported the ratification of the Constitution. Dana was a sensible choice. He had diplomatic experience as Adams's secretary to the Paris peace talks that ended the Revolution and as United States ambassador to Russia between 1780 and 1783. But Dana, too, declined. With that, Adams returned to his original choice, Elbridge Gerry—and this time he did not give in to the protest from his cabinet.[25]

Adams was frank with Gerry when he told him that "some have expressed doubts of your orthodoxy in the Science of Government—others have expressed fears, of an unaccommodating disposition and others of an Obstinancy that will risque [sic] great Things to secure Small ones." Gerry, however, pledged to cooperate fully with his colleagues on the commission and to encourage unanimity in all they did. There is little doubt that Gerry was sincere, but few who knew him would believe him capable of fulfilling this promise.[26]

In the letter promising to strive for unity and cooperation, Gerry had declared, "I think it impossible for a jealousy to be excited in my mind against either of my colleagues." But, in this, he proved disastrously wrong. The truth was that John Adams had put together a team of men whose temperaments rendered unity in the negotiations unlikely and whose inexperience in diplomacy could easily lead to disaster. Whether they succeeded or failed in forging a new, and more acceptable, relationship between the United States and France, the responsibility for the outcome rested in large part on the president's selection.[27]

3
"Talleyrand . . . could not be for war with this country."
—John Adams, October 1797

THE INSTRUCTIONS DRAFTED for the commissioners reflected the president's awareness that they would have to be flexible. They were to ask for compensation to American merchants for French depredations of US commerce as well as compensation for unpaid claims for supplies provided by merchants to agents of the French government. However, a French refusal to meet these demands was not to be grounds to end the negotiations. The commissioners' primary goal was a new treaty that could clarify—and ease—US-French relations. To accomplish this, they had the authority to place France on the same footing with Great Britain when it came to neutral shipping. In other words, America was willing to give up the "free ships / free goods" clause of the older treaty of 1778. In exchange, however, France would be asked to release the United States from the mutual guarantee of military support in that treaty. But on two points the president was unbending: the commissioners were explicitly ordered not to agree to restrictions on trade that the United States was legally entitled to under the law of nations, and they were to make no loans to France that could be used to pay for their war against Britain.[28]

These instructions were not made public until after the mission ended. But it would have made no difference to the Republican press if they had been widely published immediately. Benjamin Bache, for example, was certain that the goal of this mission was not peace but war with France. How could it be otherwise, he asked his readers, when Federalists hated France and loved England, when they were motivated by a desire for the lucrative jobs and patronage opportunities that war would bring, and when the threat of war would allow them to create a standing army and a huge national debt? "Various passions and interests will combine to drive or drag this country into a war," he declared, adding that "the ambitious and the avaricious of every shade and complexion are at this moment straining every nerve to accomplish the object; and they will accomplish it, if the people continue to sleep." Beneath the predictable rhetoric, however, was an astute reading of the situation facing the commission. It would meet with little more than cold civility, Bache argued, and the French government would simply stall until it discovered whether Britain could be forced to make peace. In other words, the envoys would find themselves powerless pawns whose fate would be decided by the struggle between France and Britain. The Federalist press was indignant at these gloomy predictions; one editor dismissed Bache's views as the "foul water which continually issues through that sewer [the *Aurora*]."[29]

Bache and his contributors did not, however, factor in the rapidly changing political situation in France. Despite the recent military victories and the expectation that England would indeed sue for peace, the Directory government was under attack by influential political opponents. These critics attacked the Directory leadership's high-handed treatment of republican governments like those in Geneva and Venice as well as in the United States. The French government attempted to placate its critics by dismissing several of the most anti-American ministers, including Delacroix. But in September 1797, a coup d'état, led by three of the directors and aided by military forces assigned by Napoleon Bonaparte, put the remaining two in prison. The three victors then cancelled the results of the 1796 elections, closed at least thirty Parisian newspapers, exiled many of the government's opponents, and called a halt to talks with England. Paul Barras, who had given the insulting speech on the occasion of Monroe's departure, now held the reins of power.[30]

Barras and his fellow directors appointed Charles-Maurice de Talleyrand as their foreign minister. It was not a post to accept lightly: of Talleyrand's fourteen predecessors, five had been executed, four had been forced into exile, and two had been imprisoned. Whether Talleyrand would have better luck was unclear, but he was willing to take his chances because the position opened up opportunities for personal profit. This chance to amass a fortune arose from the accepted practice of demanding bribes from foreign governments hoping to negotiate with France. Countries wishing to avoid invasion as well as those attempting to make peace were regularly required to line the pockets of French officials. Although this had become standard practice after the Revolution, it was far from a republican innovation. Silas Deane, sent as a purchasing agent by the Continental Congress in 1776, when France was still ruled by a king, had to pay a bribe to initiate the purchase of military supplies.[31]

Like Barras, Talleyrand was descended from a noble family. As a young man he studied for the priesthood and took orders, but there is no evidence that his religious commitment ran deep. He preferred luxury, women, and political intrigue to prayer, charitable works, and Catholic ritual. Indeed, on the evening he was installed as bishop of Autun, Talleyrand dined with his mistress. Later, as he made the transition from Royalist to revolutionary, Talleyrand was excommunicated for supporting the nationalization of Catholic Church properties. During the political upheavals of 1792, Talleyrand left France and spent two years in England and then two in America. In the United States, he formed a close friendship with Alexander Hamilton, a fellow nationalist he admired greatly. He was reported to have said, "I consider Napoleon, Pitt and Hamilton as the three greatest men of our age, and if I had to choose, I would unhesitatingly give the first place to Hamilton." Charming, cunning, and greedy: this was the man with whom the American envoys would have to deal if they hoped to establish a new relationship between his country and their own.[32]

The coup and the appointments that followed boded ill for the American mission. John Marshall, who had arrived in the Netherlands one week before Barras came to power, believed that the violence and disorder, and the use of the military to crush civilian protest, threatened the survival of the French Republic. "The constitution of France may survive the wound," he told Timothy Pickering in a letter later that month, "but the constitution of no other nation on earth could survive it. . . . A wanton contempt of rules so essential to the very being of a republic could not have been exhibited by men who wished to preserve it." Charles Cotesworth Pinckney, who had lingered in Amsterdam since leaving Paris that January, agreed with his younger colleague. The two men also shared the view that they would make little or no progress in improving American relations with France.[33]

Pinckney and Marshall nevertheless made their way to Paris. Gerry did not arrive in the Netherlands until late September, after a long trip made more unpleasant by a "slow putrid fever" he contracted. Before heading to Paris, Gerry shared his thoughts on the upcoming negotiations with the US ambassador to the Netherlands, William Vans Murray. The best strategy, he declared, was to gain time by prolonging the discussions. This, he assured Murray, would diminish the possibility of war between the two countries. He also boasted to Murray that his appointment to the commission was a serious blow to the "British party" at home and to its plot to fill all diplomatic posts with anti-French ministers. As a Federalist and a staunch supporter of the administration, Murray was unlikely to applaud Gerry's triumph.[34]

By September 27, 1797, Pinckney and Marshall were in Paris; Gerry arrived the first week of October. They moved into a large townhouse, three blocks from the foreign ministry. Pinckney, whose family had joined him, took the main floor of the house while Gerry and Marshall found themselves in a small apartment on the ground floor. Gerry was miserable. He considered their location so dangerous that he slept with not one but two loaded pistols under his pillow. Later, the trio would move to far more attractive quarters in the home of the celebrated adopted daughter of Voltaire, Madame de Villette, known as "belle et bonne" within Parisian circles. But, until the end of November, they remained in rooms a stone's throw from Talleyrand's offices.[35]

Their first encounter with Talleyrand came on October 8. It was a fifteen-minute audience that gave them time only to present their credentials and receive the necessary cards of hospitality that would allow them to remain in Paris. A week then passed with no word from the minister. During that time, Thomas Paine, who had been living in France since 1792, sent the envoys a letter urging the United States not to arm merchantmen in defense against French privateers. Although Marshall was offended by Paine's interference, the usually cantankerous Gerry took to heart Paine's underlying message: do nothing to irritate the French government.[36]

Talleyrand, like Gerry, was happy to see the negotiations move slowly. The French minister assumed that eventually a new treaty would be signed, but he saw no reason to rush. He was certain that the United States would not declare war on his country, and, as long as there was no treaty, France could continue its successful privateering against US merchantmen. Marshall took the measure of the situation almost immediately, quick to see that the delays meant money in the pockets of French ship owners, French merchants, and French government officials. Gerry, blinded by his fear that a war with France would drive the United States into alliance with Britain, was unable to see things so clearly.

Talleyrand had a second, more personal reason for delay; he intended to see American money reach his own pockets. He planned to drag out the negotiations by demanding apologies for real or imagined wrongs and then offer to facilitate matters once a bribe, or *douceur,* had been paid. Across the Atlantic, John Adams assumed that delay would be Talleyrand's strategy. "Talleyrand," he told Pickering, "I should Suppose could not be for War with this Country; nor can I apprehend that even the Triumvirate, as they begin to be called in France, will be for a measure so decided. A Continued Appearance of Umbrage, and continued Depredations on a weak defenceless Commerce, will be much more convenient." What Adams did not realize, however, was the role Talleyrand's desire for personal gain played in his strategy.[37]

On October 14, Talleyrand sent his secretary to James Mountflorence, the United States vice consul in France who had served as the primary contact between the French and American governments since the expulsion of Charles Cotesworth Pinckney. Mountflorence was to convey a message to Pinckney: the Directory was "excessively exasperated" with the United States and would not begin negotiations until the envoys explained the suggestion of French interference in American domestic politics made by John Adams in his May 1797 speech. Although Talleyrand was the actual source of this demand, he expected the vice consul to assure the Americans that he opposed it. A pattern would soon emerge: Talleyrand would present claims from the Directory that were in fact his own invention and then pose as an advocate for the envoys.

This was the first use of an intermediary by Talleyrand, but it would not be the last. In this instance, the envoys chose the appropriate response to an irregular transmission of information: no response at all. Talleyrand might not have employed this tactic again if the envoys had held firm in their refusal to deal with intermediaries or if Marshall's proposal to send a message directly to Talleyrand demanding negotiations begin at once had been agreed to by his colleagues. But Gerry vetoed Marshall's idea, urging patience and warning that putting pressure on the French government might result in no negotiations at all. Over the following months, this would become Gerry's mantra. And none of the three Americans proved able to turn away the men Talleyrand sent bearing information, threats, proposals, or suggestions on how to advance the negotiations. The result would be a succession of intermediaries, three of whom would later be known simply as X, Y, and Z.

On October 18, the second indirect contact was made. Nicholas Hubbard, an Englishman who was a partner in the Amsterdam bank that had financed the US national debt, called on Pinckney to ask whether he would receive a visit from a colleague, Jean Conrad Hottinguer. This colleague, Hubbard said, had an important message for the Americans. Hottinguer—or "X" as he was referred to in the documents President Adams would later turn over to the Congress—was a Swiss banker, a member of a European syndicate that speculated in US investments. He had lived in the United States in the 1780s and was involved with the American financial genius Robert Morris in land purchases in Pennsylvania. Hottinguer knew Pinckney and he also knew Marshall's brother James, whom he had helped with a loan. X's mission was to lay out Talleyrand's terms to Pinckney: first, the United States must assume responsibility for all the damages done to American merchants by French privateers; second, the United States must make a substantial loan to France; and third, the United States must give Talleyrand £50,000 for his troubles in negotiating the new treaty with America. The first condition reversed the demand for reparations in the envoys' instructions. The second had been expressly forbidden by those same instructions. And the third offended the envoys, who saw it as an insult to their country.

Most Americans had included British corruption among the central causes of their own revolution, and thus they would have been uncomfortable, if not repulsed, by Talleyrand's insistence on a bribe. This was Pinckney's reaction. When he shared X's message with his fellow envoys, the difference in their responses was telling: Marshall was furious; Gerry was noncommittal. In Marshall's view, the proposals made by X were tantamount to a demand for America's absolute surrender of its independence. Again, the Virginian urged that they write to Talleyrand with their own demand for a meeting with him. Yet, after some discussion, it was instead agreed that Pinckney should meet once again with X to acquire more details. This was their second major mistake, for it suggested a willingness to deal with unauthorized agents rather than the foreign minister. Talleyrand's strategy seemed to be working.

Pinckney's conversation with X the following day did little to quiet his concerns or Marshall's. X arrived with the demands of the 18th in writing. He suggested that the United States could disguise the loan by calling it an advance payment to the French for debts owed by various Americans. Sums could then be taken out of this "advance" for what he termed the "customary distribution" in diplomatic affairs, that is, the bribe. When Pinckney reported this conversation, Marshall's response was a firm no. He restated his position that the envoys should refuse to engage in any further indirect negotiations. Pinckney concurred. But Gerry did not, repeating his argument that to demand direct negotiations would be taking a hard line that would surely lead to war.

The next day, a second unauthorized agent arrived at the envoys' lodgings with X. Pierre Bellamy, or Y, introduced himself to the Americans as a close friend of Talleyrand. He too was a banker, but he was not just any banker—he was Talleyrand's personal banker. Y's task was to once again point out how offended the French government was by parts of Adams's speech and to insist that the envoys repudiate the offending comments. Above all, he made clear that official negotiations would be costly. "*Il faut de l'argent*," he said. "*Il faut beaucoup de l'argent.*" Marshall responded with a question: If we refuse to pay this money, will the Directory refuse to officially receive us? Bellamy hedged; he did not know.[38]

Once again the three envoys discussed their options. Marshall declared the situation preposterous, as neither of their visitors had any authority within the French government. He did not think it was in America's best interest to carry on these "clandestine negotiations." Gerry disagreed, and a heated argument followed. In the end, Gerry agreed that when X and Y arrived for breakfast the next morning, they would be told that the envoys would engage in no further informal discussions.

The envoys' resolve vanished, however, when their visitors arrived. X and Y told them once more that the Directory was furious about the president's speech. They assured the Americans that Talleyrand considered the repudiation essential, unless some means could be found to change the French government's mind—in other words, bribes and loans. The message was clear: the only solution to the envoys' dilemma was money. Y suggested that the United States could advance France 32 million Dutch florins. Then, when France signed a peace treaty with Holland, Holland would be required to repay the advance in full. Thus, the loan would not cost the United

States anything. When Marshall asked about the bribe to Talleyrand, Y quickly replied that it remained an additional payment.

In discussion later that day, Gerry urged his fellow envoys to delay any formal answer to this proposal. Another heated argument followed. Marshall announced that he would return to Philadelphia for instructions on the French demands, but only if France agreed to suspend its attacks on American shipping until he returned with an answer. When this offer was conveyed to Y, the banker responded with frustration. Was it not clear, he asked, that the Directory will expel you from France if you don't immediately comply?

On October 22, a dispirited Marshall sat down to write the first of two long dispatches to Secretary of State Pickering. It had been, he knew, almost two months since the three Americans had arrived in Paris, and they had no progress to report. Pinckney and Gerry signed Marshall's dispatch, but it did not reach its destination until March 1798.

4

"We experience a haughtiness . . .
unexampled in the history and practice of nations."
—Charles Cotesworth Pinckney,
October 1797

JOHN MARSHALL'S PESSIMISM was palpable as October ended. He wrote to William Vans Murray that he did not think the Directory would ever receive the envoys. And, in a letter to Charles Lee, he expressed his conviction that France "is not and never will be a republic." The United States stood alone, as it had before the French Revolution raised the hopes of Americans that liberty was spreading. "It is in America and America only," Marshall lamented, "that human liberty has found an asylum." Charles Cotesworth Pinckney was no less pessimistic. His wife, knowing her husband's mood, began to pack for a return to the United States. Elbridge Gerry, never an optimist, was equally glum. Writing to William Vans Murray, he declared, "The fact is, as I conceive it, that a small cargo of Mexican dollars would be more efficient in a negotiation at present than two

Cargoes of Ambassadors." The three men agreed, "We experience a haughtiness which is unexampled in the history and practice of nations."[39]

On the same day Marshall sent his dispatch to Pickering, Talleyrand sent a third agent, the wealthy sugar planter from Santo Domingo, Lucien Hauteval, to continue the pressure on the envoys. Hauteval, or "Z," had lived in Boston and knew Gerry. It was a mark of Talleyrand's cleverness that he chose agents who had a personal connection with one of the Americans and thus had reason to visit them. When Hauteval arrived, only Gerry was home. The planter wasted little time repeating the monetary terms allegedly set by the Directory: the loan and the bribe were essential. He assured Gerry that, unlike X and Y, he had no business connections with Talleyrand. In other words, he could be believed because he had no financial motive.

The next day, October 23, Z returned to talk to all three envoys. He suggested that they call on Talleyrand privately. Pinckney and Marshall refused, but Gerry, who had known Talleyrand during the French minister's years in America, said he would pay a personal visit on October 28. Talleyrand's patience was growing thin, however, and he sent X back to the envoys on the 27th.

The meeting was decidedly more confrontational than earlier ones. As Marshall later reported it to Pickering, Hottinguer began the two-hour conversation with boasts of recent French military successes. Austria has just made peace with France, he announced, and the French military cannot be defeated. The Americans' response to this vision of an invincible France was not what Hottinguer desired. They made clear that the French victories would not change their position on the Directory demands. In the face of this stubbornness, Hottinguer lost his temper. He resorted to an open threat: the Directory will move against any neutral nation. An equally angry Pinckney fired back that the United States would never pay tribute. "No, no not a sixpence!" he declared. Agent X, who could not fathom what he considered foolish resistance to an established practice, asked whether the US government was unaware that nothing was done in France without money changing hands. Pinckney confessed that such a practice was never suspected. To this admission, the amazed

Hottinguer observed that any American living in Paris could have told him as much.[40]

Hottinguer viewed the bribe and the forced loan as a practical matter; the Americans viewed it not only as a corrupt practice but also as a belittling assertion of domination. Perhaps if the memory of Genet and Adet and of Pinckney's own expulsion were not so fresh in the envoys' minds, they might have viewed the demands as part of a game of diplomatic chess, a move that needed to be countered by equal cunning. But attacks on the sovereignty of the federal government by Britain and France had convinced men like Pinckney and Marshall that their country was in peril. When X threatened that the failure to offer the loan and the bribe would lead to war, Marshall replied, "To lend this money under the lash & coercion of France was to relinquish the government of ourselves & to submit to a foreign government imposed upon us by force." Marshall's vow that his country would make "at least one manly struggle before we thus surrender our national independence" suggests that the Virginian saw the demand for money as a challenge to American virility. Framed in this manner, the situation brought out American bravado rather than subtle gamesmanship.[41]

On October 28, Gerry and Z went to see Talleyrand. Gerry told the foreign minister that the envoys had agreed one of them must go home to get instructions on the demand for a loan. A thoroughly annoyed Talleyrand retorted that the Directory was accustomed to dispatching business promptly and could not wait. The envoys, he declared, must assume the responsibility themselves—another challenge to their manhood—and they must do it soon. But, the following day, Talleyrand appeared to relent. X arrived with a new message and a new proposal: pay the bribe and two of you can remain in Paris while the third returns to the United States for instructions. The envoys asked whether France would agree to a moratorium on attacks on American ships while the consultation with the Adams administration took place. X replied no. Hearing this, Marshall responded that France had already taken $15 million from the United States through privateering. Despite this, he continued, we have come here to find a way to restore the harmony between our two nations. And all you can offer in return is that you might let us remain in Paris if we pay a bribe? The answer from X was yes. You must pay—or leave.[42]

Over the next few days, the visits from Talleyrand's agents continued. In addition to their old threat that there would be war if French demands were not met, they added a new one: France could easily persuade the "French Party" in America to blame the failure of negotiations on the Federalists. In effect, this was an admission of French meddling in America's domestic politics. The envoys' response to this threat was prophetic: "[France's] extreme injustice offered to our country would unite every man against her." Much hinged, Marshall knew, on whether this would prove true.[43]

November began with a decision by the envoys, once again, not to engage in indirect negotiations with the French government, a decision promptly broken when Talleyrand sent a new set of intermediaries to talk with them. The wealthy Parisian merchant Caron de Beaumarchais called on the envoys on November 8; his assignment was to discover whether their resistance to the bribe had softened. Soon afterward, James Mountflorence paid a visit to Pinckney, who succumbed to the temptation to send a message through Mountflorence to Talleyrand. Mountflorence was to tell the French minister that the envoys were disgusted with the treatment they had received. "We neither came to buy or beg a peace," Pinckney declared. Instead they were in Paris "to treat as an independent nation on the subject of differences subsisting between us." Pinckney's indignation was wasted; like the letter the envoys sent that month requesting that formal negotiations begin at once, this complaint did not receive a response.[44]

December came and with it a new strategy from Talleyrand. The French minister had decided to initiate a divide-and-conquer approach, designed to pry Gerry away from his two companions. Although Marshall was more certain than ever that Talleyrand was stalling and that France did not want a formal rupture with the United States, Gerry had grown even more anxious that war was imminent. He worried that a war between the world's only two republics would "disgrace republicanism and make it the scoff of despots." But Gerry's deepest fear was that the failure of negotiations would propel the United States into an alliance with Britain. In short, his abiding hatred of England was leading him to demand the envoys accommodate France. Certain that Gerry could be manipulated, Talleyrand invited him to dinner along with X, Y, and Z early in the month, and Y invited him to call on the foreign minister again on the 17th.[45]

Talleyrand did not, of course, relent in his pressuring of Pinckney and Marshall. They were visited several times that month by X and Y, who continued to urge them to change their minds about the bribe. While he was busy courting Gerry, Talleyrand carefully selected additional men to make the case for a bribe to the other envoys. He sent Pierre du Pont de Nemours, an old friend of the Pinckneys, to Charles Pinckney and Beaumarchais to Marshall. None of Talleyrand's agents managed to shake their resolve. Yet both men began to worry about Gerry's.

In truth, all three were restless and weary, and their letters were marked by pessimism. Gerry described their situation to his wife as "painful" and confessed to her that he had "no prospect that our mission will be of much service." And on Christmas Eve, Marshall conveyed his impatience and doubts in a letter to Rufus King, the American minister to Great Britain. He was determined, he said, to leave by mid-January if negotiations had not begun. "Submission has its limits," he declared, "and if we have not actually already passed, we are certainly approaching them." His doubts that the French could be trusted, even if a bribe were paid, were confirmed in a December 23 letter on its way to the envoys from Rufus King. Writing in cipher, King reported that England had just rejected a peace treaty offered by the Directory. The problem had not been the demand for an exorbitant bribe; it had been the English government's certainty that France could not be trusted to live up to the terms of the treaty. King strongly urged the three Americans to follow the British example. "To Ransom our country from Injustice and Power," he wrote, "would be to invite Dishonor and injury, because there can be no guaranty [sic] against them."[46]

In spite of the deadline Marshall set, January found the three Americans still in Paris. And at home, in Philadelphia, John Adams could do little but wonder about the success or failure of his efforts for peace.

5
"Shall an immediate declaration of
war be recommended?"
—John Adams, November 1797

WHILE THE ENVOYS wrestled with their predicament, Adams had been dealing with a crisis of a very different order at home. A new epidemic of yellow fever, similar to the one that had struck Philadelphia in 1793, had sent the president and much of the executive and legislative branches away from the city during October and November. At last the disease abated, and both the president and members of Congress returned to the capital. When the president addressed the reconvening Congress on November 22, he had no news to share about the negotiations. All he could report was what most congressmen surely knew: Europe was still racked by war; American ships were still vulnerable at sea. If America could do nothing to end that war, it could take steps, Adams declared, to protect its own commerce. Like the good New Englander he was, John Adams believed "Commerce has made this Country what it is." But to protect it would take money, money that must come, he said, from domestic sources rather than loans from foreign nations. This call for additional taxes was unlikely to be welcomed by the ordinary American voter.[47]

Winter began, and Marshall's October 22 dispatch had still not arrived. The apparent silence from the envoys proved more and more troubling. As George Washington wrote to Oliver Wolcott Jr., "It is somewhat singular that the Government should have received no advices from our Envoys at Paris since their arrival there." Even if the news were bad, Washington was impatient to learn it. Adams agreed. Assuming the worst because no positive news had been forthcoming, he decided to consult with his cabinet, sending it, on January 24, a long list of questions. If the envoys were refused an audience, or were ordered to depart without accomplishing their mission, what should they then do? Should they all go to Holland? Should two return to America while a third remained in Europe? Or should all of them come home? The two key questions were these: "Shall an immediate declaration of war be recommended or suggested?" And "What . . . above all . . . will policy dictate to be said to England?"[48]

Adams was worried—and he would have been more worried had he known what Talleyrand was plotting. In February, 1798, the French minister intensified his efforts to create a division among the envoys. He slyly suggested to Gerry that the French government ought to deal exclusively with him. He also asked Gerry to promise secrecy about their future meetings. Gerry was so flattered by this request that his usual wariness and suspicion wholly deserted him. He agreed to Talleyrand's insistence on confidentiality. He then compounded his error in judgment by revealing to his two colleagues that he had received several promising proposals from Talleyrand that he was not at liberty to share with them. With great drama, he added that his answer to these proposals would determine whether there would be war or peace.[49]

What were Marshall and Pinckney to make of this development? Marshall was no fool; he realized that Talleyrand planned to put the blame on the two of them if negotiations failed and to credit Gerry if they succeeded. He also concluded that Talleyrand intended to keep the suggestible Gerry in Paris and send the other two envoys home. As long as one of them remained, the likelihood of a US alliance with Great Britain was diminished. And if Talleyrand and Gerry could hammer out a treaty, this would help the Republicans—the "French Party"—in the next American presidential election. Marshall shared his insights with Pinckney. Much was at stake, including their own reputations, yet, inexplicably, the two men decided that Gerry should be free to respond to Talleyrand's proposals as he saw fit.

Two more meetings between Talleyrand and Gerry quickly followed. Marshall interceded only to remind Gerry that the French minister was not likely to offer anything the United States would accept. How, he asked Gerry, could you fail to see that all promises from Talleyrand were empty and that the foreign minister was simply stalling until the war with Britain was settled? Gerry's response was to insist that Talleyrand's offers were sincere.

The relationship between Gerry and his fellow envoys was unraveling. On February 9, Gerry reported that he had come from an "extraordinary conversation" with Talleyrand's secretary. He could not, however, report what was said. Marshall, weary of Gerry's secrets and his boasting about them, refused to ask anything about the conversation. Surprised, Gerry chose to share his extraordinary news after all: the Directory had decided to order all three envoys out of the country within twenty-four hours unless the bribe was paid. But there was more. Talleyrand, the secretary said, had managed to delay their expulsion to give them time to reconsider their position. Marshall could not hide his amazement at Gerry's gullibility. The threat, he told his colleague, was not real; it was just another of Talleyrand's tricks.

Marshall was right. February passed without any move by the French to expel the American envoys. Despite this, Gerry seemed more convinced than ever that the bribe and the loan were essential to prevent war. Talleyrand's secretary visited Gerry again on February 25, with a new proposal that America could pay the loan France demanded after the war with Great Britain was over. Gerry immediately shared the proposal with his colleagues, but Marshall just as immediately rejected it. He pointed out the obvious: there was nothing to prevent France from using the promised money as collateral for new loans during the current war. Even if prevention were possible, Marshall added, a loan granted under duress meant "we no longer acted for ourselves but according to the will of France." Pinckney agreed that France would quickly put the promised loan to use. This argument, Gerry retorted, rests on the suspicion that France would not honor its agreement. Forgetting for the moment his own reputation as the most suspicious man in American politics, Gerry declared solemnly, "It was extremely unwise for a man to deliver himself up entirely to suspicion, and the person who permitted himself to be governed by it in great national concerns would very often find himself mistaken."[50]

A long debate followed, settling nothing. The next day brought a second confrontation. Pinckney had heard a rumor that Talleyrand intended to send him and Marshall home so that he could negotiate a treaty with Gerry. This was, of course, exactly what Talleyrand intended to do. When Gerry confirmed the rumor, harsh words followed.

Marshall realized the situation had become impossible. If Talleyrand did ask for a loan payable after peace was declared with England, Marshall proposed that the envoys pledge to consult with their government before agreeing to these terms. The unspoken advantage of this pledge was that it would restrain Gerry if he were indeed left alone to negotiate with the French minister.

On the afternoon of March 2 the three envoys had their first meeting with Talleyrand in five months. They were told that the Directory now demanded an apology for George Washington's farewell address of September 19, 1796, in addition to Adams's May 16, 1797, address to Congress. They were also told that the loan to the French government was a prerequisite for any formal negotiations. Finally, the terms of that loan had changed; although it could be paid after the war, some aid must be given immediately. Marshall asked bluntly whether this was an ultimatum. Talleyrand's reply was maddeningly vague: some demonstration of friendship was required before negotiations could begin.

That night the envoys reached a stalemate. Marshall would not agree to Talleyrand's terms, and Gerry would not abandon his support for them. Gerry accused Marshall of implying that he had tried to trick them into agreeing to the French demands. Marshall dismissed the notion, insisting that no personal insult had been offered to Gerry. Gerry was not appeased. He took up the same issues the next morning. This time, Marshall was adamant: there was no point in discussing things further; neither of us is going to change our mind. There were only two alternatives: Gerry could remain in Paris and negotiate on his own, or he could return to Philadelphia for instructions. Marshall quickly added a third option. You and I, he told Gerry, could go home for instructions and Pinckney could remain in Paris. This discussion, like many other recent ones, ended with nothing decided.

The Americans scheduled another meeting with Talleyrand for March 6. As they prepared to leave for the foreign minister's office, Gerry asked Marshall whether he would be willing to insert a statement in any new treaty that the complaints Washington and Adams had made against France were "founded in mistake." At this, Marshall exploded. An equally angry Gerry announced that he wished to God that Marshall would propose something—anything!—that would accommodate French positions. Marshall coldly replied that he was not accustomed to such language. With this harsh exchange, all pretense of cordiality vanished.[51]

At the meeting, Talleyrand confirmed Pinckney and Marshall's suspicions that France would immediately use the promise of an American loan as collateral for other loans. In an effort to allay their concerns about Britain's response to the loan, the French minister suggested that the transactions between their two countries could be concealed from the public. Britain, in particular, need never know. Not surprisingly, Marshall objected. It remained clear to him that to assist France with a loan was to become France's ally in the war.

There was little more to be said. All that remained was the frantic maneuvering to place the blame for the failure of the negotiations on the other party. Would the Americans demand their passports and go home—or would the French government expel them? Realizing that it would be a blow to the Federalists if they initiated a departure, Marshall and Pinckney wisely dug in their heels. They were determined to make Talleyrand order them away. Talleyrand was just as determined to make them voluntarily depart. On March 20, he informed the Americans that the Directory was willing to negotiate only with an impartial envoy, and that man was Elbridge Gerry. The other two might just as well ask for their passports and depart.

For a brief moment, the envoys closed ranks. They agreed to tell Talleyrand that they would negotiate only as a team. In a carefully crafted message, Marshall made it clear to Talleyrand that France could not choose who would represent America at the table. While they waited for a response, Gerry repeatedly assured his colleagues that he would not remain in Paris alone. He would, he said, "sooner be thrown in the Seine than consent to stay."[52]

Yet, before the month was over, Gerry had changed his mind. On March 23, Talleyrand sent his secretary with a message: either Marshall and Pinckney submit a request for their passports within three days, or all three Americans would be ordered out of France. Marshall's response was to do nothing, which would force the French government to expel them. But Gerry, certain that their departure under any circumstances would lead to war, saw things differently. He insisted that Marshall and Pinckney must ask for their passports. He would make the sacrifice and remain in France to prevent a declaration of war. Marshall rejected this plan, but Gerry was certain it was the only viable solution. Writing home to his wife on March 26, he explained that he had to stay in Paris "to prevent a rupture." He appeared puzzled at the dynamics of his relationship with his fellow envoys. He had, he wrote, united with his colleagues on every decision, yet "their conduct to me has not been of that frank & friendly description which I expected." In Gerry's version of the mission, he was blameless. Marshall's journal and dispatches would tell a different story.[53]

For two weeks, Talleyrand and Marshall argued through surrogates over the details of the two Americans' departure. Marshall demanded a letter of safe passage to protect him from privateers. Talleyrand warned him not to stop in England on his way home. Marshall countered with the threat that he would indeed go to England if he did not receive the letter. Finally, on April 10, Marshall sent a message through Beaumarchais: the last ship bound directly to the United States was leaving soon. If Talleyrand did not want him to travel by way of England, a letter of safe conduct and a passport must be sent at once. Talleyrand replied as he had replied to Pinckney in 1797: if Marshall wanted a passport, he should apply for it from the Paris police like any other American civilian. Marshall fired back just as Pinckney had done: he was no ordinary citizen but a minister of the United States of America. In this, as in all the maneuvering that had preceded it, Marshall was determined to protect the honor and authority of the federal government.

It was perhaps inevitable that a confrontation with Gerry would take place while Marshall and Pinckney waited for the papers they needed to depart. The argument began with Pinckney's accusation that Gerry's behavior was an embarrassment to the American government. Gerry responded in kind, insisting that Pinckney and Marshall were embittered against him and had formed views and made plans that they kept secret from him. "It is false, sir," replied Pinckney, who threw back the charge of secrecy upon Gerry. Gerry defended himself, insisting he had simply honored a pledge of secrecy to Talleyrand. A livid Pinckney declared that Gerry ought never to have made such a promise![54]

On April 13, Talleyrand ended his battle of wills with John Marshall and sent a letter requesting that both he and Pinckney leave Paris. He enclosed two passports and two letters of safe conduct. On April 23, Marshall boarded the American brig the *Alexander Hamilton* for a long voyage home. Pinckney left Paris but spent several months in southern France until an ailing daughter of his was strong enough to make the Atlantic crossing. He and his family at last set sail for America on August 7. Only a day later, Elbridge Gerry began his own two-month journey home.[55]

6
"He . . . was the dupe of *Diplomatic Skill*."
—George Washington, February 1798

UPON THEIR RETURN, the three American envoys would tell wildly varied tales of their experiences in Paris. Charles Cotesworth Pinckney was openly critical of Elbridge Gerry's role in the unraveling of the negotiations. In a letter to Rufus King on April 4, 1798, Pinckney offered a harsh judgment of Gerry's character: "I never met a man of less candor and so much duplicity as Mr. Gerry." The men who had served in government with Gerry knew him to be abrasive, self-righteous, and always reluctant to compromise, but they did not doubt his patriotic intentions. If many of the choices he made as an envoy were unwise, to those who had not been in Paris, naïveté rather than cunning explained his duplicity. As John Quincy Adams would put it, "That Gentleman unfortunately was not qualified for negotiation with such men as now govern France—He was charmed with words; he was duped by professions; he had neither the spirit nor the penetration absolutely necessary for dealing with adversaries at once so bold, so cunning, and so false." George Washington agreed, although he was less charitable. "He was led astray," the former president declared, "by his own vanity & self importance, and was the dupe of *Diplomatic Skill*."[56]

Gerry, in short, like Edmond Genet, was simply out of his league as a diplomat. Yet the same could be said for Pinckney and Marshall. John Adams, who had considerable experience in such negotiations, should have known better than to send three novices to wrest concessions from a government known for its hubris—and slyness—in dealing with other countries.

Each of the three men Adams appointed had an obvious Achilles' heel. There was ample reason to suspect that Pinckney would be overly sensitive to slights after his humiliating experience in 1796.

And there was even more reason to believe that Gerry would be, as he had always proved to be uncooperative persistently annoying, and self-righteous. Finally, John Marshall, for all his obvious intelligence, lacked the gravitas to take charge of the commission when differences of opinion arose. Marshall became leader by default, and, although his analysis of the situation was usually correct, he too often appeased Gerry when he knew it was unwise.

From the beginning, Marshall's contempt for France, his rejection of its claim to be a republic, and his certainty that Talleyrand's dealings with the envoys dishonored America allowed him the distance needed to see that the Directory had more to gain by keeping the United States neutral than by making war against it. Without a new treaty, American neutrality would continue to be abused and manipulated and American supplies to be acquired without cost through privateering. Recognizing this, Marshall was able to develop an approach that was both more cynical and less frantic than Gerry's. Yet Marshall made serious tactical errors: he gave in to Gerry's pressure to treat with Talleyrand's agents, he tacitly approved Gerry's secret meetings with Talleyrand, and he foolishly agreed to let Gerry use his own judgment in responding to the French minister's proposals.

Pinckney's harsh judgment of Gerry sprang from frustration rather than a considered assessment of the latter's role in their failed mission. As a diplomat, Pinckney had no more skill than the man he accused of duplicity. Pinckney rarely asserted himself in the envoys' discussions, content to agree with Marshall except when he felt his personal honor—or his country's honor—was under direct attack. Honor was, in fact, the prism through which this South Carolina gentleman refracted much of what was proposed by Talleyrand and his agents. He may have underestimated Talleyrand's skill, for he had little respect for the French minister. He considered him to be a mere adventurer, and Talleyrand's demand for a bribe confirmed him in this judgment. When Marshall seemed willing to consider the bribe if a quid pro quo could be obtained, Pinckney's fierce declaration of "No, no not a sixpence" was less a parry to a proposal than a reflexive response to an assault upon America's honor.

And Gerry? He was a prisoner to his own intense hatred of England and all things British. That hatred prompted him to endure

French insults and to bend to French demands in order to prevent a war that might propel America into an alliance with Britain. His anxiety about this outcome blinded him to the possibility that the French did not want war with the United States and probably did not have the ability to invade America even if they wished to do so. His desire to accommodate France reflected poorly on his confidence in America's ability to defend itself and on the Federalists' willingness to avoid an alliance with Britain should war with France became a reality.

Charles Talleyrand, the fourth major player in the Paris disaster, enjoyed several advantages in dealing with the Americans. He saw no conflict in serving the interests of his country and the interests of his personal wealth. He intended to throw as many obstacles as possible in the path of the envoys until, in desperation, they acceded to his demands for a loan and a *douceur.* Unlike the American envoys, he had a clear plan to stall and mislead in order to extract concessions. He was able to keep the American envoys at arm's length through the use of intermediaries. That the Americans could not hold firm in their refusal to deal with X, Y, and Z, or Talleyrand's other agents, was their greatest mistake. Talleyrand's own misstep proved to be his belief, as Genet had believed before him, that the fundamental division in American politics was between a "French Party" and a "British Party" and that France could manipulate the outcome of that struggle. He ignored the American ministers' warning: France's extreme injustice would surely serve to unite every American against it.

In the end, Talleyrand and his agents simply outmaneuvered the three inexperienced diplomats. Only their stubbornness, born of national pride, ultimately defeated the French minister's scheme to enrich his government and, at the same time, line his own pockets. Yet, after seven months, they had fulfilled none of their instructions and never managed to bring Talleyrand into formal treaty negotiations. Their success, if it can be called that, resulted from their firm assertion that neither France nor any European power had the right to challenge American sovereignty or imperil its independence. This was a lesson the United States had been forced to teach France before, when Edmond Genet had flagrantly ignored that sovereignty and Adet had attempted to place leaders sympathetic to France in American political office.

7

"Is this the language of an American
who loves his country?"
—John Allen, spring 1798

ON MARCH 5, 1798, the long-awaited dispatches from the envoys at last reached Philadelphia. The president immediately notified the Senate, warning that it would take some time for them all to be decoded. The following day, the president and the secretary of state sat down to read the earliest reports written by Marshall in October 1797, which had been decoded. Thus, just as the final meeting between Talleyrand and the envoys was taking place, John Adams discovered that his peace mission had failed. The news was potentially devastating to American neutrality, yet Adams could hardly fail to see that exposure of French demands for loans and bribes, coupled with the disdain shown to the American envoys, might work to his political advantage. Nevertheless, he did not act to make the dispatches public. He was concerned that their publication would endanger the lives of the three American envoys who he assumed were still in France. All Adams was willing to do for the moment was report to Congress that the peace mission had failed.

Two weeks later, on March 19, he offered his blunt assessment to the legislature: "I perceive no ground of expectation that the object of [the envoys'] mission can be accomplished, on terms compatible with the safety, the honor, or the essential interests of the nation." His assessment thus placed the blame for the negotiation failure squarely on the French. The United States, he declared, must now take the necessary measures to protect its "seafaring and commercial citizens," and it must arm itself to defend America from the possibility of invasion. He accompanied this warning with the announcement of a policy that had been considered, and rejected, before the peace mission to France was undertaken: American merchantmen would be given permission to arm themselves for their defense. Soon afterward, Adams issued a recall of the envoys; by the time it reached Paris, Marshall had already departed. In effect, the president was sanctioning an undeclared war. When these steps were reported to

Thomas Jefferson, the sitting vice president and the leader of the Republican Party, he declared Adams's message "insane."[57]

Just as Adams expected, the Republican press put the blame for the failure of the negotiations on the president, members of his cabinet, and even the envoys themselves. The president, they said, had chosen the wrong men to represent the United States; Pickering had given Pinckney faulty instructions for his initial mission as the minister to France; Pinckney had been openly contemptuous of France; the Federalist press had offended the French authorities with its constant criticism. The president's call for Congress to pass major defense measures prompted newspapers like the *Aurora* to predict the ruin of American commerce and agriculture. Bache's nightmare prediction included a soaring national debt, mass deprivation for American citizens, and the imposition of crushing new taxes. The only sensible solution, the newspaper editor declared, was for Adams to resign.[58]

The response of the Republicans in Congress was far more cautious. They realized that the rejection of Pinckney and the continued attacks on American shipping had produced a rising tide of anti-French sentiment. The insulting behavior of the French government implicit in the president's message and his firm commitment to the defense of America would only increase that sentiment. Thus, the Republican minority carefully avoided a full defense of France. Instead, they vigorously opposed what one Representative called the president's effort to take the nation "step to step, until they are irrevocably involved in war."[59]

The majority of Federalists were eager to see the dispatches released to Congress, for they were confident this would increase popular support for the president and further embarrass the Republicans. But it was the Republicans themselves who made that embarrassment possible. By insisting that the president was holding back vital information, they provided an opening for Connecticut Federalist John Allen to move that Adams forward the dispatches to the House. The Republicans, still hoping to find some evidence that the administration was responsible for the failure of the mission, insisted that the instructions given to the envoys also be released. As New York Republican William Livingston put it, his constituents deserved to know that "all has been done to preserve the country in peace" before they were told that war was inevitable. On April 2, after intense debate, the House voted 65 to 27 in favor of Allen's motion. All 27 negative votes came from Federalists who did not want the envoys' instructions made public. But other, more savvy Federalists were willing to gamble that there was evidence of French contempt for America in the dispatches and that this evidence would do more damage than any flaws in the envoys' instructions.[60]

On April 3, twenty days before John Marshall safely boarded a ship headed for home, the president complied with the House demands. He submitted copies of several of Marshall's dispatches. He also provided copies to the Senate. Because of his concerns about the safety of the envoys still in France, he was careful not to disclose the names of the Frenchmen who acted as Talleyrand's agents. They were referred to simply as X, Y, and Z. Adams requested that Congress keep the dispatches confidential until they had carefully considered the consequences of their publication. The House dutifully cleared its galleries of visitors and reporters before settling in to read the chronicle of a failed mission to France. For the next few days, House members pored over John Marshall's account of demands for a bribe, a loan, and apologies for Washington's farewell address and President Adams's comments in his May 1797 message to Congress. On Friday, April 6, Delaware's James Bayard, a Federalist, moved that twelve hundred copies of the dispatches be printed. This would allow each representative a dozen copies to transmit to his constituents. Some debate followed over the number of copies that ought to be printed, although there was no challenge to making them available to the public. In the end, Bayard's proposal was accepted. The Senate also chose to publish the dispatches, ordering five hundred copies to be printed. The public was about to see for itself the French haughtiness that had so rankled John Marshall.[61]

The House then continued its debate on what defense measures the nation should take. Throughout these debates, Republicans spoke carefully: they did not want war with France, but neither did they want to appear cowardly in the face of French insults to American sovereignty. Their strategy was to focus on the cost to the nation of military preparations that they argued were unnecessary. Why burden Americans with such expenses, they asked, when no one genuinely believed France would invade America? It would be wiser to accept the French decree against American ships carrying British produce and manufactures than to declare war on France.

Federalists responded to this call for compliance with accusations of disloyalty. Alexander Hamilton's 1797 essays, "The Warning," now seemed prescient. He had warned that the American "Gallic Faction" would bring down the US government in the same manner that factions in Europe had undermined their own. The gravest danger to American independence, Hamilton had written, was the presence of a party whose "servility [was] abject enough to love and cherish the hand which despoils us, to kiss the Rod which stings us with unprovoked lashes." In the spring of 1798, representatives like John Allen took up the same theme in response to the Republican call for submission to French demands. "Is this the language of an American who loves his country?" Allen asked. "No, sir," he declared, "it is the language of a foreign agent." For Allen, the political apostasy of the Republicans was all too obvious. "I believe," he said later in the debates, "there are men in this country, in this House, whose hatred and abhorrence of our Government leads them to prefer another, profligate and ferocious as it is."[62]

Republican resistance to preparedness could not withstand such attacks. Thus Congress proceeded to prohibit the exportation of arms; took steps to procure cannon, arms, and ammunition; agreed to increase the size of the artillery and engineering forces; and decided to expand harbor defenses. By April 26, a bill to create a department of the navy had passed its third reading. Although war was not declared, warfare was beginning.[63]

Benjamin Bache did his best in the *Aurora* to counteract the growing war spirit and the explicit condemnation of the Republican Party. His argument closely followed the argument Thomas Jefferson had been making: the French Directory was not complicit in the demand for a bribe; Talleyrand acted alone when he insulted the United States by his greed. Thus, both Jefferson and Bache argued, there was no reason to go to war over the avarice of one man. Other Republican newspapers strained to associate Talleyrand with the Federalists, pointing out that during his years of self-imposed exile in America he had been a friend of Hamilton and Rufus King. This argument gained no traction. Nor did Bache's insistence that the envoys had acted precipitously and had never made a genuine effort to negotiate. Bache singled out Elbridge Gerry, alone in Paris, as the only envoy who attempted to negotiate in good faith. Nothing demonstrated how out of step Bache was with the mood of the country than his call for his readers to oust the president. "We are doomed to feel the horrors of war," he wrote, "unless the People step forward with one voice and induce the chief magistrate to retire, or their Representatives in Congress to impeach him, for having provided a war." Bache's main Federalist rival, John Fenno, was quick to realize how dramatically popular opinion had shifted. On April 12, he published a mock obituary for the Republican Party. The French faction, he wrote, "has died, as it lived, a violent and disorderly end."[64]

Despite the revelations in the dispatches, George Washington was not as ready as Fenno to celebrate the end of the opposition party. "One would think," he mused to Timothy Pickering, "that the measure of infamy was filled, and the profligacy of, & corruption in the system pursued by the French Directory, required no further disclosure of the principles by which it is actuated than what is contained in the . . . Dispatches, to open the eyes of the *blindest;* and yet, I am persuaded, that those communications will produce no change in the *leaders* of the opposition." Only a mass desertion by their followers would force men like Madison and Jefferson to abandon their support for France.[65]

The blows to the Republican Party continued with each new revelation from the president. On May 4, John Adams submitted a second set of dispatches to Congress. He released more documents on June 5, 18, and 21. In the early days of June, several of the Republican members of the House quietly left for home, resigned to the fact that anti-French sentiment dominated both in the halls of government and in the streets. Their departure allowed Congress to easily pass An Act to Suspend the Commercial Intercourse between the US and France, and the Dependencies thereof, which Adams signed on June 13. This was an embargo similar to the temporary one passed against Britain in 1795. Then, in July, the House brought to an end the years of worry over America's treaty obligations to France. It voted to abrogate the treaties of 1778, freeing the United States of any obligation to come to the defense of France or its territories if under attack.[66]

The support of Congress seemed to embolden the president. In the message accompanying the June 21 documents, Adams pledged that he would "never send another minister to France without assurances that he will be received, respected, and honored, as the representative of a great, free, powerful, and independent nation." But it was the outpouring of popular approval that most dramatically bolstered the president's confidence in his own leadership. For the first time in his life, John Adams was a popular hero.[67]

8

"Millions for defense but not one cent for tribute."
—Robert Goodloe Harper, June 1798

FOR A BRIEF—and for John Adams, glorious—moment American citizens showered their president with admiration and support. Memorials, signed by farmers as well as merchants, by working-class men of Boston and young elite gentlemen of Philadelphia, by local governments, churches, and individuals, poured in, each praising the president for his bold response to the French attack on American honor and sovereignty. Men who had sported the French cockade in their hats only a few years earlier now wore the black cockade that denoted their opposition to all things Gallic. Where once the "Marseillaise" was sung at public events, Americans now sang "Hail Columbia" and Robert Treat Paine's "Adams and Liberty." South Carolina Federalist Robert Goodloe Harper's toast "Millions for defense but not one cent for tribute," offered at a dinner honoring the president that June, became a rallying cry as stirring as "No Taxation Without Representation" had once been.[68]

The president seemed to relish the opportunity to lambast the Republicans in his replies to the memorials flooding his office. After almost two years of constant assault and insult in the Republican press, Adams allowed himself the satisfaction of venting against his critics and their party. "Woe to that country," he declared to the inhabitants of Harrison County, Virginia, "which supinely suffers malicious demagogues to excite jealousies, ferment prejudices, and stimulate animosities between [political parties]." Responding to a memorial from the mayor, aldermen, and citizens of Philadelphia, he pointed to the domestic dangers "when these Agitations of the human Species, have affected our People, and produced a Spirit of Party, which Scruples not to go all Lengths of Profligacy, falsehood, and malignity in defaming our government." James Madison considered the president's replies to his admirers "grotesque." Even Alexander Hamilton, not known for measured views of a party that had opposed every facet of his economic and fiscal plan for the country, worried that Adams had gone too far. But other Federalist leaders offered their own lavish praise for the president. From Massachusetts, for instance, George Cabot found the president's replies to the memorials "manly, just, spirited, and instructive."[69]

For the moment, even in the stronghold of Jefferson and Madison, anti-French sentiment predominated. Although a war with Virginia planters' best customer, France, would wreak havoc on tobacco prices, Virginians as much as Connecticut men resented the French contempt shown to their country. The old Antifederalist firebrand Patrick Henry urged unity in the wake of the XYZ affair. Many Virginians joined the rush for war preparedness, fearful that a war with France would mean an invasion from the Caribbean by black revolutionary Toussaint L'Ouverture and a wave of slave revolts throughout the southern states. Cities in the Old Dominion raised private funds to build frigates and sloops of war, and voluntary militia brigades were formed in the coastal city of Norfolk. Similar support for defense measures prompted South Carolina to build a fort that it named in honor of its native son, the envoy Charles Cotesworth Pinckney.[70]

Despite the bellicose posturing in his replies to the memorials, Adams remained reluctant to act. He shared with his predecessor a firm belief that France would not attempt to invade America. Although Washington had no doubt that France was capable of "any Species of Despotism and Injustice," he insisted that, in the face of a nation whose citizens were united to oppose it "with their lives & fortunes," an invasion would be folly.[71]

But if Adams was hesitant to declare war, members of his cabinet and the Congress were not. By May, war hawks like Pickering and Secretary of War James McHenry had seized control of military preparations. Ignoring the president's conviction that a buildup of naval forces was essential, these men pressed for the increase in

ground troops that Alexander Hamilton desired. Federalists in the
Senate were eager to comply with the hawks' requests. On Tuesday,
April 24, the House read for the first time a Senate bill that authorized the president to raise a provisional army of 20,000 men. This
triggered a fierce debate over the dangers Republicans saw in this
move. Granting the president this authority, they argued, was unconstitutional; raising an army was a legislative, not an executive, power.
If this bill were passed, what, Albert Gallatin asked, would prevent
the president's co-optation of other legislative powers? Running
through the debate was the fear of a standing army that lay deep in
the American psyche and had prompted an earlier Congress to include the preservation of state militias in the Bill of Rights. Despite
Gallatin's concerns that such a large federal army might be used domestically "for dangerous purposes," the Federalist-dominated Congress approved its creation.[72]

There was some basis for Gallatin's concern, for by July the new
army was effectively under the control of Alexander Hamilton. Although Washington had been chosen to command the provisional
army, it was understood that his participation would be minimal.
Actual army leadership was to fall on three major generals. For these
posts, the former president recommended Hamilton, Pinckney, and
Henry Knox. Both Knox and Pinckney had outranked Hamilton in
the Revolutionary War, yet Pickering and other cabinet members
pressed Adams to give Hamilton ultimate authority with the rank of
inspector general. In the face of secret maneuvering and overt pres-
sures from his cabinet, Adams bowed to their demand that the man
he most hated, Hamilton, take pride of place over the other major
generals.[73]

Hamilton had been a steady voice of moderation in the XYZ crisis, opposing both a declaration of war against France and a formal
alliance with England. But his appointment as inspector general of
a greatly expanded army prompted visions of empire in his head.
Sounding disturbingly like an American version of Citizen Genet,
Hamilton suggested using the army for an invasion of Louisiana and
Florida, both still held by France's ally Spain. He saw other uses for
the army as well: it could be an effective weapon against future domestic insurrections. In short, Hamilton and his supporters were
willing to use preparedness as an excuse not only for conquest but

also for the very suppression of protest that Gallatin feared. John Adams wanted nothing to do with Hamilton's ideas. Later, Adams would describe the difference between Hamilton and him by declaring, "This man is stark mad or I am."[74]

Despite the war hawks' enthusiasm, neither the president nor the Congress proved willing to issue an official declaration of war. In July, at the height of popular anti-French feeling, Fisher Ames advised Secretary of State Pickering that it would be best to simply proceed *as if* we were in war." Whether this was the best strategy remained to be seen. How long could the American public accept the costs of preparedness when its government seemed content with a mere approximation of war?[75]

9

"There is reason to believe that the XYZ delusion is wearing off."
—Thomas Jefferson, January 23, 1799

POPULAR PATIENCE, IT turned out, was not infinite. As summer turned to autumn and no declaration of war was made, war fever began to fade. The price of indecision was dramatized that winter as news was released of the bizarre actions of a private citizen, Dr. George Logan, who had gone to France on an unauthorized peace mission. Armed with a certificate of introduction from his good friend Thomas Jefferson and carrying letters from the French consul in Philadelphia to members of the Directory, Logan, a Pennsylvania Republican, had somehow managed to meet with Lafayette in Hamburg and to talk with members of the Directory and Talleyrand in Paris. In these conversations, Logan had urged the French to lift their embargo on US vessels and release the imprisoned American sailors captured by French privateers. These steps, he assured them, would make the renewal of cordial relations between the two countries possible.[76]

Philadelphia's Federalist press had learned of Logan's "mission" when he departed for Europe in June, responding to it with indignation and horror. The Philadelphia *Gazette* labeled the doctor "a noted and violent democrat" and condemned his mission as "a species of conspiracy, most fatal to freedom." The *Gazette* warned that Logan's goal was to see France forcefully—"with bayonet and guillotine"—reorganize America's government. On his return that September, Logan faced a second firestorm of criticism. Pickering condemned Logan's actions, and Washington treated the doctor with icy restraint when Logan visited to pay his respects. Logan's supporters, however, praised him for his efforts to lay the foundation of peace between France and America that the Adams administration had failed to do. At the end of January 1799, Federalists passed legislation forbidding unauthorized citizens from negotiating with any foreign governments involved in a dispute with the United States. The act quickly became known as the Logan Act.[77]

Logan was not alone in his frustration with the government's indecision about war with France. Complaints about the cost of preparedness grew as government spending nearly doubled, and there was palpable anger at the direct property tax on houses and slaves passed by Congress to cover military and naval expansion. In early 1799, this discontent would lead to violence in Pennsylvania once again, as hundreds of armed German farmers from the eastern part of the state, led by John Fries, freed a dozen men held as tax evaders. As the rebellion spread, both the governor and the president hurried to act. The uprising, like the Whiskey Rebellion, which it closely resembled, ended only in the face of state militia and a federal military force.[78]

Concern about the presence of an idle but greatly expanded army was also spreading. In Kentucky, where resistance to federal government had begun with the excise tax, "A Friend to Peace" tapped into the pervasive fear of a standing army. He warned that these newly assembling troops would be used not to defend the country against France but to oppress American citizens. They would "dragoon the . . . multitude" and "force them to bend their necks to the yoke." By January 1799, Jefferson, who had continued to believe that the XYZ affair was a "dish cooked up by Marshall," urged Republicans in Congress to distribute thousands of handbills exposing the "dupery" practiced on the public. Included in this "dupery" was most of the legislation passed by the Federalist Congress, including the repressive Alien and Sedition Acts, the Stamp Act, the direct tax, the additional army, a huge navy, and the millions of dollars used in the name of preparedness. It was clear that a policy of preparedness no longer convinced: the president either had to declare war or seek a new peace.[79]

As 1799 began, a now discontented John Adams assessed his situation. He had been stung and humiliated by his own cabinet, forced to appoint a man he despised to lead an army he did not believe necessary. He had witnessed the waning of his own popularity, as petitions demanding an end to direct taxation replaced flattering memorials. And he had come to fear that the steady outpouring of slander and criticism aimed at him by Republican newspapers could not be staunched, even by legislation. It was time, he concluded, to take control of his administration. He resolved that he would be his own man—and that meant he would be a statesman rather than a politician. He would act in the best interests of the nation, not the narrow interests of the party. He would not abandon the policy of preparedness, but he would repurpose it: he would use the nation's enhanced military and naval strength as bargaining chips in negotiations with France.

Adams was emboldened by his knowledge that, on the other side of the Atlantic, the political climate had changed. For many months he had doubted a French invasion of America was possible; after the crushing defeat of the French navy by the British in the August Battle of Aboukir Bay, he had declared to James McHenry that "there is no more prospect of seeing a French army here, than there is in Heaven." The emergence that winter of a new coalition among France's enemies made a war with the United States even more unlikely. It was no surprise, therefore, that Talleyrand was sending out feelers to William Vans Murray, the American minister to The Hague, in the hopes of rapprochement.[80]

On December 8, 1798, in a speech to the new session of Congress, John Adams declared himself ready to entertain the possibility of a new peace mission to France. Two months later, on February 18, 1799, he stunned Congress by announcing his nomination of William Vans Murray as minister plenipotentiary to that country. Describing himself as a president "always disposed and ready to embrace every plausible appearance of probability of preserving or restoring tranquility," he expressed his confidence that the new minister would receive the respect and honor that "the representative of a great, free, powerful, and independent nation" deserved. These were the very words Talleyrand had used to persuade Murray that the French desired to reopen negotiations.[81]

Suddenly months of war preparation, taxes, and bellicose rhetoric seemed precipitous, even foolish. Small wonder that Massachusetts Federalist Theodore Sedgwick declared the decision ruinous or that Timothy Pickering proclaimed himself thunderstruck. Pickering took pains to assure Alexander Hamilton that the president had "peremptorily determined (against our unanimous opinions) to leave the door open for the degrading and mischievous measure of sending another minister to France, even without waiting for *direct* overtures from her." The nomination of Murray now left the members of the cabinet "shocked and grieved." Republicans, however, quietly rejoiced. Thomas Jefferson captured their response perfectly in a letter to James Madison. The president's decision, he wrote, "silences all arguments against the sincerity of France, and renders desperate every further effort towards war."[82]

Federalist leaders in Congress tried to rally. They insisted that William Vans Murray was not up to the task and pressed Adams to add two more commissioners. At first, Adams stood firm, declaring they were interfering with his power to determine diplomatic policy. But he eventually complied. On March 8, 1800, three Federalists— William Vans Murray, Connecticut's Oliver Ellsworth, and William Richardson Davie of North Carolina—were greeted by Napoleon in Paris. On September 20, after seven months of negotiations, an agreement known as the Convention of 1800 was reached. The US Senate approved the treaty on February 3, 1801. The quasi-war with France was over. So too was John Adams's political career.[83]

Epilogue

THE XYZ AFFAIR and the quasi-war it prompted were the defining events of the Adams administration. The president's decision to end rather than escalate the hostilities between the United States and France led to the revival of the Republican Party and contributed to the end of Federalist hegemony. But perhaps the most important consequence of the XYZ affair was the revelation that loyalty to the federal government had become the sine qua non of patriotism. The growth of this loyalty had been slowly emerging since Washington's first term as president. In the Whiskey Rebellion, citizens had rallied to defend a man they loved and admired; in the Genet affair, they had defended the powers of the office he held. In the XYZ affair, it was not the president as much as the nation entrusted to his care whose honor Americans consciously rose to defend. They hailed John Adams for defending the honor of their country, and, in doing so, they discovered an identity they shared as Americans. Despite the many and deep ideological and policy differences between Federalists and Republicans, Americans of both parties were determined to show they were not, as the French Directory had claimed, a "divided people" who could be separated from one another or from their government. Instead, they insisted that their country had a national character that bound them together. "We ought all to be Americans," wrote one Virginian, giving evidence that Americans were learning that no disagreements should run so deep as to permanently divide them from one another and no criticism they might have of their government should destroy their loyalty to it.

In 1812, the nation would wage another war, this time against its former mother country. During that war, the tune to Robert Treat Paine's "Adams and Liberty" was recycled by Francis Scott Keyes and became "The Star-Spangled Banner." When peace returned, the nationalism that had been growing during the 1790s truly flowered. Instead of simply defending their sovereignty and independence, Americans created art and literature as well as political policies that proudly celebrated what they considered their exceptional destiny.

Part IV

THE ALIEN AND
SEDITION ACTS

IN THE WAKE of the XYZ revelations, America began to prepare for what President John Adams would call "the half war with France." But for the Federalist Party, there were other wars to be waged, too: first, a war with those "internal disturbers," members of the Republican Party whose relentless criticism of the administration and its policies threatened to undermine popular support for their government; and, second, a war against foreigners whose radical ideas or loyalties to other nations fostered division within American society. As long as "the temple of our freedom," as Charles Pinckney called the Union, was under siege, Federalists could not rest.[1]

The Republican Party was no less involved in a war to save the United States, but it located that danger within the government itself. Republicans were convinced that the "monocrats" in power wished to take the country down the path to tyranny. They believed Federalists intended to so erode state sovereignty that Americans would find themselves living under a consolidated government run by a monarch and his minions.

This Manichaean struggle between the two parties—a rhetorical and ideological battle for the soul of the country—allowed the eighteenth-century men involved to make sense of their political universe. It brought an intellectual order to disparate and complex events, to economic and fiscal policies, and to diplomatic decisions. It allowed both Federalists and Republicans to believe that their political stances and even their personal quests for power were synonymous with the welfare of their country. It also ensured that the eradication of one's opponents seemed the only option.

Historians have generally condemned the Federalists for their effort to eradicate, or at least greatly wound, their oppositions through the Alien and Sedition Acts. The party's anti-immigrant bias and its effort to suppress dissent and the freedom of the press have been portrayed as a challenge to American values. These acts are seen as the forerunners of such modern abuses of American rights and liberties as twentieth-century immigration quotas, the Red Scare, Japanese internment camps, and minority voter suppression. The defeat of the Federalists in 1800 and the demise of the party soon afterward are interpreted as a well-deserved rejection of men determined to hold back the progress of democracy.

But harsh judgment can sometimes obscure more than it reveals. History might be better served by a closer look at the context for these acts, an analysis of their actual impact on immigration and freedom of the press, and a consideration of their positive role in establishing American nationalism. Above all, it would be wise to recast the nature of the crisis the Alien and Sedition Acts produced. It was, after all, a crisis in two parts, each with long-term consequences in American history: the first, the attempt to suppress liberties; the second, arising from the Virginia and Kentucky Resolutions that defied these laws, the introduction of the concept of nullification that would eventually threaten the survival of the nation the Federalists had nurtured and sustained. If the first was the work of the Federalists, the second was the work of Jefferson's Republicans.

1
"Many Jacobins and vagabonds."
—James Bayard, 1798

THE SUMMER OF 1798 seemed an ideal time for Federalists to mount their crusade to wipe out the Republican opposition. In the spring, news of the infamous treatment of the American envoys by the French, and the fear of an invasion by that nation, had produced a strong outpouring of nationalism. With this came an outpouring of support for both President Adams and his administration. Republican popularity, by contrast, was at its nadir, diminished by the party's Francophile reputation and its ineffectual attempts to defend the French Directory's treatment of the envoys. In the midst of enacting legislation aimed at military and naval preparedness, the Federalist-dominated Congress struck: it passed a series of bills known collectively as the Alien and Sedition Acts.

The first of these acts, the Naturalization Act of 1798, was intended to address what Federalists considered the disturbing growth of support for the Republican Party among immigrants, especially the Irish. They saw that much of the opposition's recruitment success was due to the work of Irish, English, and Scottish radicals. These men, whose anti-British activism had sometimes led to charges of treason in their home countries, condemned a Federalist agenda they believed closely mimicked the oppressive policies of the British government. On arrival in the United States, they gravitated quickly to the Republican Party and worked effectively to persuade rank-and-file Irish and even German immigrants to join them. Their recruiting success helped a party that had been based in the South make inroads into New England and northeastern cities like Philadelphia. As editors of newspapers or as regular contributors to the partisan press, Irishmen like Matthew Carey, Matthew Lyon, John Binns, and William Duane, along with English radicals James Callender and Thomas Cooper, became leading propagandists for the Republican Party. In urban and country newspapers, these writers frequently published criticism and invective against Hamiltonian economics, Federalist foreign policies, and the character of individual Federalist officeholders. Meanwhile, the Irish and German immigrants created ethnic and nationalistic organizations that encouraged unity and reinforced anti-Federalist ideas. Federalists decided that delaying citizenship for these foreigners, and for the French refugees already residing in the United States, was their best hope to stem the rising membership of the opposition party.[2]

Naturalization laws were not new, nor were they unconstitutional. Article 1, section 8, clause 4 of the Constitution granted Congress the power to establish a uniform rule of naturalization. The first application of this power had come on March 26, 1790, when Congress passed a liberal naturalization act. By its terms, immigrants could apply for citizenship after a two-year residence in the United States. The only restriction was that the applicants be "free white persons" of "good moral character." On January 29, 1795, the Third Congress produced a revised naturalization act, increasing the residence requirement to five years. It also required applicants to give three years' notice of their intent to apply for citizenship and to renounce any allegiance to a foreign prince or state. In the spring of 1798, Federalists in both houses of Congress declared it time to revise the process once again.[3]

The debate in the House was acrimonious. South Carolina Federalist Robert Goodloe Harper preferred that there be no path to citizenship at all for an alien. Immigrants, he declared, simply caused trouble in the United States. Although New Englander Harrison Gray Otis was not prepared to go that far, he did want restrictions imposed on immigrants who had already attained citizenship. Although he was ready to allow them to own property, he thought it best to bar them from any participation in politics. They should neither be allowed to hold office, Otis argued, nor vote for legislators. Although neither of these two extreme positions was seriously considered, by May 21, the House had resolved to extend the waiting period for naturalization to fourteen years.

The debate over what the former aliens' rights as citizens would entail was not over, however. Federalist James Bayard of Delaware recommended that all new citizens should be restricted from voting in federal elections or serving in federal office. He alleged that "many Jacobins and vagabonds" had immigrated in recent years. His extremism, like Harper's and Otis's, reflected the Federalists' genuine fear that the United States would fall to the French, not in battle but in the erosion of support for the Constitution and its federal government. Although the restrictions on political participation proposed by Bayard and Otis did not pass, Federalist fears of a coalition of immigrants and Republicans did win out. On Tuesday, May 22, the new House naturalization bill was read for the third time and passed.[4]

On June 18, 1798, the same day that the president forwarded additional dispatches from the envoys to the Congress, President Adams signed into law the new Naturalization Act, which almost tripled the waiting time for citizenship. Under the new law, applicants were required to announce their intention to seek citizenship five years in advance of formal application to the courts. In addition, all white aliens, other than foreign ministers, consuls, or agents and their families and staff, were required to register within six months of arrival with the clerk of the district court or an equivalent government official. Any alien failing to register would be subjected to a fine, and any alien who drew complaints for being disruptive would be required to give surety of good behavior. The refusal to provide this surety would result in commitment to the common gaol (jail).[5]

At the same time that the Federalist majorities in the Congress were delaying citizenship—and suffrage—for immigrants, they were contemplating how to protect the country from those aliens who might be directly "dangerous to its peace and safety." On April 25, Connecticut senator James Hillhouse called for a bill that would include a provision for the deportation of those found dangerous to the security of the country. Throughout the month of May, the Senate debated the resulting bill and several amendments to it. At one extreme, it was proposed that the scope of the president's power be enlarged to include the ability to expel any alien who had been imprisoned for "speaking, writing, or printing" dangerous ideas. At the other, it was proposed that the president be reined in by requiring him to provide the basis for any deportation and deposit a record of his actions in the office of the secretary of state for Congress's perusal. Both amendments were voted down. But, as the debate progressed, the bill did take on a decidedly harsh tone. On Wednesday, May 30, the Senate agreed by a vote of 16 to 6 that any alien who refused or evaded an order to leave the United States should be punished with a term of life imprisonment and hard labor. On June 8, after several

postponements and several proposed amendments, the Senate final-
ized its draconian version of what would come to be known popularly
as the Alien Friends Act by a vote of 16 to 7.[6]

Throughout May and June, the House engaged in overlapping debates on how to deal not only with troublesome aliens from friendly
countries but with aliens from countries at war with, or threatening
war with, the United States. At the same time, it had begun to discuss
how to define, and to punish, sedition. But discussions of war preparedness issues such as the size of the provisional army and direct
taxes overshadowed these issues of sedition. It was not until Tuesday,
June 19, that a sustained House debate on the alien friends bill began in earnest.[7]

In the course of the long and dense argument over the constitutionality of such a bill that followed, the fractures and fault lines
that separated the two parties emerged with startling clarity. The
concerns that divided Republicans and Federalists echoed older arguments over the nature of the Union. Was it a consolidation of the
states, as nationalists like Hamilton and Ames believed? Or was it a
voluntary compact among sovereign states, as Gallatin and Abraham
Baldwin would argue? The House debate revived old disagreements,
voiced first during the ratification struggle, over which government,
state or federal, best protected the people's liberties. And it pitted
those who believed restrictive, even punitive measures were necessary to keep the country safe against those who saw claims of vul-
nerability as ruses to increase the power of the executive branch and
open the way to monarchy and tyranny.

Pennsylvania's Albert Gallatin, one of the leading voices of the
Republican Party, opened the debate with a challenge to the bill's
constitutionality. The bill, he argued, infringed the right of habeas
corpus and denied immigrants due process. With what crimes were
the targeted aliens to be charged? Gallatin asked. Why were they
subject to the discretion of the president rather than to the judicial
process? But Gallatin's central argument focused on which government, state or federal, had authority over the admission of aliens. Every country, he conceded, had the right to permit or exclude aliens,
but it was his understanding that the Tenth Amendment to the Constitution ensured that this power "does solely belong to each individual State." Gallatin buttressed his argument for state regulation

of aliens by citing the constitutional prohibition against interference with the "migration or importation of such persons as any of the States now existing shall think proper to admit" until 1808. Europeans might migrate and Africans might arrive against their will, but Gallatin held that the Constitution placed the regulation of both in the hands of the states until that year.[8]

Gallatin's argument thus exposed the fundamental disagreement between the two parties over the nature of the Constitution, a disagreement that would continue into the nineteenth century with violent and bloody consequences. The Republicans insisted that the Constitution was a compact and that the states and the people had only granted specific and limited powers to the federal government created by that compact. Federalists disagreed. The Preamble to the Constitution, they argued, established the "sovereignty of the United States and its government" and committed the federal government to provide for the common defense and general welfare. This interpretation placed legislation designed to protect the country from dangerous aliens well within the scope of Congress. Even when conceding that the states controlled the *admission* of aliens to the country, Federalists insisted the federal government had a clear right to regulate their continued residence in the United States.[9]

For southern slaveholders in particular, the stakes were high in this battle over the relative authority of the federal government and the states. And Gallatin had unintentionally roused their anxiety when he read immigrants into the prohibition clause generally understood to apply only to the importation of slaves. If, as Federalists argued, Congress could legislate the deportation of dangerous immigrants, could it also deport a black labor force that many thought was equally dangerous? This possibility had led Georgia's Abraham Baldwin to protest against *any* legislation based on the peoples' "general welfare." To grant the federal government this authority, Baldwin warned during a debate on sedition that raised the same issues, was to ensure that the state governments would "fall prostrate before it."[10]

Federalists gave no evidence that they intended to remove enslaved blacks from the country. Their focus remained on the threat to American sovereignty posed by radical aliens who might have conspired with foreign governments or with domestic opponents of the administration to weaken American political institutions. Federalist congressmen rose on the floor of the House to remind their colleagues of the fate of Venice, of Switzerland, of Holland, and of all the independent states and countries that had fallen to France through such conspiracies. It was well known, Harrison Gray Otis declared, that France caused their downfall by organizing bands of aliens and native citizens to topple their governments.[11]

New York's Edward Livingston, who shared leadership of the Republicans in the House with Gallatin, rejected the examples Otis presented. It was not foreigners, he said, but domestic "factions" that fatally weakened these European nations. In an attempt to stress the extremism of the legislation Federalists were proposing, Livingston stumbled into a suggestion he would soon regret: "We ought to banish not aliens," he said, "but all those who did not approve of the Executive acts!" Pennsylvania Federalist John Kittera chose to take the suggestion seriously. It was his hope, he declared, that passage of this bill to curb aliens would be followed by passage of a strong sedition bill to curb the actions of citizens.[12]

On June 21, despite the continued protest by Republicans that the bill ran roughshod over states' rights, the Federalist majority in the House passed the alien friends legislation by a vote of 46 to 40. On June 25, John Adams signed the alien friends act, officially entitled An Act Concerning Aliens, into law. By its terms, the president had the authority to order "all such aliens as he shall judge dangerous to the peace and safety of the United States, or shall have reasonable grounds to suspect are concerned in any treasonable or secret machinations against the government thereof, to depart out of the territory of the United States." Punishment for remaining in the United States was far milder than the Senate had once wished: imprisonment for a term not exceeding three years plus the denial of the right of citizenship forever. The president was given discretion not only in removing a dangerous alien but also in allowing him to remain. This privilege could be rescinded if the president found it necessary. Through its third section, the act required the captains of ships arriving in a US port to provide the name, age, and place of birth of any alien on board their vessels. Significantly, jurisdiction over cases arising from the act fell to US circuit and district courts rather than to state courts. Section 5 of the act reflected the respect for the rights of property that Federalists and Republicans shared. If deported, an alien would be allowed to take with him "such part of his goods, chattels, and other property as he may find convenient" and any property left in the United States would remain under his control. Despite the threat Federalists believed aliens posed to the security of the country, they were not willing to permanently grant a president the powers provided by this law. An Act Concerning Aliens was to remain in force for only two years, a period coinciding with the end of John Adams's term in office.[13]

As a counterpart to this Alien Friends Act, legislation dealing with aliens from enemy countries soon followed. There was little opposition to legislation that allowed aliens from countries at war with the United States to be "apprehended, restrained, secured and removed." On July 3, the Senate passed this bill with minor amendments, and the House concurred with these changes.[14]

The president signed An Act Respecting Alien Enemies into law on July 6, 1798. In its final form, this act gave the president great latitude in deciding "the manner and degree of the restraint to which [alien enemies] shall be subject." Those alien enemies who might become hostile but had not yet engaged in any hostile action would be entitled to retain and remove their property. This act, unlike the one dealing with alien friends, gave state courts the same authority as federal courts to hear complaints against alien enemies.[15]

Federalists hoped the passage of this law would protect against the rise of new plots that challenged the sovereignty of the United States. They wanted no new Genets enlisting Americans to invade Louisiana or Spanish Florida and no new Frenchmen like Andre Michaux pretending to be on scientific explorations in the West while working secretly for the French. But surely war hawks like Otis and Pickering also hoped that the act would prompt a formal declaration of war against France.

Despite any sense of satisfaction passage of these two alien acts gave the Federalists, the powers they granted to the president remained dormant under John Adams. As president, Adams deported no one. At most, these laws applied psychological pressure on immigrants who had not begun the naturalization process. The Alien Enemies Act no doubt played a role in the decision of many members of the French Caribbean community who had taken refuge in the United States to leave America voluntarily. The Alien Friends Act expired in 1801 without any actual application; the Alien Enemies Act, whose impact was first felt in the twentieth century, remains in force today.[16]

2

"Deliver us from . . .
the public floods of falsehood and hatred."
—John Allen, July 1798

THE FEDERALISTS SAW the naturalization law and the two alien acts as part of the broader war preparedness efforts to protect the nation from external and internal threats. During the debates on these acts, John Kittera's concern about the dangers of verbal and written attacks on public figures hummed just below the surface, occasionally making its way into suggested amendments. Finally, on Saturday, June 23, James Lloyd, a Federalist Senator from Maryland, announced his intention to bring a bill to "define more particularly the crime of treason, and to define and punish the crime of sedition." The target of this bill was immediately obvious to all: the Republican press.[17]

Much of the Federalists' enthusiasm for curbing the opposition press came, of course, from a desire to end the relentless ad hominem attacks and the often wild accusations that had been aimed at them throughout the decade by newspapers like the *Aurora* and the *Time-Piece.* John Adams, who had felt the sting of newspaper criticism even as vice president, might be excused for wishing that Republican papers could be silenced. Over the course of his years in federal office, he endured descriptions of himself as a "mock Monarch," a "blind, bald, toothless, querulous" old man, "a repulsive pedant," and a "gross hypocrite." Often enough, the attacks contained violent imagery. A contributor to the *Richmond Examiner* had suggested that President Adams should be hurled "headlong, with as little ceremony as we would run an invading enemy through with a bayonet."[18]

The president's wife, Abigail, hated the Republican press even more than her husband did. In June 1797, after reading a particularly hostile piece in the Boston *Independent Chronicle,* she vented her anger to her sister. The editor of the *Chronicle,* she declared, "has more of the true spirit of Satan, for he not only collects the Billingsgate of all the Jacobin papers but he add[s] to it the Lies, falsehoods, calumny and bitterness of his own."[19]

Federalists conceded that their supporters were sometimes equally unrestrained. The prime example was English-born William Cobbett, a seemingly affable, portly autodidact who nevertheless was responsible for an unending string of personal insults and attacks in his popular *Porcupine's Gazette.* Cobbett's criticism of the British government had forced him to seek refuge from English authorities in France, although he had no sympathy for the French Revolution. By 1792, he had made his way to America. He declared an immediate distaste for his new country, finding its climate detestable and its people "a cheating, sly roguish gang." Yet, for the next eight years, he used his newspaper to skewer radical refugee intellectuals like Joseph Priestley, native-born Republicans, and the immigrants who flocked to the Republican banner. In one outburst he described these primarily Irish immigrants as "frog-eating, man-eating, blood-drinking cannibals."[20]

Cobbett's writing was so engaging and his venom so entertaining that many Philadelphia residents who disagreed with him nevertheless eagerly read each edition of *Porcupine's Gazette.* Yet Cobbett was an iconoclast at heart and did not confine his attacks to Republicans; he insulted anyone he considered pompous or puritanical. Some of his targets fought back. Thomas McKean, who rose to be chief justice of Pennsylvania, sued Cobbett for criminal libel in the summer of 1796 and had the satisfaction of serving as both judge and witness at his trial. Philadelphia's leading physician, Dr. Benjamin Rush, also sued Cobbett for his criticisms of the use of bloodletting to battle yellow fever and won a judgment of $5,000 in damages. And Noah Webster tried to have Cobbett arrested for sedition. By 1800, Cobbett had made so many prominent enemies in America that he thought it best to return to England.[21]

To Federalists, the flood of what Connecticut's John Allen called Republicans' "falsehood and hatred of everything sacred, human and divine" was far more dangerous than the ethnic insults of an irrepressible cynic whom Federalists generally disavowed. It was patently obvious to men like Allen that Republicans were waging a war in the press against the domestic and foreign policies of the administration, accusing Federalists of plots to establish an American monarchy, bringing charges of bribery and embezzlement against members of the cabinet, and insisting that Adams and Pickering were guilty of a concerted effort to provoke a war with France. Without the concept of a loyal opposition to frame these disagreements over domestic and foreign policies, Federalists could perhaps be excused for seeing Republicans as agents of social anarchy and political upheaval.[22]

Recent history served as the context for their alarm. There had, after all, been powerful opposition to the ratification of the Constitution in the 1780s. When that battle was lost, opponents of the new government hoped to strip its powers of taxation and regulation of commerce by calling a second constitutional convention. And during Washington's first administration, extragovernmental organizations like the Democratic Societies had been staunch supporters of Genet, and, in the Federalist view, they encouraged western insurgents to reject the whiskey tax and deny the authority of the president and the Congress. As Federalists saw it, concerted efforts to weaken, or even destroy, the Constitution and the government it created had been a constant in American political life.

Like George Washington, most Federalists believed the press had become a dangerous political weapon, wielded by "internal disturbers" whose goal was to "destroy all confidence in those who are entrusted with the Administration." As war with France loomed, Virginia Federalist Charles Lee voiced his party's conviction that the peril America faced was domestic as much as—or more than—it was foreign. Our frame of government, Lee wrote, depends upon "the affections and respect of the people; take that away and the government is at an end." In short, words mattered. And because of this, Federalists were convinced that many of the words appearing in the partisan press should be considered seditious.[23]

The Federalist move to rescue the Republic began in earnest on Tuesday, June 26, when James Lloyd made good on his promise and proposed a sedition bill. The vote to bring in the bill passed by a comfortable 14 to 8 vote along party lines. The next day, a committee made up exclusively of Federalists was appointed to report the bill. By July 4, the third reading had taken place. No disagreement seemed to arise over the first section of the bill, which labeled as high misdemeanors the unlawful combination or conspiracy to oppose any measure of the federal government, the impeding of the operation of any federal law, the intimidating or preventing an officer of the government from executing his duties, or the advising of insurrection, riot, or unlawful assembly. Nor did any Republican senator appear to protest section 3 of the bill, which allowed a person accused of writing or publishing libel to use truth as a defense. But Republicans did protest section 2, which would subject to prosecution the writing, printing, uttering, or publishing of anything "false, scandalous and malicious" against the government, either house of Congress, or the president. Anyone found guilty of bringing the government or its leaders into contempt or disrepute, exciting the hatred of the people against those leaders, stirring up sedition within the United States, resisting a federal law or a constitutional act of the president, or abetting hostile designs of a foreign nation could be tried and, if convicted, fined up to $2,000 and imprisoned for up to two years. The Republican attempt to expunge this entire section—and thus protect the press—failed by a vote of 18 to 6. A second 18 to 6 vote led to the passage of the bill. Thus, on the date Americans would come to celebrate as Independence Day, the upper house of Congress approved An Act in Addition to the Act, Entitled An Act for the Punishment of Certain Crimes Against the United States.[24]

On July 5, the House of Representatives read the Senate bill for the first time. Harrison Gray Otis of Massachusetts moved that it should be read a second time, while the Republican spokesman, Edward Livingston, moved to reject the bill immediately. In the long and heated discussion that ensued, Federalists and Republicans staked out their positions on the need for and the constitutionality of a sedition bill. Federalists argued that the partisan press as well as certain Republican members of Congress were creating a crisis of confidence in the government by spreading lies about the administration's policies and slandering the character of the president and other key members of the federal government. They defended the constitutionality of the bill on two grounds, arguing, first, that the federal government—and, for that matter, any government—had the right to defend itself against sedition and libel; and, second, that the Constitution allowed legislation that was necessary and proper to assure the government's ability to serve the people. Republicans built their opposition around three central points. First, no such crisis of confidence existed. Second, the sedition bill went beyond the legislative powers enumerated in the Constitution. And, third, it was in defiance of the First Amendment right to a free press.[25]

John Allen opened the debate with a vigorous defense of the bill. No one, he said, could deny that it was needed, for there was a "warrantable and dangerous combination to overturn and ruin the government" through the publication of "shameless falsehoods against the Representatives of the people." Allen had brought with him examples of falsehood found in the *Aurora* and the New York *Time-Piece,* and he read these to the chamber. Allen then warned that the "dangerous combination" had spread to the House itself. He accused Edward Livingston, who had hoped to squelch the bill, of giving speeches declaring that insurrection was a duty in the face of an unconstitutional law. Allen quoted Livingston's statement that "whenever our laws manifestly infringe the Constitution under which they are made, the people ought not to hesitate which they should obey." Allen also cited a Virginia representative who had sent a letter to his constituents accusing the federal government of a tendency toward abuses similar to those of England. Here was proof, Allen asserted, that the press and the Republican politicians meant to endanger the Republic and transform the people into a mob. To encourage resistance to the law was to "produce divisions, tumults, violence, insurrection and blood," all of which are the end result of the instigators' "recurrence to first revolutionary principles." From such principles, Allen hoped that "God [may] preserve us."[26]

Republicans fired back. What evidence was there of an imminent threat of insurrection? And where exactly did the threat come from? Virginia's John Nicholas observed somewhat wryly that the Federalists seemed more afraid of speeches and letters by their fellow congressmen than those newspaper essays and editorials the bill was intended to suppress. He was opposed, he said, to creating a "*domestic tyranny,*" for he had confidence that the people were competent to judge for themselves the truth or falsehood of what they read. Other Republicans warned that bills like this one would actually drive people into opposition to the government. Like Nicholas, they were confident the people had good judgment. And if left alone, the press was self-correcting; if one paper said something untrue, another would be there to point it out.[27]

The bigger question remained: Did the federal government have the authority to suppress the supposed threat? Federalists said yes. North Carolina's Nathaniel Macon, a devoted follower of Thomas Jefferson and a pithy commentator on political issues, conceded that the protection of the federal government might indeed be necessary; however, the responsibility for that protection could just as easily fall to the state governments. In response, the often verbose Otis proved equally pithy: that notion, he said, was "absurd."[28]

Federalist members of the House shared Otis's cynicism. In past crises, states had proven less than dependable in protecting the authority of the federal government. Pennsylvania had allowed the whiskey rebels great latitude. Kentucky authorities had turned a blind eye when their citizens ignored the excise law. And the governors of Kentucky and South Carolina had allowed French intrigues against America's allies and had permitted French officials to mock the federal government's policy of neutrality. To Federalists like Otis, state governments could not be trusted to uphold the Constitution.

Republicans pressed their opposition to the sedition bill, asking where, specifically, the authority to pass such an act was to be found in the Constitution. Nathaniel Macon said no such authority could be found. The Constitution did grant the federal government the power to define and punish piracies and felonies committed on the high seas and offenses against the law of nations, but it had been given "no power to define *any other crime whatsoever.*" Hence, his suggested solution remained: if the federal government was in need of protection, it must rely on the states to protect it from sedition. Federalists dismissed Macon's argument and ignored his solution. The Constitution might not have explicitly granted the power to punish sedition, but it had given the federal government the power to make all laws necessary to execute the powers that *were* enumerated within it. Without a Sedition Act, they again asserted, there would be such chaos and tumult that the government could not fulfill its duties.[29]

Republicans doubted this reading of the necessary and proper clause, but they had no doubt the Constitution explicitly guaranteed freedom of speech and the press. They were certain that the sedition bill presented a clear challenge to the First Amendment. Federalists dismissed the claim angrily. Connecticut's Samuel Dana articulated their position when he asked whether anyone really believed that the Bill of Rights intended to "guarantee as a sacred principle the liberty of lying against the government?"[30]

Once again, these arguments brought to the surface the profound, long-standing differences over the nature of the Union. Albert Gallatin voiced the Republican understanding that "the Government of the Union was not a consolidated one, possessing general power; it was only a federal one, vested with specific powers." Only a decade before, Antifederalists had warned that the men who drafted the Constitution intended to create a consolidated government, one that would enjoy dominion over the states. Now, in 1798, Republican leaders from Gallatin to Madison to Jefferson, men protective of the sovereignty of their individual states and fearful of losing that sovereignty to a single, unrestrained government, insisted that the Constitution was only a compact among the states, not an act of consolidation.[31]

In the end, Livingston's motion to reject the bill failed by a vote of 47 to 36. On July 9 the House resolved itself once again into a committee of the whole, and, after a series of amendments was proposed, the bill was ordered read for a third time on July 10. As the debate wound down, it was Harrison Gray Otis, the nephew of a Massachusetts icon who gave no quarter to the British government in the 1770s, who recognized the significance of the moment. Otis looked beyond the bitter disagreements to comment on a shared acceptance of the primacy of the Constitution. Both sides, after all, had defined their position within the framework of that document. After a long speech by his opponent John Nicholas, Otis remarked that Nicholas's "professions of attachment to the Constitution . . . are certainly honorable to him; and he could not believe that an attachment so deeply engrafted, as he states his to be, would be shaken by this bill." The battleground had definitively shifted since the clashes over ratification, moving from whether to support the Constitution to who had the power to interpret its meaning. In this instance, a vote of 44 to 41 on July 10 gave that power to the Federalists.[32]

Of the forty-one men who voted against what would quickly become known as the Sedition Act, only three were Federalists. Twenty-nine came from southern or southwestern states and six from Pennsylvania, a state dominated by Republicans and, of course, the home of the most violent whiskey rebels. These were regions long lost to the party of Washington and Hamilton. But the remaining six nays came from a combination of New York, Massachusetts, and Vermont Republicans, and they reflected the rising fortunes of the party in the northeast. It was this incursion into their heartland, perhaps more than any other danger, that the Federalists hoped the Sedition Act would halt.

In its final form, An Act in Addition to the Act, Entitled An Act for the Punishment of Certain Crimes Against the United States declared it a high misdemeanor to do any of the following: unlawfully combine or conspire together with the intent to oppose measures of the government of the United States; impede the operation of any law of the United States; intimidate or prevent any person holding a place or office in or under the government of the United States from performing his trust or duty; or to counsel, advise, or attempt to procure insurrection, riot, unlawful assembly, or a combination of them, whether these efforts were successful or not. If convicted, the guilty party or parties would be punished by a fine not exceeding $5,000 and by imprisonment for a term not less than six months nor more than five years. The court could also demand sureties for the offender's good behavior. Section 2 of the act made it illegal to write, print, utter, or publish or cause to be written anything false, scandalous, and malicious against the government of the United States, the president of the United States, or either house of Congress. Anyone who knowingly and willingly assisted in these acts would also be subject to arrest and trial. No person could bring the government, president, or Congress into contempt or disrepute or excite against them the hatred of the good people of the United States. No person could excite any unlawful combinations to oppose or resist any law of the United States or any act of the president done in pursuance of such laws or of the powers vested in him by the Constitution. No one could oppose, through the written or spoken word, any such law or act, nor could anyone aid, encourage, or abet any hostile designs of any foreign nation against the United States, its people, or its government. If convicted of any such crime, a person would be punished with a fine not to exceed $2,000 and by imprisonment not to exceed two years. In section 3, the defendant was given the right to use truth as a defense. The jury trying the case had the right to determine the law and the fact, under the direction of the court. The final section declared that the act would continue in force until the third day of March 1801—the day John Adams's first term came to an end—although any pending prosecutions and punishments would remain in force.[33]

The breadth and depth of the act was impressive—and, to Republicans, draconian. They pointed to the fact that, under its terms, anyone who simply read seditious newspapers or declared support for their sentiments and opinions could be found guilty of a high misdemeanor. Federalists, however, emphasized the act's liberality, for it guaranteed truth as a defense, a provision that the common law did not allow. The Federalists also argued that nothing in the act abridged the freedom of the press; this freedom, they insisted, applied only to the protection of writers from censorship *before* publication. Regardless of their evaluation of the law, both parties realized that the passage of the Sedition Act could severely limit the Republicans' ability to expand public support through the press.

3

"Much good may . . .
result from the investigation of Political heresies."
—George Washington, June 1798

ON JULY 14, 1798, the House received the news that the president of the United States had approved and signed the Sedition Act. Reaction by leaders of both parties was predictably partisan. Vice President Jefferson, who early on had predicted the government would take steps to suppress the Republican press, declared the law "so palpably in the teeth of the constitution as to shew they mean to pay no respect to it." But Washington, who had been a target of Bache and company, had already given his imprimatur for a crackdown on the Republican press. Writing to Judge Alexander Addison of western Pennsylvania on June 3, the former president had observed that "much good may, & I am persuaded will result, from the investigation of Political heresies, when the propagation of them is intended, evidently, to mislead the multitude."[34]

The "investigation of Political heresies" that Washington considered wise had actually begun even before the debates over the sedition bill ended. John Adams and his secretary of state Timothy Pickering had been so eager to rid themselves of the constant, often vicious attacks by Bache that they had not waited for the Sedition Act to make its way to the president's desk. Two weeks before the president signed the act into law, the Adams administration arrested Benjamin Bache in a common law, rather than a statutory, prosecution for seditious libel. The grand jury indictment accused the man Adams considered his bête noire of "libeling the President and the Executive Government, in a manner trending to excite sedition, and opposition to the laws, by sundry publications and republications." The possibility of the more serious charge of treason also arose, based on his publication of a letter from a French official before the administration had an opportunity to make it public. The assumption was that Bache possessed the correspondence because he was a French spy, but the government could not muster evidence to make the treason charge stick. Instead, Bache was charged with seditious libel and released on bail until the October term of the federal circuit court. Hearing of his arrest, the Republican Boston *Gazette* sounded a death knoll for liberty. "The period is now at hand when it will be a question difficult to determine *whether there is more safety and liberty to be enjoyed at Constantinople or Philadelphia*."[35]

Throughout the summer, Bache nevertheless continued to attack the president and the administration in the pages of the *Aurora*. Yet when the court sat once more in Philadelphia, the Bache trial was not on its docket. Nothing had ever deterred Bache from frequently baseless and usually hyperbolic partisan journalism. He had kept his paper going despite the death threats he and his wife Peggy had received, despite mob vandalism of his home, and despite physical assaults by the son of a rival newspaper editor and the son of a local shipbuilder. But he could not ward off or stand resolute in the face of the yellow fever that had become a familiar summer scourge of Philadelphia. Benjamin Franklin Bache died on September 10, 1798, silenced not by a jury but by a painful fatal disease. The *Aurora*, however, lived on, operated by Bache's widow and by his assistant, the Irish radical William Duane.[36]

Pickering initiated two other common law cases against newspaper editors early in July. On July 6, John Daly Burk, editor of the influential New York *Time-Piece*, was arrested and charged with seditious libel. Burk, who had been born in Ireland in 1775, fled to America in 1796 as a wanted man as a result of a futile attempt to rescue a political prisoner from execution. He had managed to elude the pursuing authorities by disguising himself in the clothes of a woman he met in a bookstore. In appreciation for her help, he took her last name as his middle name. Only two years after arriving in the United States, Burk became the editor of the *Time-Piece,* a paper critical of Adams and his foreign policies. Three weeks into his editorship, Burk accused the president of deliberately falsifying a letter to Congress from Elbridge Gerry to promote a war with France.

Pickering originally initiated an inquiry into Burk's citizenship status, hoping that the editor might be a good subject for deportation under the Alien Friends Act. But he wound up having Burk arrested and charged with sedition under the common law. With the help of donations from prominent New York Republicans, including Aaron Burr, Burk posted the $2,000 bail and was free until his case came to court in October. In the interim, he continued to publish attacks on the administration until his newspaper went out of business in September. October came and went with no trial, and, sometime in 1799, Burk offered to end the case out of court. He vowed to leave the country if the charges were dismissed and his bail money returned. Adams agreed to these terms. Burk, however, did not honor his promise; instead, he went to Virginia where he lived under an assumed name, got a job as an academic, and waited until Jefferson was elected president to reveal his identity.[37]

Bache and Burk edited urban newspapers with considerable influence on popular opinion, but Pickering's third target that July, William Durrell, published an obscure upstate New York paper called the *Mount Pleasant Register.* Durrell had attracted Pickering's attention when he reprinted a paragraph from a neighboring Ulster County paper that criticized Adams. On July 17, three days after the president signed the sedition bill into law, the secretary of state had Durrell taken into custody. Durrell was not formally indicted until September, when he pleaded guilty before a US circuit court to having published "false scandalous malicious and defamatory libel of and concerning John Adams." Because the action he was indicted for occurred before the Sedition Act passed, Durrell was charged under common law doctrine; the truth contained in the paragraph was not, therefore, a defense. Even before his indictment, Durrell had closed down his press, a decision probably prompted by the $4,000 bail he had been required to post. For two years, he lived under the threat of a trial and without employment of any kind. When at last, in 1800, he appeared before a judge, Durrell pleaded for clemency as the sole support of his family. The judge was apparently unmoved by Durrell's circumstances and sentenced him to four months in jail and a $50 fine. He was to remain in jail until the fine was paid and he had posted $2,000 in security for good behavior. Adams, however, pardoned Durrell, and the former editor was released after serving two weeks of his sentence.[38]

On July 30, the government brought the first case to be tried under the Sedition Act. The man indicted was William Duane, the successor to Benjamin Bache at the *Aurora*. Duane was an American citizen, born in Vermont in 1760, whose widowed mother took him to Ireland when he was fourteen. He eventually returned to the United States and took a job at Bache's newspaper. After Bache's death, Duane carried on the partisan attacks that had made the *Aurora* such a thorn in the side of the administration. Duane was indicted once again in February 1799, this time for circulating a petition calling for the repeal of the Alien Friends Act. In the indictment, he was accused of "deliberately procuring an assembly of people with the determination of subverting the government of the US." It took a Philadelphia jury only thirty minutes to acquit Duane, either a sign that an impartial body believed the government had not made its case or of the support for the Republican Party in the nation's capital. A month later, however, a band of thirty fervent Federalists, all members of Philadelphia's volunteer cavalry, engaged in vigilante justice worthy of frontier whiskey rebels. They dragged Duane out of his office and beat and whipped him unconscious.

Despite the legal and physical attacks, Duane remained as dedicated to his mission as his predecessor had been. He continued to wage a print war on the Adams administration, claiming in July 1799 that the British exercised undue and improper influence in Pickering's State Department. Before the month was out, he found himself indicted a third time. His trial began on October 15, 1799; the case was heard by George Washington's brother, associate Supreme Court justice Bushrod Washington, and by District Judge Richard Peters.

But, before the case went to the jury, the trial was suspended for several months. Although the government cited "procedural reasons" for the suspension, the actual cause appeared to be that Duane had evidence to back up his accusations: a letter from John Adams to Tench Coxe that allegedly impugned the integrity of President Washington. The letter, written in May 1792, said that "our new ambassador [Thomas Pinckney] has many powerful old friends in England." Adams added his suspicion that the Pinckney family had played a role in limiting his own tenure as ambassador to Great Britain to create the opportunity for a Pinckney to be appointed to the post. "Knowing as I do the long intrigues, and suspecting as I do, much British influence in the appointment," Adams told Coxe, who was then undersecretary of the treasury, it would be wise to "keep a vigilant eye upon them." Suspicion was one thing, however, and proof was another; the letter contained no real proof.[39]

Washington's response to Duane's use of the letter captured the genuine frustration—and resentment—Federalists had for the unrestrained criticism they faced in the Republican press. In a letter to Charles Cotesworth Pinckney, Washington vented that frustration, asking, "When—where—and how such things are to terminate." But the real question, Washington conceded in a letter to Pickering, was how to effectively respond to charges like Duane's of bribery at the highest level of government. Should we be "quiescent under the direct charge of bribery?" To do so, Washington told Pickering, would have dangerous consequences. And yet, Washington continued, perhaps the direct frontal attack made possible by the Sedition Act was a poor strategy. "I am persuaded that if a rope, a little longer had been given [Duane], he would have hung himself in something worse."[40]

While Duane waited for his trial to resume, he continued his assault on the government. In 1800, he criticized a proposed Senate bill to settle disputed presidential and vice presidential elections, claiming—this time, with considerable truth—that it was designed to give the Federalists an advantage in the upcoming election. Although the bill did not pass, the Senate decided to summon Duane to answer questions about how he acquired information on a discussion behind the closed doors of the upper chamber. When his own lawyers refused to accompany him for the interrogation, Duane decided not to appear before the senators. Vice President Thomas Jefferson, the presiding officer of the Senate, had no choice but to sign a contempt warrant against Duane. Pickering, however, delayed indicting Duane for libeling the Senate until after Congress adjourned. The opportunity was thus lost to bring him to trial, for, as president, Jefferson dismissed the suit. Duane thus escaped all prosecution. His only apparent punishment was to suffer attacks in the Federalist press like the doggerel verse that appeared in the New York *Evening Post* on November 16, 1801: "Lie on Duane, lie on for pay / and Cheetham, lie thou too / ore against truth you cannot say / Than truth can say 'gainst you."[41]

The rash of indictments in July 1798, the month the acts were passed by Congress and signed into law by Adams, prompted popular outrage in the Republican stronghold of Virginia and in its sister state of Kentucky where whiskey rebels had once reigned. In these two states, the support for President Adams that had followed the revelations of the XYZ affairs had evaporated. By September, Virginia newspapers like the *Norfolk Herald* applauded the signs of resistance beginning to appear in many local counties. "The real friends to the liberties and the happiness of America," the paper declared, would rejoice upon reading the resolutions passed by the "respectable county of Goochland." There, some four hundred people voted to request their delegates in the state legislature demand that the Alien and Sedition Acts be repealed. On September 19, the *Virginia Gazette and General Advertiser* carried the resolutions passed in Powhatan County that labeled the Alien and Sedition Acts "tyrannical and unconstitutional" and affirmed the right of the people to demand their representatives take action to "suspend, alter, or abrogate those laws"—and to punish "their unfaithful and corrupt servants." By October, the freeholders of Prince William County had petitioned Adams for redress of grievances resulting from the Alien and Sedition Acts. Adams never saw this petition because Pickering intercepted it and returned it to its authors.[42]

Public meetings soon followed in Virginia's Prince Edward, Orange, Augusta, Amelia, Louisa, and Caroline Counties. Almost all were organized and orchestrated by local elites, who not only set the

agenda for discussion but also often wrote the petitions and resolutions the meetings produced. Attendance numbers were frequently
exaggerated; in Dinwiddie, for example, a Petersburg lawyer drafted
the resolutions the "meeting" of only a few people produced. Yet what
the protests lacked in spontaneity, they made up for in fervor. Public
feeling ran so high in parts of the Old Dominion that not even the
state's most famous resident, George Washington, could escape the
public's wrath. In Virginia, "A Speedy Death to General Washington"
became a popular toast.[43]

In Kentucky, local leaders also carefully nurtured popular outrage, cleverly scheduling rallies to coincide with court days and militia muster days, thus ensuring large crowds. Wealthy landowner and
lawyer George Nicholas established the tone for these well-attended
Kentucky protest meetings when, on August 1, he published his response to the Alien and Sedition Acts in the *Kentucky Gazette*. "I do
verily believe," he wrote, "that the majority of the legislature of the
US, who voted for the [Acts] have violated that clause of the Constitution of the United States, which declares that 'Congress shall
make no law respecting an establishment of religion, or prohibit the
free exercise thereof, or abridging the freedom of speech, or of the
press, or of the right of the people peaceably to assemble and to petition the government for a redress of grievances.'"[44]

It was, however, Nicholas's protégé, thirty-eight-year-old John
Breckinridge, who organized the major Kentucky protests, in
Bourbon, Fayette, Franklin, Mason, and Woodford Counties. The
petitions produced at these demonstrations, many drafted by Breckinridge himself, were filled with radical sentiments, mixing declarations of states' rights with assertions of the rights of individuals
to disobey any law they considered unconstitutional. Clark County's resolutions were representative. They went beyond an opposition
to the Alien and Sedition Acts to address foreign relations and the
Adams administration's war-preparedness programs. Although they
condemned the Sedition Act as "the most abominable that was ever
attempted to be imposed upon a nation of free men," they also denounced any war with France as ruinous to the nation, rejected the
idea of an alliance with Great Britain, and voiced serious concern
that the powers given to the president to raise armies and borrow

money were dangerous to the people's liberty. The Alien and Sedition Acts had brought to the surface a general popular discontent with Adams and the Federalist agenda.[45]

On August 13, Kentucky's protest moved to Lexington. An ailing George Nicholas lectured on the dangers of the Sedition and the Alien Acts for four hours to a crowd numbering between 4,000 and 5,000. In his stirring peroration Nicholas declared that "as long as my country continues free, I care not who watches me; I wish all my thoughts, words, and deeds, so far as they concern the public, to be known. He who has not political objects, but the happiness and liberty of his country need not fear having them exposed to the eyes of the world." After Nicholas finished, twenty-one-year-old Henry Clay, a recent transplant to Kentucky from Virginia, stood in a wagon and addressed the throng for another hour. When a Federalist in the crowd attempted to defend the legitimacy of the Alien and Sedition Acts, he was shouted down. The arguments made by Nicholas and Clay echoed those made in Congress by Edward Livingston: the federal government had gone beyond its enumerated powers, and, as a result, the states and individual citizens had a right to resist these laws. Before disbanding, the crowd passed ten resolutions that declared the acts "unconstitutional, impolitic, unjust and a disgrace to the American name." They also ominously urged their fellow Kentuckians to arm themselves—not in defiance but in defense of the Republic.[46]

Kentucky's spirited defense of the Constitution and its citizens' determination to resist any abuse of its guarantees was a measure of the steady growth of popular nationalism during the era. In 1793 and 1794, Kentucky residents who opposed the excise tax preferred to simply ignore the Constitution and any authority its federal government had to intervene in their lives. Now, in 1798, they spoke of the Constitution as the bulwark of their liberties and declared their willingness to defend it against abuse by the men in office. Nicholas captured this shift in attitude when he wrote that "no constitution affords any real security to liberty, unless it is considered sacred and preserved inviolate."[47]

4

"I do not care if they fire thro' his arse!"
—Luther Baldwin, July 1798

DESPITE THE EMERGENCE of protest against the Alien and Sedition Acts, Timothy Pickering had no intention of abandoning the
power the acts gave him to protect the federal government. Far more
than Adams or Hamilton, Pickering was an ideologue, and he believed it his mission to save the Federalist hegemony, the Republic,
and the Constitution itself. He had no qualms about applying the Sedition Act whenever and wherever possible, no matter the price the
administration paid in public indignation.

August and September seemed to bring a hiatus. Both months
passed without arrests or indictments. But in October, Thomas Adams and Abijah Adams, brothers living in Cambridge, Massachusetts, found themselves charged with sedition. Thomas was the
editor of the Boston *Independent Chronicle,* a newspaper that had
earned Abigail Adams's deepest contempt for its relentless criticism
of her husband. Massachusetts Federalists, who described Thomas
Adams as "a flaming minister of anarchy" had burned copies of the
Chronicle at their Fourth of July picnic that year. A campaign to os-
tracize Adams led to his expulsion from the New Relief Fire Society
of Cambridge on the grounds that he disgraced the American character. Despite all the efforts of his political enemies, Adams showed
no signs that he would temper his criticism of the president and his
policies.

On October 23, 1798, Thomas Adams was arraigned before
the federal circuit court in Boston, where he pleaded not guilty of
"sundry libelous and seditious publications." Like all the other men
brought before the courts for libel and sedition, he was released on
bail. He was not to go to trial until June 1799. New charges awaited,
however. In February 1799, both Thomas and his brother Abijah, the
bookkeeper for the newspaper, were indicted under Massachusetts
common law. Abijah was tried on March 1, 1799, but by then Thomas
was too ill to appear in court. Abijah was found guilty, sentenced to
thirty days in county jail, and required to post a $500 surety bond
against any further offenses. Thomas, too sick to continue publishing

the *Chronicle,* sold it. On May 13, he died. Republican newspapers hailed Thomas Adams as a hero, even as Federalists declared that justice had been served with his demise. Harrison Gray Otis offered a dark epitaph: Thomas Adams was "finally arrested . . . by that grim messenger whose mandate strikes terror in the heart of the false and malicious libeler."[48]

Not everyone indicted in the immediate aftermath of the passage of the Sedition Act was a newspaper editor. As the pilot of a garbage scow named Luther Baldwin learned in the summer and fall of 1798, even a spontaneous comment uttered by a man with no influence in his community could result in an indictment under the Sedition Act. Baldwin was drinking without much restraint on a warm July day when President John Adams passed through his hometown of Newark, New Jersey, on the way to his family home in Quincy, Massachusetts. Newark heralded the president's arrival with a full parade and a cannon salute. But Baldwin did not share this local enthusiasm. When one of his drinking companions commented, "There goes the president and they are firing at his a—," Baldwin expressed his sour opinion of both the cannon salute and the president. "I do not care," he boasted, "if they fire thro' his arse!" The local Republican newspaper, the *Centinel of Freedom,* printed this exchange between the two less-than-sober commentators, and Baldwin wound up indicted that September. The charge was speaking "seditious words tending to defame the President and the Government of the United States." Two of the men drinking with him were also indicted. On October 3, 1798, all three pleaded guilty, although Baldwin and one of his friends soon changed their pleas. The three men were fined, and the two who had pleaded not guilty were committed to jail until their fines and court fees were paid.[49]

The most dramatic case in October began only three days after Luther Baldwin and his hapless drinking buddies found themselves convicted of seditious comments. On October 5, a highly controversial member of the House of Representatives, Matthew Lyon, was arrested in Fairhaven, Vermont. Lyon, a former printer, had emigrated from Ireland to Connecticut as an indentured servant. He made his way to Vermont before the Revolution and was among Ethan Allen's Green Mountain Boys who captured Fort Ticonderoga. His military career ended badly; he was discharged when the troops under his command mutinied. After the Revolution, Lyon became a successful mill owner and paper manufacturer, and, by the 1790s, he had entered politics. In 1797, after three failed campaigns, he was finally elected to the House of Representatives.

It was immediately clear to many in Congress that Lyon was a combative personality. He saw himself as the voice of the common man, and he did not mince words in his criticism of the Federalists. He openly accused Alexander Hamilton of "screwing the hard-earnings out of the poor people" so that the federal government could "vie with European Courts in frivolous gaudy appearances." His hostility to his opponents' alleged elitism was not tempered by the tendency of Federalist congressmen to make fun of his Irish accent. In January 1798, Lyon shocked his fellow representatives by spitting in the face of Connecticut's Roger Griswold on the floor of the House. Griswold was certainly guilty of provocation, for in an angry exchange he accused Lyon of being a scoundrel. The patrician Griswold repeated an old but false charge that Lyon had been cashiered from the military for cowardice and given a wooden sword to symbolize his shame. After the incident in the House, it was not long before some wit dubbed the novice congressman "The Spitting Lyon." Although Lyon apologized to his fellow representatives for his behavior, he did not directly apologize to Griswold. This may explain why, on February 15, the aggrieved Griswold attacked Lyon with his wooden cane, beating him on his head and shoulders in full view of the House members. Lyon managed to defend himself with a pair of tongs taken from a fireplace. Congressmen finally pulled Griswold away by his legs. The House debated the appropriate action to be taken in the Lyon-Griswold episodes for almost a month; in the end it voted against the censure of either man. Nevertheless, the confrontations between Lyon and Griswold seemed to many to be a physical embodiment of the intense party hostility in American politics.[50]

Although the Lyon-Griswold altercation was sensational, it was not the basis for Lyon's arrest. On June 20, Lyon had published an open letter in *Spooner's Vermont Journal,* written in response to a scathing attack made on him. In the letter, Lyon accused John Adams of engaging in a "continual grasp for power" and described the president as a man with an "unbounded thirst for ridiculous pomp, foolish adulation, and selfish avarice." He went on to denounce what he considered a trumped-up threat of French invasion and unnecessary and costly war preparations. This letter was the basis for the first count of the indictment against him. Lyon also published, and read aloud at rallies, a letter written by Joel Barlow to Barlow's brother-in-law in which the poet harshly condemned the war preparations. The printing and reading of the Barlow letter and the criticism of the president were the bases of the second and third counts of the indictment.

Lyon's October trial in the US Circuit District Court of Vermont was closely followed by supporters and detractors alike. The Federalist congressman John Allen was one of the many prominent men who crowded the courtroom. In his opening remarks, Justice William Patterson told the grand jury that seditious libel was a crime against the people who elected government officials. The jury agreed that domestic licentiousness was a greater threat than invasion by a foreign country. Later, Republican supporters of Lyon would argue that indictment for his letter, published before the Sedition Act was passed, was a blatant example of ex post facto prosecution. Lyon, who defended himself at his trial, argued that the Sedition Act was unconstitutional and that there was no evidence he intended to undermine the federal government; he claimed his criticism was nothing more than "a legitimate opposition." The judge instructed the jury to ignore the issue of the act's constitutionality; the only question before it was whether Lyon published the letter and whether his intent was sedition. Patterson went on to remind the jurors that "unlawful combinations, conspiracies, riots and insurrections strike at the being of our political establishment" and that "written or printed detraction, calumny, and lies are odious and destructive vices in private, and still more so in public life." These crimes, he added, threaten a government that is the "creation and work of the people, emanating from their authority and declarative of their will." After that charge, the jury took only an hour to return a guilty verdict.[51]

Matthew Lyon was fined $1,000 and sentenced to four months in jail. The *Aurora* declared that the Vermont congressman "had the honour of being the first victim of a law framed directly in the teeth of the Constitution of this federal republic." Prison did little to soften Lyon's views. While locked up, he wrote an account of his trial and also conducted his reelection campaign. To the consternation of

the Vermont Federalists, he won a second term by an overwhelming majority. And upon his release from prison, he was treated to a
parade. Supporters called him "a martyr to the cause of liberty and
the Rights of Man." Clearly, the Sedition Act was failing to control
opposition to the Adams administration.[52]

The justice system was not finished with Lyon, however. At the
October 1799 term, Lyon was once again arrested, this time for criticizing his fine, the jury selection process, and the marshal's alleged
abuse of him while he was in prison. But Lyon could not be arrested,
for he was nowhere to be found in Vermont. He was safely in Congress in Philadelphia. When Congress adjourned in March 1801,
Lyon wisely did not return to Vermont. Instead, he moved to Kentucky and won election to Congress from his new home in 1802.
Despite all the efforts of the Federalist officeholders and judges and
despite several seditious libel cases against others in Vermont, nothing could silence the critics of the administration and the Alien and
Sedition Acts. Even worse, from the Federalist point of view, nothing
and no one seemed able to prevent the growth of the Republican
Party in its own New England backyard.[53]

5

"The nullification of all unauthorized acts . . .
is the rightful remedy."
Kentucky Resolutions, 1799

AS 1798 DREW to an end, the administration had little to show for
itself in the battle against Republican sedition and libel. Three working men from Newark, New Jersey, had been convicted for drunken
comments; William Duane was out on bail and busy publishing
new attacks on Adams and his policies; and three other newspaper
editors, along with a bookkeeper, still awaited trial. The administration's victory in the Matthew Lyon case appeared to be pyrrhic,
because Lyon had used his time in jail to paint himself as a hero and
the judge and jury as villains.

A more serious problem was that each effort to apply the new
laws seemed to spur more protests, not only in Virginia and Kentucky
but in Pennsylvania, New Jersey, and New York as well. While militia

units in Kentucky toasted "trial by jury, the liberty of the press, and no standing army," local newspapers including the *Centinel of Freedom* in New Jersey and the *Herald of Liberty* in Washington, Pennsylvania, were carrying on the same print crusade against the Alien and Sedition Acts as had the *Aurora*. Opposition was voiced through poetry and song as well as prose. In the poem "War-worn Soldier," for example, the author urged, "Then freemen assemble at 'Liberty's Call' / Resolve—and to congress petition / That the law called Alien, to nothing may fall / And also the bill of sedition." Where only a few months before memorials praising John Adams had flooded Congress and the president's office following the revelations of the XYZ affair, now petitions had begun to pour in, calling for the repeal of the acts. By February 1799, Republican congressmen had presented several hundred petitions from across Pennsylvania alone.[54]

Even more ominous for the Federalists was the fact that, by November, the call for repeal had moved off the streets and the pages of newspapers and into the legislatures of Kentucky and Virginia. As early as August 22, a newspaper writer calling himself "Philo-Agis" had suggested that the Kentucky legislature take up the cause, arguing that "united and official action" would carry more weight than would the disparate petitions from obscure towns and villages of the West. When the Kentucky legislature met in November, Governor James Garrard delivered his address in person to the state assembly. Garrard, a farmer and Baptist minister, echoed the view of "Philo-Agis" that a legislative protest was necessary. He considered Kentucky uniquely suited to defend the people's freedoms because it was, in his words, "remote from the contaminating influence of European politics." Aware that his state had a reputation for being "if not in a state of insurrection, yet utterly disaffected to the federal government," Garrard urged the assembly to declare Kentucky's full support of the US Constitution even as it entered its protest "against all unconstitutional laws and impolitic proceedings."[55]

The Kentucky legislators were more than ready to act. The next day, the entire assembly sat as a committee of the whole to begin its debate on a set of resolutions proposed by John Breckinridge but secretly drafted by Thomas Jefferson. Jefferson's resolutions had originally been intended for North Carolina, but the fall elections there had gone badly for the Republicans and it was decided to bring them to Kentucky instead. The resulting Kentucky Resolutions, passed by the lower house on November 10 and unanimously concurred in by the state senate three days later, were more than a statement condemning the Alien and Sedition Acts; they were an attempt to revive—and settle—an argument that began when the Constitution was first proposed: Was the Constitution and the government it established a union of the people or a compact entered into by the states?

The first of the Kentucky Resolutions made clear where Jefferson stood on this fundamental issue. "Resolved," it said, "that the several States composing, the United States of America, are not united on the principle of unlimited submission to their general government; but that, by a compact under the style and title of a Constitution for the United States, and of amendments thereto, they constituted a general government for special purposes—delegated to that government certain definite powers, reserving, each State to itself, the residuary mass of right to their own self-government . . . that to this compact each State acceded as a State, and is an integral part, its co-States forming, as to itself, the other party . . . each party has an equal right to judge for itself, as well of infractions as of the mode and measure of redress." In other words, the states do not lose their separate and independent identities through the creation of the union; as sovereign political entities, they created the general government and gave it limited, special powers while preserving their own authority in all other instances. As Jefferson argued, the sovereign states gave birth to the federal government, and they alone had the right to judge whether it had exceeded the powers granted to it.[56]

For Jefferson, this debate over the nature of the federal government should have been settled by the Tenth Amendment, which spelled out the limits and the source of federal power: "The powers not delegated to the United States by the Constitution, nor prohibited by it to the States, are reserved to the States respectively, or to the people." This statement coupled with the First Amendment restriction on the federal government regarding freedom of speech and the press were the two pillars upon which the Kentucky Resolutions declared not only the Sedition Act but also the Act to punish frauds committed on the Bank of the United States and the Alien Friends Act to be "altogether void and of no force." Resolutions 5 and

6 reflected the sectional base of the party of Jefferson and Madison. Resolution 5 echoed the House concern that the Alien Friends Act endangered slave ownership as much as immigrant right of residence. It declared the act illegal, based on the constitutional provision that prohibited any interference with the migration or importation of persons by the states until 1808. Resolution 6 used the Fifth Amendment guarantee of due process to bolster Kentucky's position that the alien acts were unconstitutional.

In resolution 7, Jefferson returned to a critical question of interpretation, first raised during the early years of the Washington administration: What was the legitimate extent of the federal government's power to "make all laws which shall be necessary and proper for carrying into execution the powers" that had been vested in it by the Constitution? Alexander Hamilton had defended the constitutionality of the Bank of the United States on this necessary and proper clause in 1791; at the time, Jefferson had disagreed with his interpretation. Now, in 1798, Jefferson made his argument once again, through the Kentucky Resolutions, declaring that this clause was intended to facilitate the execution of only the *limited powers* granted to the federal government. It was not, that is, an avenue for the expansion of those powers.

Taken together, the arguments presented in the first and the seventh resolutions embodied key elements of the credo of the Republican Party. The Kentucky legislators were more than ready to endorse them. But Breckinridge, like Kentucky's governor, was not ready to follow Jefferson's argument to its logical conclusion. Jefferson's eighth resolution asserted that "where powers are assumed which have not been delegated a *nullification* of the act is the rightful remedy." Although Kentucky's political leaders retained Jefferson's Cassandra-like warning that the Alien and Sedition Acts, and future acts resembling them, might "drive these states into revolution and blood," they were unwilling at this juncture to threaten nullification. Nor were they willing to follow Jefferson's conclusion that it was up to the state governments, not the federal government itself, to find a remedy to the unconstitutional Alien and Sedition Acts. Instead, Breckinridge inserted a resolution that honored the wishes of local petitions and memorials that the fight for repeal be waged by Kentucky's representatives and senators in the federal Congress.

This was a tacit acknowledgment that the federal government, not the state legislatures, had the authority to determine whether its actions had overstepped constitutional boundaries. In other words, Breckinridge, unlike Jefferson, preferred to rely on the Congress to mend its ways. The practical consequences were as significant as the theoretical implications: the revised eighth section in the Kentucky Resolutions meant that the fate of the acts would be determined by the party politics of Congress rather than by that grand debate over the relationship of the states and the federal government that Jefferson desired. Jefferson hoped to establish the primacy of the states. Kentucky's legislators wanted to make it clear that, despite their deep concern and resentment of the Alien and Sedition Acts, they remained attached to the federal Constitution. Their duty was not to destroy it but "to preserve it inviolate."[57]

Less than seven weeks later, Virginia followed suit with its own set of resolutions. These resolutions were drafted by Jefferson's closest ally, James Madison. Madison's early nationalism had been eroded by the government's adoption of Hamilton's financial and economic programs and by what Madison considered the abuse of the necessary and proper clause. Where once he had labored to protect and energize the federal government, by 1798 he shared Jefferson's commitment to blocking that government's encroachment on the authority and power of the states. Although he had retired from Congress in 1797, the Alien and Sedition Acts prompted Madison to return to the political fray as a champion of states' rights. Jefferson had forwarded the Kentucky Resolutions to Madison in mid-November and encouraged his old friend to write a set of resolutions for their home state.

The language of Madison's resulting resolutions was far less provocative and combative than was Jefferson's; although they agreed that the Constitution was a compact among the states, condemned the Federalists' use of a loose construction to expand the powers of the federal government, and considered the Alien and Sedition Acts as infractions of the Constitution, Madison's resolutions contained no talk of "revolution and blood" and no threat of nullification. Madison refused to declare the Alien and Sedition Acts "void & of no force" and would go only so far as to propose that the states should "interpose for arresting the progress of the evil." Finally, he focused his critique narrowly on the Alien and Sedition Acts and urged other states to take proper measures to advance their repeal. Madison forwarded his draft to Wilson Cary Nicholas, who he assumed would introduce the resolutions when the Virginia legislature convened on December 3. Nicholas, however, showed Madison's handiwork to Jefferson, who in turn persuaded Nicholas to add the more incendiary claim that the Alien and Sedition laws were "not law, but utterly null, void and of no force or effect." On December 10, Nicholas handed the resolutions to John Taylor of Caroline, who introduced them to the Virginia assembly. Madison's authorship of the resolutions was not widely known for more than a decade.

After a long and contentious debate, the legislature approved the eight resolves that made up the Virginia Resolutions, but Jefferson's description of the Alien and Sedition Act was expunged from the final version. Although this ensured that the Virginia Resolutions were more restrained than the Kentucky Resolutions, they were so closely linked in the minds of the public that Madison's effort to be measured and conciliatory was ultimately ineffective. These resolutions passed on December 21, but the vote was far from unanimous. The vote of 100 in favor and 63 opposed made it clear that there was a strong Federalist presence in Virginia's lower house. Republicans enjoyed firm control in the state senate, however, and that body passed the resolutions by a vote of 14 to 3.[58]

By the end of 1798 both the Virginia and the Kentucky Resolutions had made their way to the governments of other states. There was nothing left to do but wait for their responses. When they came, those responses were disheartening to the Republicans and a cause for celebration and relief among Federalists everywhere. Seven states—Delaware, Rhode Island, Massachusetts, New Hampshire, New York, Connecticut, and Vermont—spoke with one voice: any legislature that expressed such "inflammatory and pernicious sentiments and doctrines" must stand alone. In their official responses, these legislatures repeated most of the Federalist arguments made on the floor of the House of Representatives. Rhode Island, for example, took pains to lecture Virginia on the provisions of the Constitution that gave the federal courts exclusive authority to decide the constitutionality of any act or law of Congress. For a state legislature to assume that authority, the Rhode Islanders pointed out, would be to blend legislative and judicial powers—precisely the infraction Virginia had attributed to the provisions of the Alien Acts. Most of the statements expressed concern that the extreme stance taken by Virginia and Kentucky was dangerous, disruptive in a time when a foreign invasion was still possible, and likely to produce "many evil and fatal consequences." Several insisted that their own legislatures would not deign to judge the constitutionality of the Alien and Sedition Acts, but they were willing to offer their *opinions* that the laws fell within the powers delegated to Congress. Massachusetts, which submitted the longest reply, declared that Virginia misunderstood the compact that had created the Constitution; it was the consent of the people that gave the federal government its power, not the state governments. Vigilance was admirable, the Massachusetts legislators continued—but, in a direct attack on the Republican leadership, they added that an "unreasonable jealousy" of the men chosen to lead the nation, and a resort to extreme measures, "upon groundless or trivial pretexts," was not.[59]

Maryland, New Jersey, and even Pennsylvania also passed resolutions disapproving of the Virginia and Kentucky Resolutions, but they did not forward them to the governors of those states. In these states, as in the seven who did reply, the votes followed party lines.

With the exception of Maryland, no southern legislature produced or submitted formal statements. But if these southern states chose not to critique or criticize the positions taken by Virginia and Kentucky, neither did they volunteer to join them in open protest.

The combination of criticism and silence led Kentucky to issue a new and even bolder set of resolutions in December 1799. The state admitted the futility of presenting its arguments again. The legislators had made their case "with decency and with temper," but the answers they received were awash in "unfounded suggestions" and "uncandid insinuations," and they were "derogatory of the true character and principles of the good people of this commonwealth." Yet, because silence might be taken for an acceptance of the arguments made by other states, Kentucky considered it necessary to issue new resolutions. These were more radical than the ones issued a year before, for they now asserted that *the nullification of all unauthorized acts done under colour of that instrument [the Constitution], is the rightful remedy.*[60]

Only a few years before, when Kentucky was still part of Virginia, the people of the region had greeted a federal excise tax with an almost casual contempt, ignoring the law that imposed it without making any reference to its constitutionality. But now, in 1799, Kentucky felt compelled to justify its opposition to a set of federal laws out of respect for the Constitution. As the legislature (and Jefferson) saw it, nullification was a mechanism for preserving the integrity of that founding document, not a rejection of the government it created. Yet Kentucky was not ready to stand alone in defiance of an illegitimate federal law. It resolved instead to bow to the laws of the Union but to continue to oppose, "in a constitutional manner," the violation of the compact that created the federal government. Nevertheless, the concept of nullification had entered the political vocabulary of the nation.

6
"No Stamp Act, No Sedition Act. No Alien Bills, No Land Tax, downfall to the Tyrants of America."
—David Brown, 1798

IN 1799, WHILE state governments discussed the merits of the Virginia and Kentucky Resolutions and President Adams moved toward a diplomatic solution to the problems with France, Timothy Pickering and the courts continued their arrests and trials under the Sedition Act. Many of the cases begun in 1798 were still pending, including the prosecution of the Adams brothers of Massachusetts and William Durrell and John Daly Burk of New York. There were new offenders to prosecute as well. In March 1799, the law finally caught up with an itinerant philosopher, David Brown, who had persuaded a group of Republicans in Dedham, Massachusetts, to construct a "liberty pole" in 1798. The liberty pole was a familiar symbol of defiance of government authority; it had been used by American revolutionaries in the years before independence was declared and again by the whiskey rebels in the early 1790s. But it was not the Dedham pole itself but the placard attached to it that sealed Brown's fate. The sign read "No Stamp Act, No Sedition Act. No Alien Bills, No Land Tax, downfall to the Tyrants of America; Peace and retirement to the President; Long Live the Vice-President." Local Massachusetts

Federalists in this most Federalist of Federalist states had quickly chopped the pole down and mounted a statewide search for Brown. They had the satisfaction of seeing him and one of his allies indicted and convicted in June 1799.[61]

The fall of that year brought several additional new cases. Matthew Lyon was indicted for the second time, and Charles Holt, the editor of a Connecticut paper, the New London *Bee,* was charged with sedition for writing an article critical of Alexander Hamilton and the provisional army Hamilton commanded. Jedidiah Peck, a member of the New York State Assembly from Oswego County, was brought to court for collecting signatures on a petition that demanded repeal of the Alien and Sedition Acts. And, in November, Pickering struck a blow against the leading Republican newspaper in New York City, the *Argus, or Greenleaf's New Daily Advertiser,* charging the widow of its editor and the paper's foreman with seditious libel for announcing that Hamilton planned to silence the *Aurora* by purchasing it.[62]

But Pickering's most ambitious new cases came in 1800, just as Adams's three new Federalist commissioners were negotiating a détente with France. The first case was brought against Thomas Cooper that April. Cooper had immigrated to America in 1794, leaving behind a reputation as an opponent of the Church of England and a Jacobin. He settled in Pennsylvania, where he became part of a circle of likeminded English dissenters. By 1799, he was editing a small newspaper and launching written attacks on the president, calling him a "power-mad despot." In an effort to silence—or at least embarrass—Cooper, the Federalist champion Fenno printed an anonymous letter in his *Gazette* that revealed that this adamant critic of John Adams had once applied to the president for a government post. The clear implication was that the rejection of his request lay behind Cooper's hostility. An enraged Cooper responded that he had applied for the job before Adams became an opponent of liberty. He then accused Adams of interfering in a court case involving a sailor whom the British government accused of participating in a mutiny aboard a navy vessel. The president's willingness to turn the man over to the British, despite the sailor's claim to US citizenship, was, Cooper suggested, clear evidence that Adams was a tool of Great Britain. This accusation earned Cooper an arrest and indictment by a grand jury.

Cooper chose to serve as his own counsel. As part of his defense, he demanded to subpoena Adams, Timothy Pickering, Pickering's clerk, and a member of Congress. Justice Samuel Chase, presiding over the trial, was astonished at the notion of the president of the United States being cross-examined and refused to allow it. Cooper, however, was nonplussed; Was the president above the law? he asked the judge. Antagonizing the judge did not help him. Chase repeatedly challenged Cooper and in his charge to the jury declared that Cooper was attempting to poison the minds of the people. It took the jury less than an hour to return a guilty verdict. Thomas Cooper was sentenced to six months in prison and fined $600. After his release, he would be required to post a $2,000 surety bond for good behavior.

Pickering, who had sat in the courtroom throughout the trial, was surely pleased with the verdict. Cooper, an intelligent man and a gifted writer, was a particularly dangerous foe of the administration; Pickering believed his conviction and imprisonment sent a stern message to the partisan press. In reality, however, the Cooper case testified to the futility of the Sedition Act. Once in jail, Cooper passed the days writing political letters and continuing his assault on Federalist policies. When he was released in October 1800, the totally unreformed man went to New York City where he called upon the courts to prosecute Alexander Hamilton for sedition, based on the former secretary of the treasury's lengthy, and damning, 1800 account of the failures of the Adams administration.[63]

A month after Thomas Cooper was sentenced to jail, James Thomson Callender was indicted by a grand jury in Virginia. The Callender indictment was perhaps the most important of all the cases tried under the Sedition Act. Unlike Matthew Lyon or Cooper, Callender stood for few political or ethical principles; he was a libelist for hire, with no loyalty to any party or to any patron. His was the voice the Federalists most desperately wanted to banish from public discourse.

Callender was born in Scotland. At the age of thirty-four he published *Political Progress in Britain,* which purported to be an "impartial history of abuses" in the British government. This led to an indictment for sedition and prompted him to flee to America. Settling in Philadelphia, he worked as a recorder of the debates in the House of Representatives. In 1797, he exposed the affair between Alexander

Hamilton and Maria Reynolds to the press. While the Sedition Act was being debated, a cautious Callender decided to protect himself from expulsion by becoming a US citizen. But when Benjamin Bache was indicted, Callender decided it was best to leave Philadelphia. A Federalist newspaper in the nation's capital sarcastically announced his departure, saying, "Envoy Callender left this city on a tour to the westward—destination unknown." But Callender had not gone west; he had gone south to Virginia.

Callender was initially welcomed and assisted by Virginia Republicans, including George Mason and Thomas Jefferson. In 1800 he published a pamphlet titled *The Prospect Before Us,* a ringing endorsement of Jefferson's bid for the presidency, which Callender cavalierly forwarded to John Adams. In it, Callender described the Adams administration as "one continued tempest of malignant passions," claiming that Adams "never opened his lips, or lifted his pen without threatening and scolding." The choice in the upcoming presidential election, he declared, was between "Adams and beggary, and Jefferson, peace and competency." By May 1800 he was under indictment by the US circuit court.

While Callender's excellent lawyers fought a losing battle with Justice Samuel Chase, John Marshall sat in the courtroom, listening with satisfaction. In his instructions to the jury, Chase rejected the defense's argument that the jury could consider the constitutionality of a law. It came as no surprise that Callender was convicted or that Chase sentenced him to a relatively long incarceration—nine months—and to a $200 fine. Yet, like Cooper, Callender used his time in jail to continue his attack on the government. While serving his term, he completed a second volume of *The Prospect,* in which he called Justice Chase "the most detestable and detested rascal in the state of Maryland." Callender emerged from prison on March 3, 1801, the same day that the Sedition Act expired.

Callender's story did not end well. As a free man, he soon applied to President Jefferson for appointment as postmaster of Richmond. Jefferson, who now considered Callender too radical and too divisive, refused. In response, Callender abandoned all loyalty to the Republican Party and its president, and in 1802 he published a report that Jefferson kept a slave mistress and had children by her. By 1803, Callender was a broken man, consumed with bitterness and troubled by alcoholism. On July 17, 1803, a witness reported seeing him in a drunken stupor; by the end of the day Jefferson's ally-turned-nemesis had drowned in the James River.[64]

Epilogue

IN RETROSPECT, THE Federalists could claim little success in their determined effort to silence the opposition press and punish all those whose lies and exaggerations diminished the administration in the eyes of the public. In total, only twenty-one arrests were made, and only eighteen of these led to indictments. Three of those indictments, including Bache's, were under existing common law rather than the Sedition Act. Only eleven of the seventeen men and one woman indicted actually went to trial, and most of the editors, released on bail, continued to publish their newspapers in the interim. Those sent to prison spent their time writing damning accounts of the conduct of their trials and continuing their fierce criticisms of the administration's war-preparedness policies. They had been incarcerated but not silenced.

The vast majority of Republican newspaper editors escaped prosecution under the Sedition Act, although some of the most influential partisan writers and editors were among those successfully targeted by the Adams administration. The strategy devised by Pickering and his supporters, if a strategy could be said to exist, was to force the closure of the influential newspapers whose editorials and essays were frequently reprinted—and thus disseminated—by small, local newspapers across the country. If the *Aurora* and the *Time-Piece* could be forced to close up shop, it was thought, the arguments made by Benjamin Bache and John Daly Burk would no longer find their way into the small communities outside Philadelphia and New York. Occasionally, the administration did prove willing to prosecute editors of smaller presses, using them as object lessons of the dangers of attacking the federal government and its officers. It was also sometimes willing to make examples of ordinary citizens who insulted the character of the president or members of his administration. But the main targets were men like Bache, Duane, and Callender. Perhaps the most telling point about these prosecutions is that all but one of the men targeted operated in the Northeast. This is evidence that the Federalists had conceded the South to the opposition but hoped to prevent its spread in New England and the middle states. Despite these efforts, Pickering and company failed to prevent the growth of the Republican Party. It is likely that this failure of the Sedition Act, rather than the response to its passage, played some role in the triumph of the opposition in 1800.

The failure of the Sedition Act to suppress free speech was an ironic tribute to the Federalists' respect for due process and the restraints this respect imposed on them. Although a judge like Samuel Chase might take actions that hampered the defense strategy of the accused, there was no attempt to replace the legal process that allowed the defendant the right to know the charges against him, to win release on bail, to have legal counsel, and to be judged by a jury of his peers. There would be no executions, no wholesale destruction of presses, no censorship of publication—the abuses John Marshall had observed in Paris in 1798 would not be replicated in the United States under the Federalists.

The Republicans fared no better with their precipitous move to define the nature of the Constitution and delineate the powers of its government. The response to the Virginia and Kentucky Resolutions by the remaining state governments was overwhelmingly negative. Although opposition was not unanimous in most states, the fact that the Federalists were able, in every instance, to ensure that their legislatures rejected Jefferson and Madison's challenge is evidence that the Federalists remained the dominant force in American politics until the end of the decade. Neither the Alien and Sedition Acts nor the Virginia and Kentucky Resolutions were decisive in determining the Republican victory in the election of 1800; this transfer of power owed more to the two parties' differing approaches to American voters: throughout the 1790s, Federalists had sought only affirmation from these voters; Republicans offered them a role as active participants in the nation's politics.

Perhaps the success or the failure of these two efforts is not the most significant measure of their importance. Instead, that importance lies in the acceptance by both parties of the legitimacy of the Constitution and the federal government it created. Only a decade earlier, the Antifederalist-Federalist battle had been over whether the Constitution ought to be accepted as the establishment of a lasting political relationship among the states. Even after the Constitution was ratified, acceptance of its legitimacy was not complete. It was possible in 1794 for western Pennsylvanians to reject the right of the federal government to tax them and for the people of Kentucky to simply ignore that taxation without bothering to defend their right to do so. But in 1798, the leaders of the opposition party and the legislatures of two states considered it necessary to do more than reject or ignore particular legislation. Instead they felt compelled to offer an interpretation of the Constitution itself. Their protest against the Alien and Sedition Acts operated within the context of a loyalty to the Constitution and to the government it created. The resolutions passed by the legislatures of Kentucky and Virginia were not a challenge to the Constitution but a challenge to a particular interpretation of that document; they were not challenging the federal government but a particular set of alleged abuses of its powers. At issue was how to interpret the relationship the Constitution created between a federal government and the states, not whether it had the right to establish one. Thus, "nullification" and "interposition" were offered as a remedy, not a renunciation. The men who wrote these resolutions and the men who approved them saw themselves as loyal citizens of the Union. The tragedy of the Republicans was that they did not realize the destructive potential these remedies had if they became uncoupled from a loyalty to this union of the states.

The tragedy of the Federalists, meanwhile, was that they did not recognize their mission had been accomplished: the government they had designed in 1787 was no longer an experiment but an institution. Federalists misread the challenges to their leadership late in the decade as yet more in the long line of challenges to the legitimacy of the government and to its survival. They read the repressive legislation they passed as an essential defense of the Constitution, not of the men who held the reins of government or their policies. Republicans saw the Alien and Sedition Acts as their opponents' desperate effort to remain in power. Like Samuel Adams, who believed the American Revolution was necessary to save the principles of the British Constitution from a corrupt king and Parliament, Thomas Jefferson would see himself, and his party, as crusaders to restore the principles they believed were embodied by the Constitution.

CONCLUSION

I N THE SAME inaugural address to the First Federal Congress
that introduced this book, George Washington showed himself
keenly aware of the weighty responsibilities he and the Congress
faced together. It was, he said, his duty to preside over the "preservation of the sacred fire of liberty," a fire that he, like all Federalists,
believed depended on the survival of the Constitution and the federal government it created. He knew as well as they did that many
Americans had opposed this new federal government and that their
voices had still not been silenced. He could only pray that the members of this government would have "the enlarged views, the temperate consultations, and the wise measures" needed for it to succeed.
Over the course of the next eight years, Washington would have reason to wonder whether that success was a chimera, existing only in
his imagination and impossible in the realities of the decade ahead.

Not all the measures taken by Washington, Adams, and the Federalists were wise, and not all of their consultations were temperate.
And although men like Alexander Hamilton had what Washington
would surely consider enlarged views, the Pickerings and Wolcotts of

his party did not. Nevertheless, success did not prove an impossible dream, and both the Constitution and the federal government survived the crises of the 1790s—and the new crises that would follow for two centuries.

The belief of men like Washington and Hamilton that the Constitution and its government was the best, if not the only, means to save the Republic lay at the core of their nationalism. They were certain that the states, acting as separate sovereign governments, could not effectively negotiate with foreign nations, protect and extend the country's borders, or unleash the economic potential of a young and ambitious population blessed with the natural resources available to them. This is what drove them to replace the loose "league of friendship" created by the Articles of Confederation with an "energetic government" whose authority came not from the states but from the American people. They never doubted that the Republic needed such a government, and they saw themselves as its guardians and its champions. Leading Federalists like Hamilton were simultaneously anxious about the American people's full acceptance of this new government and full of optimism about what it could achieve with their support. America, Hamilton told a British ambassador, was "a young and a growing Empire, with much Enterprize and vigour." To the Federalists' relief and pride, the bond between the people and the government, the citizens and their constitution, grew stronger with each new crisis they faced.[1]

The four crises covered in this book challenged different aspects of federal authority and legitimacy. The Whiskey Rebellion, for example, denied the federal government's authority to tax its citizens. Its participants laid claim to the legacy of the American Revolution, with its justification of armed rebellion against oppression. They coopted the symbols of that revolution, but the analogy they drew was false: the government they opposed gave them a vote and a voice in the legislature that passed the excise tax. In many ways, of course, the response of the Kentucky distillers was an even greater blow to the sovereignty of the federal government; they did not bother to rebel, they simply ignored the law. Washington's handling of the crisis carried a critical message: the federal government was neither arbitrary nor tyrannical. The men placed in charge of it respected the law and the rights of the people, but they would fulfill their obligations to protect government agents and enforce the legislation passed by the people's representatives. The public accepted this message in large part because of the widespread admiration and love Americans felt for Washington himself. Their trust in him had not yet transferred to a trust in the office he held; that shift came in the next crisis, the Genet affair.

In the Genet affair, the exclusive authority of the federal government to set foreign policy was challenged. When France attempted to turn the United States into a satellite and a pawn in its war with Britain, Edmond Charles Genet and his government exposed the weakness of the United States on the world stage. Yet, despite his country's military and naval weakness, Washington steadfastly asserted his policy of neutrality. In the end, Washington managed to frustrate Genet sufficiently that the impulsive and impolitic French minister embarrassed himself by threatening to make his appeal for assistance directly to the people. This flagrant rejection of protocol justified the American government's request that Genet be recalled.

The Federalist resistance to what amounted to a recolonization of its country produced important gains for the government's reputation at home. First, it reinforced the idea that it was the role of the federal government to represent American interests to the wider world. The kind of meddling in diplomacy by individual state governments like Kentucky and South Carolina would no longer be tolerated. Second, Genet's threat to appeal directly to the people prompted an expression of support not simply for Washington but for the authority of the executive branch itself. The Constitution had placed foreign diplomacy and policy in the hands of the executive of the federal government. After the Genet affair, it was widely accepted that this, in fact, was where it belonged.

In the third crisis, the XYZ affair, one of the essential elements of nationalism emerged: the recognition of a shared American identity. In the face of the French government's insult to American honor, citizens who had long thought of themselves primarily as citizens of their states now identified themselves as Americans. They met the French claim that they were a divided people with the assertion that, in fact, we are all Americans. The patriotic toast, "Millions for defense, but not one cent for tribute," was thus more than a response to an insult; it was a pledge that no disagreement should ever run so deep as to permanently divide Americans from one another and no criticism they might have of their government should ever destroy their loyalty to it.

The Federalists were themselves the instigators of the fourth and final crisis examined in this book. Caught up in a combination of war fever and political self-interest, the Federalists moved to weaken their political opponents and solidify a guardianship of the Constitution and its government that they feared was slipping away. Their passage of the Alien and Sedition Acts prompted a challenge to federal authority mounted by the legislatures of Virginia and Kentucky. This crisis was clearly a party struggle between Federalists and Republicans, but there is no compelling evidence that the acts or the resolutions played a definitive role in the election of 1800 that ended Federalist hegemony.

The issues raised in this crisis did, however, have important consequences for American nationalism. With the Virginia and Kentucky Resolutions, Republicans were challenging the Federalists to define the union the Constitution had created, to clarify the powers it had given the federal government, and to weigh the relative sovereignty of that government and the states. In these resolutions, states' rights advocates struck a blow at the nationalism Federalists had nurtured for a decade. The men who drafted the resolutions and the legislators who passed them rejected the Federalist argument that the necessary and proper clause and the Preamble's charge to ensure domestic tranquility justified the acts. But, more than this, the resolutions asserted that the states, not the people, were the source of the Constitution's authority, and therefore the states retained the right to judge the constitutionality of any federal legislation.

Despite the intractable disagreement over the nature of Constitution and the powers of the federal government, the most striking aspect of this debate was this: both sides accepted the legitimacy of the Constitution and the government it created. The Virginia and Kentucky Resolutions were a challenge to a particular interpretation of the Constitution, not to the Constitution itself. The legislators responsible for the resolutions repeatedly expressed their loyalty to the Constitution and to its federal government; their goal was not to deny its validity but to better define its powers in order to prevent further abuses.

The arc of nationalism can thus be traced through the crises of the 1790s. The trust placed in Washington as an individual, so critical in the approval of his handling of the Whiskey Rebellion, was transformed during the Genet affair into a respect for the office he held. The XYZ affair helped Americans recognize their shared identity, a national identity that limited the power of provincialism to shape their views and their political choices. And the challenge to the Alien and Sedition Acts demonstrated that there was no longer an anti-Constitution movement but a loyalty to the Constitution that could withstand a difference in interpretation of the powers it invested in the federal government. This loyalty was fundamental to the acceptance of the notion of a loyal opposition in politics. And this idea of a loyal opposition helped sustain the Union until the struggle over the survival of slavery created a breach too broad and too deep to be mended without bloodshed.

Not even the crisis of the Civil War solved the problem of defining federalism, however. It remains with us in the twenty-first century. The government the Federalists created did not then, nor does it today, fully consolidate sovereignty. Thus, the challenge of localism to nationalism continues, with its drive to strengthen state sovereignty, to rein in the ability of the federal government to direct the economic growth and shape the social norms of American society—in short, to constrain the "enterprize and vigour" of the federal government. Nevertheless, the Federalist achievement must be acknowledged: its guardianship of the Republic succeeded. The government it designed in 1787 was no longer an experiment in 1800; it was the national government of a sovereign people.

ACKNOWLEDGMENTS

SOMEWHERE, USUALLY IN the middle of researching and writing a book, an author's thoughts turn to those few pages entitled "Acknowledgments." Thinking about all the people you have relied upon does more than make you feel fortunate; it reminds you that the lone historian, toiling away in the solitude of her study, is a myth. Writing history is collaborative work. Archivists and librarians—the people who have preserved and collected, inventoried, indexed, published primary sources on paper or, these days, online—have provided the treasure chests of information you plunder as you write. A thousand times a day, you realize that Founders Online, the Pennsylvania archives, JSTOR, and the *Annals of Congress* have put the past at your fingertips. Just as often you are reminded that the authors of the biographies, monographs, and articles piled high beside your desk are your guide to the past you are exploring. Without them, you would be wandering in the dark. Unlike Oscar winners, historians cannot thank every one of these people individually; we must be content to provide a bibliography as our thank-you note.

There are individuals, however, who must be acknowledged. Cindy Lobel, Angelo Angeles, Phillip Papas, and Rebecca Dresser are the members of a group still affectionately called the "dissertation salon," although these former students have gone far beyond that stage of their career and are now professors and historians. We have been meeting at my home for more than fifteen years now, discussing each other's work, offering criticism and praise, reminding one another to do more "sign posting" or to clarify and elaborate, while we indulge in croissants, bagels, and assorted other brunch delights. They are, for me, that fabled community of scholars, and I am ever grateful to them. Although Meg Berlin and Cecelia Hartsell live too far away to be members of our salon, they too patiently read versions of chapters, listen to me moan and groan when work is not going well, and provide insightful and tactful suggestions for improving the text. Among my usual suspects—those friends and colleagues I turn to when I can't track down a source, need technical advice ("Michael, why won't my printer print??"), and need to talk through an idea or interpretation for the ninetieth time—I must include three future stars of my profession, Michael Hattem, Christopher Minty, and Sarah Shapiro, along with current scholars of impeccable credentials, Richard Bernstein, Mary-Jo Kline, and Stuart Blumin. I am indebted to Sarah, who helped me organize the footnotes to this book. A special thanks also to Michael Ryan, the chief archivist at the New-York Historical Society, for his assistance and for serving as a model of erudition and intelligence.

My agent, Dan Green, has once again done double duty; he not only finds the right press and the right editor for me, he also reads the drafts of each chapter. After all these years I am still bowled over by the acuity of his comments, by his encouragement, and by his tolerance for both my corny jokes and my lengthy reviews of cops and robbers movies. As the editor for this book, I have the good fortune of another remarkable Dan, Dan Gerstle. His careful reading and keen analysis played a major role in shaping the manuscript. I dread to think what I would have done without his advice.

As always, family members, both human and feline, have provided me the laughter and delight that sustain me. Mr. Magoo did his part by purring loudly and soothingly while he blocked my view of the computer screen. And my daughter Hannah and her husband Eamon and my son Matthew and his wife Jessica have given me the most wonderful of gifts: my granddaughters, Talulla Thomas Joyce and Noa Grey Berkin. The last book was yours, Miss T; this one is for Noa.

Carol Berkin
New York City 2017

NOTES

Abbreviations

AC	Annals of Congress
ASP	American State Papers
FOL	Founders Online, National Archives (founders.archives.gov)
PA	Pennsylvania Archives
PJA	Papers of John Adams
PAH	The Papers of Alexander Hamilton
JMP	The Papers of James Madison
PJM	The Papers of John Marshall
PGW	The Papers of George Washington
PTJ	The Papers of Thomas Jefferson

Part I: The Whiskey Rebellion

1. Alexander Hamilton to George Washington, July 30–August 3, 1792, PAH, Vol. 12, pp. 137–139; Alexander Hamilton to John Jay, September 3, 1792, PAH, Vol. 12, pp. 316–317; George Washington to Alexander Hamilton, September 7, 1792, PAH, Vol. 12, pp. 331–333.

1: "The debt of the United States . . . was the price of liberty."

2. Fisher Ames to George R. Minot, March 25, 1789, in *Documentary History of the First Federal Congress, 1789–1791*, Vol. 15, ed. Charlene Bangs Bickford et al. (Johns Hopkins University Press, 2004), 126.

3. First Inaugural Address: Final Version, April 30, 1789, PGW, Presidential Series, Vol. 2, pp. 173–177.

4. AC, House, 1st Congress, 2nd Session, Appendix, pp. 2041–2074; *Report Relative to a Provision for the Support of Public Credit,* January 9, 1790, PAH, Vol. 6, pp. 65–110.

5. Alexander Hamilton, "Conversation with George Beckwith" [October 1789], PAH, Vol. 5, pp. 482–490.

2: "There is perhaps nothing so much a subject of national extravagance, as these spirits."

6. *The Federalist No. 21,* "Other Defects of the Present Confederation," in *The Documentary History of the Ratification of the Constitution,* Vol. 14, ed. Gaspare J. Saladino and John P. Kaminski (Wisconsin Historical Society Press, 1983), pp. 414–418. It can also be found online in *The Avalon Project,* Documents in Law, History, and Diplomacy, Yale Law School.

7. *The Federalist No. 12,* "The Utility of the Union in Respect to Revenue," *The Avalon Project.* See also Cynthia L. Krom and Stephanie Krom, "The Whiskey Tax of 1791 and the Consequent Insurrection: 'A Wicked and Happy Tumult,'" *Accounting Historians Journal,* Vol. 40, No. 2 (December 2013), pp. 91–114, 95.

8. Ed Crews, "Rattle-Skull, Stonewall, Bogus, Blackstrap, Bombo, Mimbo, Whistle Belly, Syllabub, Sling, Toddy, and Flip: Drinking in Colonial America," online in *Colonial Williamsburg Journal* (Holiday 2007).

9. Ibid.

10. See *Report of the Secretary of the Treasury, Relative to a Provision for the Support of Public Credit,* AC, 1st Congress, Appendix, pp. 2065–2066. For the full report, see the Appendix, pp. 2041–2074.

11. AC, House of Representatives, 1st Congress, 2nd Session, May 25, 1790, p. 1666.

12. See Hamilton's December 13, 1790, *Report on Public Credit,* AC, 1st Congress, Appendix, pp. 2074–2082; see also PAH, Vol. 7, pp. 225–236.

13. For the debate in the House, see AC, 1st Congress, 3rd Session, House of Representatives, pp. 1890–1934; AC, 1st Congress, 3rd Session, House of Representatives, pp. 1890–1893.

14. AC, 1st Congress, 3rd Session, House of Representatives, January 24, 1791, p. 1931.

15. AC, 1st Congress, 3rd Session, House of Representatives, March 3, 1791, p. 2027.

16. For the act, see *The Public Statutes at Large of the United States of America,* Vol. 1, ed. Richard Peters, Esq. (Charles C. Little and James Brown, 1850), pp. 199–214.

3: "The law is deservedly obnoxious to the feelings and interests of the people."

17. For the problems facing western farmers and the impact of the excise tax on them, see Krom and Krom, "The Whiskey Tax," pp. 97–102.

18. Ibid., pp. 102–105.

19. See Mary K. Bonsteel Tachau, "The Whiskey Rebellion in Kentucky: A

Forgotten Episode of Civil Disobedience," *Journal of the Early Republic*, Vol. 2, No. 3 (Autumn 1982), pp. 239–259.

20. Ibid., p. 246.

21. See Thomas Jefferson to William S. Smith, November 13, 1787, PTJ, Vol. 12, pp. 355–357.

22. For a review of the protests and the violence against the tax collectors, marshals, and other supporters of the federal excise tax, see Alexander Hamilton to George Washington, August 5, 1794, PGW, Presidential Series, Vol. 16, pp. 478–508. For the best collection of documents on the Whiskey Rebellion, see "Papers Relating to What is Known as the Whiskey Rebellion in Western Pennsylvania, 1794," *Pennsylvania Archives*, Second Series, Vol. 4, ed. John B. Linn and William H. Egle, MD (Clarence M. Busch, State Printer of Pennsylvania, 1896). For contemporary accounts, see H. H. Brackenridge, *Incidents of the Insurrection in the Western Parts of Pennsylvania, in the Year 1794*, Classic Reprint (Forgotten Books, 2016); H. M. Brackenridge, *History of the Western Insurrection in Western Pennsylvania Commonly Called the Whiskey Insurrection, 1794*; reprinted (Heritage Books, 2009); and William Findley, *History of the Insurrection in the Four Western Counties of Pennsylvania in the Year MDCCXCIV; with a Recital of the Circumstances Specially Connected therewith, and an Historical Review of the Previous Situation of the Country* (Philadelphia 1796). For modern accounts of the Whiskey Rebellion, see William Hogeland, *The Whiskey Rebellion: George Washington, Alexander Hamilton, and the Frontier Rebels Who Challenged America's Newfound Sovereignty* (Simon and Schuster, 2010); Leland D. Baldwin, *Whiskey Rebels: The Story of a Frontier Uprising.* (University of Pittsburgh Press, 1939); and Thomas P. Slaughter, *The Whiskey Rebellion: Frontier Epilogue to the American Revolution* (Oxford University Press, 1988).

23. The account of the attack on John Connor can be found in Alexander Hamilton to George Washington, August 5, 1794, PAH, Vol. 17, pp. 24–58.

24. Hogeland, *The Whiskey Rebellion*, p. 105.

4: "What occasion is there for such violent and unwarrantable proceedings?"

25. George Washington to David Humphreys, July 20, 1791, PGW, Presidential Series, Vol. 8, pp. 358–361.

26. Alexander Hamilton to George Washington, April 10, 1791, PAH, Vol. 8, p. 269.

27. To The United States Senate and House of Representatives, October 25, 1791, PGW, Presidential Series, Vol. 9, pp. 110–117.

28. For the report, see AC, 2nd Congress, 1st Session, Appendix, pp. 1077–1098; see also *Report on the Difficulties in the Execution of the Act Laying Duties on Distilled Spirits* (March 5, 1792), PAH, Vol. 11, pp. 77–106.

29. AC, 2nd Congress, 1st Session, House of Representatives, March 8, 1792, pp. 450–451.

30. AC, 2nd Congress, 1st Session, April 30, 1792, pp. 584–586.

31. AC, 2nd Congress, 1st Session, House of Representatives, April 26, 1792, p. 580, and May 5, 1792, pp. 593–594.

5: The *"great* and *real* anxiety is . . . the ability to preserve the national government."

32. AC, 2nd Congress, 1st Session, House of Representatives, April 30, 1792, p. 588.

33. See Ron Chernow, *Alexander Hamilton* (Penguin Press, 2004), pp. 39, 425–430; Stanley Elkins and Eric McKitrick, *The Age of Federalism: The Early American Republic, 1788–1800* (Oxford University Press, 1993), pp. 293–302. See also George Washington to Alexander Hamilton, August 26, 1792, and Hamilton's reply, Alexander Hamilton to George Washington, September 9, 1792, PGW, Presidential Series, Vol. 11, pp. 38–40, 91–94.

34. Alexander Hamilton to Edward Carrington, May 26, 1792, PAH, Vol. 11, pp. 426–445.

35. Alexander Hamilton to Edward Carrington, July 25, 1792, PAH, Vol. 12, pp. 83–85.

36. Hogeland, *The Whiskey Rebellion,* p. 117.

37. Alexander Hamilton to Tench Cox, September 1, 1792, PAH, Vol. 12, pp. 305–310.

38. See George Clymer to Alexander Hamilton [October 4, 1792], PAH, Vol. 12, pp. 517–522; George Clymer to Alexander Hamilton, September 28, 1792, PAH, Vol. 12, pp. 495–497; see also, Hogeland, *The Whiskey Rebellion,* pp. 126–127.

39. Alexander Hamilton to John Jay, September 3, 1792, PAH, Vol. 12, pp. 316–317.

40. George Washington to Alexander Hamilton, September 7, 1792, PAH, Vol. 12, pp. 331–333.

41. Ibid.

42. John Jay to Alexander Hamilton, September 8, 1792, PAH, Vol. 12, pp. 334–335.

43. Alexander Hamilton to George Washington, September 11, 1792, PAH, Vol. 12, pp. 365–368; Edmund Randolph to George Washington, September 10, 1792, PGW, Presidential Series, Vol. 11, pp. 106–108. The account was published in the Philadelphia *Gazette of the United States* on September 25, 1792.

44. Proclamation of September 15, 1792, *Avalon Project*; George Washington to Thomas Mifflin, September 29, 1792, PAH, Vol. 12, pp. 508–509; Alexander Hamilton to George Washington September 23, 1792, PGW, Presidential Series, Vol. 11, p. 147.

45. Richard Henry Lee to George Washington, September 26, 1775, PGW, Revolutionary War Series, Vol. 2, pp. 51–53; George Washington to Edmund Randolph, October 1, 1792, PGW, Presidential Series, Vol. 11, p. 187.

6: "Where the law ends, there tyranny begins."

46. George Washington to the Ministers and Members of the Methodist Episcopal Church in Fayette County, Pennsylvania, January 30, 1793, PGW, Presidential Series, Vol. 12, p. 63.

47. George Washington to Alexander Hamilton, September 17, 1792, PAH, Vol. 12, pp. 390–391.

48. PA, Second Series, Vol. 4 (1896), pp. 28–32.

49. George Clymer to Alexander Hamilton, October 10, 1792, PAH, Vol. 12, pp. 540–542.

50. PA, Second Series, Vol. 4 (1896), pp. 35–39.

51. AC, 2nd Congress, 2nd Session, House of Representatives, November 10, 1792, p. 677.

52. William Findley to Governor Mifflin, November 21, 1792, PA, pp. 41–44.

53. William Findley to Governor Mifflin, November 21/92, PA, pp. 41–44; Thomas Mifflin, Annual Message, PA, 44–46.

7: "It is the duty of the general government to protect the frontiers."

54. Gilder Lehrman Institute Collection, New-York Historical Society, #GLCO2437.05942, October 11, 1793. For a full discussion of the yellow fever epidemic, see J. H. Powell, *Bring Out Your Dead: The Great Plague of Yellow Fever in Philadelphia in 1793* (University of Pennsylvania Press, 1993).

55. Alexander Hamilton to Henry Knox, June 25, 1793, PAH, Vol. 15, p. 26.

56. Proclamation on Violent Opposition to the Excise Tax, February 24, 1794, PGW, Presidential Series, Vol. 15, pp. 275–277.

57. Kentucky, formerly part of Virginia, became the fifteenth state on June 1, 1792; Cabinet Meeting: Opinion on Expeditions Being Planned In Kentucky for the Invasion of the Spanish Dominions, March 10, 1794, PAH, Vol. 16, p. 136–140; "Proclamation on Expeditions against Spanish Territory, March 24, 1794, PGW, Presidential Series, Vol. 15, pp. 446–447. For a full discussion of Genet's invasion plans, see Part 2 of this volume.

58. See George Muter, *On Saturday the 24th instant a numerous meeting of respectable citizens from different parts of this state assembled in Lexington . . .* (Printed by John Bradford, 1794); see also Edmund Randolph to William Bradford, Alexander Hamilton, and Henry Knox, July 11, 1794, PAH, Vol. 16, pp. 588–590. Edmund Randolph would eventually manage to win a truce with the distillers in 1795 by offering to forgive all whiskey tax arrears and by announcing that a treaty with Spain had been signed. For a brief moment, the problem of Kentucky seemed to be solved, but the distillers reneged on their promise to obey the law when Spain dragged its feet on honoring the treaty. It would not be until 1799, when president-elect Thomas Jefferson promised to repeal the excise tax, that Kentucky's distillers at last voluntarily paid their taxes. Bonsteel Tachau, "The Whiskey Rebellion," pp. 239–259.

59. Alexander Hamilton to George Washington, July 13, 1794, PAH, Vol. 16, pp. 600–602; Edmund Randolph to William Bradford, Alexander Hamilton and Henry, July 11, 1794, note 2, in PAH, Vol. 16, pp. 588–590; see also ASP, Indian Affairs, Vol. 1, p. 500.

8: "Finding the opposition to the revenue law more violent than I expected . . . "

60. See notes from Thomas Mifflin to George Washington, April 18, 1794, PGW, Presidential Series, Vol. 15, pp. 612–614; Alexander Addison to Thomas

Mifflin, March 31, 1794, and May 12, 1794, PA, pp. 50–51, 53–54; Alexander Hamilton to George Washington, June 4, 1794, PGW, Presidential Series, Vol. 16, pp. 184–185.

61. See US Statutes at Large, Vol. 1, 3rd Congress, 1st Session, Library of Congress 49; Alexander Hamilton to John Jay, PAH, Vol. 16, pp. 456–457.

62. For the correspondence on the Whiskey Rebellion, see "Opposition to the Excise Law in Pennsylvania," AC, 4th Congress, Appendix, pp. 2791–2868; for additional accounts of these attacks and the rebellion in general, see Hogeland, *The Whiskey Rebellion*; Brackenridge, *Incidents of the Insurrection*; and Slaughter, *The Whiskey Rebellion*; see also "Papers Relating to What is Known as the Whiskey Rebellion," pp. 1–47.

63. Deposition of Francis Mentges, August 1, 1794, PAH, Vol. 17, pp. 2–6.

64. General Gibson to Governor Thomas Mifflin, July 18, 1794, PA, pp. 58–60; Major Thomas Butler to Gen. Knox, July 18, 1794, PA, pp. 63–64.

65. Hogeland, *The Whiskey Rebellion,* pp.167–173.

66. "Circular of the Western Insurgents to the Militia Officers," July 28, 1794, in PA, p. 67.

9: "The crisis is now come, submission or opposition."

67. Deposition of Francis Mentges, August 1, 1794, PAH, Vol. 17, pp. 2–6.

68. Conference at the President's, Saturday, August 9 [2?], 1794, PA, pp. 122–124.

69. Alexander Hamilton to George Washington, August 2, 1794, PAH, Vol. 17, pp. 15–19.

70. Ibid.

71. James Wilson to George Washington, August 4, 1794, PA, p. 70; Opposition to the Excise Law, AC, 4th Congress, Appendix, p. 2796.

72. Circular to the President Judges, July 25, 1794, PA, pp. 65–66; Governor Thomas Mifflin to George Washington, August 5, 1794, AC, 4th Congress, 1795–1797, Appendix, pp. 2825–2830; Gen. John Wilkins to Col. Clement Biddle, August 1, 1794, PA, p. 69.

73. Alexander Hamilton to George Washington, August 5, 1794, PAH, Vol. 17, pp. 24–58; AC, 4th Congress, Appendix, p. 2796; Edmund Randolph to George Washington, August 5, 1794, PGW, Presidential Series, Vol. 16, pp. 523–530.

74. Appointment of United States Commissioners, August 8, 1794; Instructions to the United States Commissioners, August 8, 1794, in PA, pp. 116–118.

75. Thomas Mifflin to Judge (Thomas) McKean and Gen. William Irvine, August 6, 1794, PA, pp. 93–94.

76. David Bradford to the Inhabitants of Monongahela, Virginia, August 6, 1794, PA, p. 95.

10: "Such disorder can only be cured by copious bleedings."

77. Proclamation, August 7, 1794, PGW, Presidential Series, Vol. 16, pp. 531–537.

78. Secretary of War to Governor Mifflin, August 7, 1794, PA, pp. 104–105.

79. Secretary of State to Governor Mifflin, AC, 4th Congress, Appendix, pp. 2829–2837.

80. Thomas Mifflin to the President of the United States, August 8, 1794, AC, 4th Congress, 1795–1797, Appendix, pp. 2837–2843.

81. Secretary of War to Governor Mifflin, August 7, 1794, PA, pp. 104–105; Second Proclamation of Governor Mifflin, August 7, 1794, PA, p. 114.

82. H. H. Brackenridge to Tench Coxe, in Brackenridge, *Incidents of the Insurrection*, Appendix, pp. 130–131, also in PA, pp. 119–122; see also Samuel Hodgdon to Isaac Craig, July 26, 1794, in Kenneth A. White, "Such Disorder Can Only Be Cured by Copious Bleedings: The Correspondence of Isaac Craig During the Whiskey Rebellion," *The Western Pennsylvania Historical Magazine*, Vol. 67, No. 3, pp. 213–242; and for another account of the attack on Neville, see David Lenox to Alexander Hamilton, September 8, 1794, PAH, Vol. 17, pp. 203–209.

83. For an account of the meeting at Parkinson's Ferry, see PA, pp. 135–136.

84. Hogeland, *The Whiskey Rebellion*, pp. 190–192; The United States Commissioners to the Secretary of State, August 17, 1794, PA, pp. 138–141; and also PGW, Presidential Series, Vol. 16, pp. 592–593.

85. Isaac Craig to Henry Knox, August 17, 1794, in White, "Such Disorder Can Only Be Cured by Copious Bleedings," pp. 224–225; The United States Commissioners to the Secretary of State, August 17, 1794, PA, pp. 138–141; Gen. William Irvine to Secretary Dallas, August 17, 1794, PA, pp. 142–143.

86. Proceedings of the First Conference, August 20, 1794, PA, pp. 155–158; Ross, Yeates, Bradford to the Committee of Conference, Assembled at Pittsburg [sic], August 21, 1794; Edward Cook, Chairman to the Commissioners, August 22, 1794; Ross, Yeates, Bradford to the Committee of Conference, August 22, 1794; Edward Cook to the Commissioners, August 23, 1794; Ross, Yeates, and Bradford to the Committee of Conference, August 23, 1794; Robert Stephenson, William Sutherland, William McKinly to Commissioners, August 23, 1794; Ross et al. to Stephenson et al., August 23, 1794; Stephenson et al. to Commissioners, August 23, 1794, all in AC, 4th Congress, Appendix, pp. 2809–2816.

87. Minutes of a Meeting Concerning the Insurrection in Western Pennsylvania, August 24, 1794, PAH, Vol. 17, pp 135–138.

88. Proceedings of the Second Conference, August 29, 1794; Col. Cook to the US Commissioners, August 29, 1794; The Committee of Conference to the US Commissioners, September 1, 1794; US Commissioners to the Committee of Conference, September 1, 1794, all in PA, pp. 180–182, 183, 197, 198–201.

89. Judge Addison's Charge to the Grand Jury of Allegheny, September 1, 1794, PA, pp. 201–209.

90. The Committee of Conference to the US Commissioners, September 2, 1794, PA, p. 219.

11: "An amicable accommodation [is] so very doubtful."

91. Gen. Wilkins to Gen. Clement Biddle, September 5, 1794, PA, p. 222; Judge Addison to Thomas Mifflin, September 5, 1794, PA, pp. 222–225; Secretary of War to Governor Mifflin, PA, p. 226.

92. Alexander Hamilton to Thomas Sim Lee, September 6, 1794, PAH, Vol. 17, pp. 201–202; For news of a liberty pole in Milton, Pennsylvania, see Jasper Ewing, of Northumberland, to Charles Hall, of York, September 27, 1794, PA, pp. 319–320.

93. Declaration of David Bradford et al., September 13, 1794, PA, p. 251.

94. Westmoreland Declaration, September 16, 1794, PA, p. 252.

95. Fayette County Declaration, September 16, 1794, PA, pp. 252–253.

96. Resolves of Ohio County, Virginia, September 8–9, 1794, PA, pp. 228–229.

97. Alexander Hamilton to Rufus King, September 22, 1794, PAH, Vol. 17, pp. 258–259; Alexander Hamilton to Rufus King, September 17, 1794, PAH, Vol. 17, pp. 241–242.

98. Special Message of Governor Mifflin to the Assembly, September 10, 1794, PA, pp. 229–230; Col. Josiah Crawford to Gen. Harmar, September 4, 1794, PA, pp. 219–220; Address of Gov. Mifflin to the Militia of Philadelphia, September 10, 1794, PA, pp. 231–233; Secretary Dallas's Report to the Senate, September 10, 1794, PA, pp. 237–238.

99. Alexander Hamilton to Thomas Sim Lee, September 24, 1794, PAH, Vol. 17, pp. 266–267; see annotations to Alexander Hamilton to George Washington, August 12, 1794, PAH, Vol. 17, pp. 86–88, for excerpts from the letters of John Stagg to Henry Knox and Isaac Craig to Henry Knox detailing these proscriptions and threats.

100. Proclamation, September 25, 1794, PGW, Presidential Series, Vol. 16, pp. 725–727.

12: "To arms once more."

101. Alexander Hamilton to George Washington, September 19, 1794, PAH, Vol. 17, pp. 254–255.

102. Alexander Hamilton to General Henry Lee, October 20, 1794, AC, 4th Congress, 1795–1797, Appendix, pp. 2866–2868.

103. Alexander Hamilton to Jared Ingersoll, October 10, 1794, PAH, Vol. 17, pp. 315–317; Alexander Hamilton to Thomas Mifflin, October 10, 1794, PAH, Vol. 17, pp. 317–319.

104. George Washington to Edmund Randolph, October 9, 1794, PGW, Presidential Series, Vol. 17, pp. 45–46; George Washington, Diary, October 9, 1794; PGW, *The Diaries of George Washington*, Vol. 6, ed. Donald Jackson and Dorothy Twohig, pp. 183–186.

105. Ibid.

106. Report of the Committee of Conference with Gen. Lee's Reply, November 1, 1794, PA, pp. 367–369; notes on the march from September 30 until October 29, 1794, PA, pp. 362.

107. Resolves of the Inhabitants of Greensburgh, October 23, 1794, PA, pp. 354–355; Deposition of Judge Addison, n.d., PA, pp. 328–329; H. H. Brackenridge to Governor Mifflin, October 3, 1794, PA, p. 331; Resolutions of the Second Meeting at Parkinson's Ferry, October 3, 1794, PA, pp. 327–328; David Bradford, of Washington, to Governor Mifflin, October 4, 1794, PA, pp. 333–334.

13: "We are very strong & the Insurgents are all submissive."

108. H. H. Brackenridge to the Army, October 26, 1794, PA, p. 359.

109. General Henry Lee to General Wm. Irvine, November 9, 1794, PA, p. 376; Alexander Hamilton to George Washington, November 11, 1794, PAH, Vol. 17, pp. 366–367.

110. Alexander Hamilton to George Washington, November 11, 1794, PAH, Vol. 17, pp. 366–367.

111. H. H. Brackenridge, *Incidents of the Insurrection*, pp. 75–78.

112. For one account of these interrogations, see William Findley, *History*, pp. 228–235, 240–245; see also Ron Chernow, *Alexander Hamilton*, pp. 476–477.

113. Alexander Hamilton to William Rawle, November 17–19, 1794, PAH, Vol. 17, pp. 378–381; William Rawle to Alexander Addison, July 17, 1795, PA, p. 448; Capt. D'Hebecourt to Gen. Henry Lee, November 15, 1794, PA, pp. 378–379.

114. General Lee's Proclamation of Pardon, November 29, 1794, PA, pp. 402–403.

14: "The spirit inimical to all order."

115. See Findley, *History,* pp. 164, 218, 226; H. M. Brackenridge, *History of the Whiskey Insurrection*, p. 21.

116. See the (Philadelphia) *General Advertiser,* November 9, 1794.

117. AC, 3rd Congress, 2nd Session, Proceedings of the Senate, November 19, 1794, pp. 787–791.

118. Thomas Jefferson to James Madison, December 28, 1794, PJM, Vol. 15, pp. 426–429; AC, 3rd Congress, 2nd Session, House of Representatives, November 28, 1794, pp. 947–948.

Part II: The Genet Affair

1: "France is on the high-road to despotism."

1. Gouverneur Morris to William Carmichael, May 14, 1792, in *The Diary and Letters of Gouverneur Morris: Minister of the United States to France, Member of the Constitutional Convention, Etc.*, Vol. 1, ed. Anne Cary Morris (Charles Scribner's Sons, 1888) p. 533; Gouverneur Morris to Thomas Jefferson, September 10, 1792, PTJ, Vol. 24, pp. 364–365.

2. Thomas Boylston Adams to John Adams, April 7, 1793, *Adams Family Correspondence,* Vol. 9, ed. Margaret A. Hogan et al. (Harvard University Press, 2009) pp. 421–422; Samuel Allyne Otis to John Adams, April 17, 1793, FOL.

3. James Madison to the Minister of the Interior of the French Republic, April 1793, PJM, Vol. 15, p. 4; Thomas Jefferson to William Smith, November 13, 1787, PTJ, Vol. 12, pp. 355–357.

4. Elkins and McKitrick, *The Age of Federalism*, p. 322.

5. John Adams to Tench Coxe, April 25, 1793, FOL.

2: "I find him to be a great treasure to sustain and employ."

6. For a discussion of the various proposed instructions to the minister to the United States, see Regina Katharine Crandall, "Genet's Projected Attack on Louisiana and the Floridas, 1793–94," PhD Dissertation, University of Chicago, 1902; Eugene R. Sheridan, "The Recall of Edmond Charles Genet: A Study in Transatlantic Politics and Diplomacy," *Diplomatic History,* Vol. 18 (Fall 1994), pp. 463–488; Harry Ammon, *The Genet Mission* (W. W. Norton, 1973); Albert Hall Bowman, *The Struggle for Neutrality: Franco-American Diplomacy During the Federalist Era* (University of Tennessee Press, 1974), pp. 42–55.

7. Ammon, *The Genet Mission,* pp. 7–8.

8. George Clinton Genet, *Washington, Jefferson, and "Citizen" Genet, 1793* (New York Public Library, 1905), p. 7.

9. Crandall, "Genet's Projected Attack," p. 9.

3: "FREEMEN, WE ARE YOUR BROTHERS AND FRIENDS."

10. Thomas Jefferson, "Notes on the Opinions regarding the Reception of Edmond Genet," March 30, 1793, PGW, Presidential Series, Vol. 12, pp. 392–393.

11. James Parton, "The Exploits of Edmond Genet in the United States," *The Atlantic Monthly: A Magazine of Literature, Science, Art and Politics,* Vol. 31, No. 186 (April 1873), pp. 385–405, 390.

12. C. L. Bragg, *Crescent Moon over Carolina: William Moultrie and American Liberty* (University of South Carolina Press, 2013), pp. 249, 253–261; Harlow Giles Ungar, *The French War Against America: How a Trusted Ally Betrayed Washington and the Founding Fathers* (John Wiley & Sons, 2005), pp. 145–146. For continued infractions of neutrality in South Carolina, see Alexander Hamilton to Isaac Holmes, June 2, 1794, PAH, Vol. 16, pp. 446–447.

13. George Washington to the Cabinet, April 18, 1793, PGW, Presidential Series, Vol. 12, pp. 452–454.

14. Alexander Hamilton to John Jay, April 9, 1793, PAH, Vol. 14, pp. 297–299.

15. Minutes of a Cabinet Meeting, April 19, 1793, PGW, Presidential Series, Vol. 12, pp. 459–460.

16. For the Proclamation of Neutrality of 1793, see *The Avalon Project,* Documents in Law History and Diplomacy, Yale University.

17. [Alexander Hamilton], Enclosure: Answer to Question the 3d. Proposed by the President of the U. States, May 2, 1793, PAH, Vol. 14, pp. 367–396.

18. [Thomas Jefferson], IV. Opinion on the Treaties with France, April 28, 1793, PTJ, Vol. 25, pp. 608–619.

19. See, for example, Conversation with George Hammond, March 7–April 2, 1793, PAH, Vol. 14, pp. 193–195; Conversation with George Hammond, June 10–July 6, 1793, PAH, Vol. 14, pp. 525–528; Thomas Jefferson to James Madison, July 7, 1793, PJM, Vol. 15, p. 43.

4: "The Republics of France and America: may they be forever united in the cause of liberty."

20. George Washington to the Earl of Buchan, April 22, 1793, GWP, Presidential Series, Vol. 12, pp. 468–471.

21. Bernard, Mayo, ed. "Instructions to the British Ministers to the United States, 1791–1812," No. 3, American Historical Association, (1941), pp. 37–39.

22. John Steele to Alexander Hamilton, April 30 [1793], PAH, Vol. 14, pp. 358–360.

23. Alexander Hamilton, On the Reception of Edmond Charles Genet in Philadelphia, May 14–16, 1793, PAH, Vol. 14, pp. 449–450.

24. Parton, "The Exploits of Edmond Genet in the United States," pp. 391–393.

25. Ibid., p. 393.

26. Ibid., p. 394.

27. Thomas Jefferson to Jean Baptiste Ternant, May 14, 1793, PTJ, Vol. 26, pp. 42–44.

28. William Vans Murray to Alexander Hamilton, May 8, 1793, PAH, Vol. 14, pp. 425–428; Memorandum from Alexander Hamilton, May 15, 1793, PGW, Presidential Series, Vol. 12, pp. 577–584.

29. See The Provisional Executive Council of France to George Washington, January 1793, PGW, Presidential Series, Vol. 12, pp. 77–79; see also Enclosure: Letter of Credence from the Provisional Executive Council of France, December 30, 1792, PTJ, Vol. 26, pp. 48–49; The French National Convention to George Washington, December 22, 1792, PGW, Presidential Series, pp. 538–540.

30. Alexander Hamilton to ——, May 18, 1793, PAH, Vol. 14, pp. 473–476.

31. Thomas Jefferson to James Madison, May 19, 1793, PJM, Vol. 15, pp. 18–20.

32. Ibid.

33. Notes on the *Citoyen Genet* and Its Prizes, May 20, 1793, PTJ, Vol. 26, pp. 71–73.

34. Ibid.

5: "Our common enemies are trying to dampen American zeal for liberty."

35. Translation: Edmond Genet to Thomas Jefferson, May 22, 1793, PTJ, Vol. 26, pp. 86–87.

36. Edmond Charles Genet to Thomas Jefferson, May 23, 1793, PTJ, Vol. 26, pp. 98–99; ASP, Foreign Relations, Vol. 1, p. 147.

37. Notes of a Conversation with George Washington, May 23, 1793, PTJ, Vol. 26, pp. 101–102.

38. Citizen Genet, Minister Plenipotentiary of the Republic of France, to Mr. Jefferson, Secretary of State of the United States, May 27, 1793, ASP, Foreign Relations, Vol. 1, pp. 149–150; PTJ, Vol. 26, pp. 124–129.

6: "No one has a right to shackle our operations."

39. Edmond Charles Genet to Thomas Jefferson, June 1, 1793, PTJ, Vol. 26, p. 159; Translation, ASP, Foreign Relations, Vol. 1, 151.

40. Thomas Jefferson to Edmond Charles Genet, June 1 [June 4], 1793, PTJ, Vol. 26, pp. 160–161; ASP, Foreign Relations, Vol. 1, p. 151.

41. Thomas Jefferson to Edmond Charles Genet, June 5, 1793, PTJ, Vol. 26, pp. 195–197.

42. Edmond Charles Genet to Thomas Jefferson, PTJ, Vol. 26, pp. 231–234; Translation, ASP, Foreign Relations, Vol. 1, p. 151.

43. Conversation with George Hammond, June 10–July 6, 1793, PAH, Vol. 14, pp. 525–528.

44. Thomas Jefferson to Edmond Charles Genet, June 11, 1793, PTJ, Vol. 26, p. 252.

45. Thomas Jefferson to Gouverneur Morris, June 13, 1793, PTJ, Vol. 26, pp. 274–277.

46. Henry Lee to George Washington, June 14, 1793, PGW, Presidential Series, Vol. 13, pp. 77–78.

47. Edmond Charles Genet to Thomas Jefferson, June 14, 1793, PTJ, Vol. 26, pp. 283–284; Translation, ASP, Foreign Relations, Vol. 1, pp. 156–157.

48. Edmond Charles Genet to Thomas Jefferson, June 14, 1793, PTJ, Vol. 26, pp. 281–283; Translation, ASP, Foreign Relations, Vol. 1, pp. 152–153; Edmond Genet to Thomas Jefferson, June 15, 1793, PTJ, Vol. 26, pp. 290–292; ASP, Foreign Relations, Vol. 1, p. 157. The case in New York referred to by Genet concerned the ship *Republicain*, a vessel owned by one Frenchman and commanded by another. According to an affidavit by the French consul in the city, Alexandre Maurice Blanc de Lanautte, Comte d'Hauterive, the governor of New York had ordered a detachment of state militia to detain the *Republicain* until the president had the facts of the case. At issue was how long a belligerent's ship must wait in a neutral port before undertaking pursuit of a departed ship belonging to the enemy. Genet insisted that the pursuing ship did not have to honor the customary European twenty-four-hour truce. It had only to commit no hostile action against the enemy on American territory or in American territorial waters. Although the question was submitted to a cabinet meeting on June 17, no decision was made. The US policy on a truce would not be set until six months after Jefferson left office. In June 1794, the new secretary of state, Edmund Randolph, gave the British minister President Washington's decision: all belligerent warships and privateers would be required to wait twenty-four hours before pursuing an enemy ship that had reached a point "beyond the jurisdictional line of the United States on the ocean." See Cabinet Opinion on French Privateers, June 17, 1793, PGW, Presidential Series, Vol. 13, pp. 90–91; and Edmund Randolph to George Hammond, June 19, 1794, PGW, Presidential Series, Vol. 16, pp. 253–255.

49. For the use of the term "anglomancy," see, for example, James Madison to Thomas Jefferson, June 19, 1793, PTJ, Vol. 26, pp. 323–324.

50. George Hammond to Thomas Jefferson, June 14, 1793, PTJ, Vol. 26, pp. 284–285; Cabinet Opinion on French Privateers, June 17, 1793, PTJ, Vol. 26, pp. 296–297; Thomas Jefferson to George Hammond, June 19, 1793, PTJ, Vol. 26, p. 321.

51. Thomas Jefferson to Edmond Genet, June 17, 1793, PTJ, Vol. 26, pp. 297–300.

52. Edmond Charles Genet to Thomas Jefferson, June 18, 1793, ASP, Foreign Relations, Vol. 1, p. 158; Thomas Jefferson to Edmond Charles Genet, June 23, PAH, Vol. 15, p. 17; see also Citizen Genet, Minister Plenipotentiary of the

French Republick, to the Citizens of the United States, June 17, 1793, ASP, Foreign Relations, Vol. 1, p. 158. This address to the citizens of the United States was not published.

7: "[Genet] has threatened to appeal from The President of The United States to the People."

53. For Genet's comments on Washington, see Francois Louis Michel Chemin Deforgues's reply to Genet's Dispatch No. 4, quoted in Crandall, "Genet's Projected Attack," pp. 88–91. Edmond Charles Genet to Thomas Jefferson, June 22, 1793, PTJ, Vol. 26, pp. 339–342; Translation, ASP, Foreign Relations, Vol. 1, p. 155; Edmond Charles Genet to Thomas Jefferson, June 22, 1793, ASP, Foreign Relations, Vol. 1, p. 155.

54. Thomas Jefferson to Edmond Charles Genet, June 23, 1793, PTJ, Vol. 26, p. 344; Edmond Charles Genet to Thomas Jefferson, June 25, ASP, Foreign Relations, Vol. I, p. 159.

55. Thomas Jefferson to Edmond Charles Genet, June 29, 1793, PTJ, Vol. 26, p. 399; Thomas Mifflin to George Washington, June 22, 1793, PGW, Presidential Series, Vol. 13, pp. 126–127; Thomas Mifflin to George Washington, June 22, 1793, PGW, Presidential Series, Vol. 13, p. 127; George Washington to Henry Knox, June 23, 1793, PGW, Presidential Series, Vol. 13, pp. 131–132; Thomas Mifflin to George Washington, June 22, PGW, Presidential Series, Vol. 13, p. 128; Thomas Jefferson to the Minister Plenipotentiary of France, June 29, 1793, ASP, Foreign Relations, Vol. 1, p. 162; Memorandum from Alexander Hamilton and Henry Knox, July 8, 1793, PGW, Presidential Series, Vol. 13, pp. 185–191; Cabinet Opinion on the *Little Sarah* (*Petite Democrate*), July 8, 1793, PGW, Presidential Series, Vol. 13, pp. 180–185; [Thomas Jefferson], Dissenting Opinion on the *Little Sarah,* July 8, 1793, PTJ, Vol. 26, pp. 449–452; Enclosure: Thomas Jefferson's Notes on a Conversation with Edmond Genet, July 10, 1793, PGW, Presidential Series, Vol. 13, pp. 202–207; I. Alexander Hamilton's Questions for the Supreme Court (c. July 18, 1793), PTJ, Vol. 26, pp. 527–530.

56. For Mifflin's account of the Dallas and Genet meeting, see Thomas Mifflin to George Washington, July 8, 1793, PGW, Presidential Series, Vol. 13, pp. 191–194; see also John Jay and Rufus King, November 26, 1793, in *The Historical Magazine: And Notes and Queries Concerning the Antiquities, History and Biography of America*, Vol. 10 (Henry B. Dawson, 1866), pp. 333–335; see *The Works of Thomas Jefferson*, ed. Paul Leicester Ford (G. P. Putnam's Sons, 1904), Vol. 1, Anas, July 10, 1793.

57. Enclosure: Thomas Jefferson's Notes on a Conversation with Edmond Genet, July 10, 1793, PGW, Presidential Series, Vol. 13, pp. 202–207; Thomas Jefferson to James Madison, July 7, 1793, JMP, Vol. 15, p. 43.

58. Memorandum from Alexander Hamilton and Henry Knox, July 8, 1793, PGW, Presidential Series, Vol. 13, pp. 185–191.

59. Cabinet Opinion on the *Little Sarah* (*Petite Democrate*), July 8, 1793, PGW, Presidential Series, Vol. 13, 180–185.

60. [Thomas Jefferson], Dissenting Opinion on the *Little Sarah,* July 8, 1793, PTJ, Vol. 26, pp. 449–452.

61. Enclosure: Thomas Jefferson's Notes on a Conversation with Edmond Genet, July 10, 1793, PGW, Presidential Series, Vol. 13, pp. 202–207.

8: "Is the Minister of the French Republic to set the Acts of this Government at defiance—*with impunity?*"

62. The Citizen Genet, Minister Plenipotentiary of the French Republic, to Mr. Jefferson, Secretary of State, July 9, 1793, ASP, Foreign Relations, Vol. 1, p. 163.

63. This is the second letter on July 9, 1793, regarding the British privateer, the *Jane*. See The Citizen Genet, Minister Plenipotentiary of the French republic, to Mr. Jefferson, Secretary of State of the United States, July 9, 1793, ASP, Foreign Relations, Vol. 1, p. 163.

64. George Washington to Thomas Jefferson, July 11, 1793, PGW, Presidential Series, Vol. 13, pp. 211–212; [Thomas Jefferson], Memorandum of a Conversation with Edmond Charles Genet, July 10, 1793, PTJ, Vol. 26, pp. 463–467. For the letters and documents Jefferson forwarded to Washington, see Memorandum from Thomas Jefferson, July 11, 1793, PGW, Presidential Series, Vol. 13, pp. 200–202.

65. Cabinet Meeting, Opinion on Vessels Arming and Arriving in United States Ports, July 12, 1793, PAH, Vol. 15, pp. 87–88; Thomas Jefferson to Edmond Genet and George Hammond, July 12, 1793, PTJ, Vol. 26, pp. 487–488; I. Alexander Hamilton's Questions for the Supreme Court, c. July 18, 1793, PTJ, Vol. 26, pp. 527–530.

66. Thomas Jefferson to James Madison, July 14, 1793, JMP, Vol. 15, p. 44; James Madison to Thomas Jefferson, July 18, 1793, JMP, Vol. 15, pp. 44–45.

67. Thomas Jefferson to Edmond Charles Genet, c. July 16, 1793 [not sent], PTJ, Vol 26, pp. 510–514.

68. [Thomas Jefferson], Notes of Cabinet Meeting on Edmond Charles Genet, July 23, 1793, PTJ, Vol. 26, pp. 553–556.

69. "Pacificus," June 29, July 3, 6, 10, 13–17, 27, 1793, PAH, Vol. 15, pp. 33–43, 55–63, 65–69, 82–86, 90–95, 100–106, 130–135. "No Jacobin," No. 1, July 31, 1793, PAH, Vol. 15, pp. 145–151.

70. [Thomas Jefferson], Notes of Cabinet Meeting on Edmond Charles Genet, July 23, 1793, PTJ, Vol. 26, pp. 553–556; George Washington to Henry Lee, July 21, 1793, PGW, Presidential Series, Vol. 13, pp. 260–262.

9: "He will sink the republican interest if they do not abandon him."

71. Memorial From Edmond Charles Genet, May 27, 1793, PTJ, Vol. 26, pp. 130–131; Edmund Randolph's Opinion on the Case of Gideon Henfield, May 30, 1793, ASP, Foreign Relations, Vol. 1, p. 152; Citizen Genet to Mr. Jefferson, June 1, 1793, ASP, Foreign Relations, Vol. 1, p. 151; Mr. Jefferson to Mr. Genet, June 1, 1793, ASP, Foreign Relations, Vol. 1, p. 151. For the record of the indictment and trial, see *State Trials of the United States during the Administrations of Washington and Adams, With References, Historical and Professional, and*

Preliminary Notes on the Politics of the Times, ed. Francis Wharton (Carey and Hart, 1849), pp. 49–89.

72. Notes of Cabinet Meeting on Neutrality, July 29, 1793, PTJ, Vol. 26, pp. 579–580; Cabinet Opinion on the Rules of Neutrality, August 3, 1793, PGW, Presidential Series, Vol. 13, pp. 325–327; Cabinet Meeting: Opinion Respecting Certain French Vessels and Their Prizes, August 5, 1793, PAH, Vol. 15, pp. 181–184.

73. Cabinet Meeting: Notes Concerning the Conduct of the French Minister, August 2, 1793, PAH, Vol. 15, pp. 159–162; Ford, *The Works of Thomas Jefferson,* Vol. 1, Anas, Aug. 1, 2, 3, 6.

74. Ford, *The Works of Thomas Jefferson,* Vol. 1, Anas, Aug. 1, 2, 1793, pp. 305–308.

75. Charles Francis Adams to John Quincy Adams, July 29, 1793, AP, Adams Family Correspondence, Vol. 9, pp. 440–442; Thomas Jefferson to James Madison, August 3, 1793, PJM, Vol. 15, pp. 50–51.

76. Thomas Jefferson, Notes of a Conversation with George Washington, August 6, 1793, PTJ, Vol. 26, pp. 627–630.

10: "We stand united and firm."

77. Cabinet Opinion on the Recall of Edmond Genet, August 23, PGW, Presidential Series, Vol. 13, pp. 530–531; Cabinet Meetings, Proposals Concerning the Conduct of the French Minister, August 1–23, 1793, PAH, Vol. 15, pp. 157–158.

78. Genet wrote his own call to arms for the Frenchmen in Spanish-held territory. See Marco Sioli, "Citizen Genet and Political Struggle in the Early Republic," in "Crise et Crises," special issue, *Revue Française D'Études Americaines,* No. 64 (May 1995), pp. 259–267; on spies, see Pis-Gignouse to Spanish Ambassador, *Correspondence of Clark and Genet, Selections from the Draper Collection in the Possession of the State Historical Society of Wisconsin, to Elucidate the Proposed French Expedition under George Rogers Clark Against Louisiana in the Years, 1793–94* (Government Printing Office, 1897), p. 1002.

79. George Rogers Clark to French Minister, February 5, 1793, *Correspondence of Clark and Genet,* pp. 967–971.

80. For Jefferson's minutes of the conversation, see *Correspondence of Clark and Genet,* pp. 984–985; Elkins and McKitrick, *The Age of Federalism,* pp. 349–350.

81. Robert Troup to Alexander Hamilton, August 8, 1793, PAH, Vol. 15, pp. 208–209; *Gazette of the United States,* August 14, 1793; *Daily Advertiser* (New York), August 9, 1793.

82. Thomas Jefferson to James Monroe, June 28, 1793, PTJ, Vol. 26, pp. 392–393; Thomas Jefferson to James Madison, August 11, 1793, JMP, Vol. 15, pp. 56–59.

83. For Genet's public denial of the threat, addressed to Governor William Moultrie, see *The New-York Journal & Patriotic Advertiser,* October 23, 1793; Thomas Jefferson to James Madison, September 1, 1793, PTJ, Vol. 27, pp. 6–8; Alexander Hamilton to Rufus King, August 13, 1793, PAH, Vol. 15, pp. 239–242; [Thomas Jefferson], Memorandum of a Conversation with Edmond Charles Genet, July 10, 1793, PTJ, Vol. 26, pp. 522–523.

84. Edmond Charles Genet to George Washington, August 13, 1793, PGW, Presidential Series, Vol. 13, pp. 436–438.

85. Thomas Jefferson to Edmond Charles Genet, August 16, 1793, PTJ, Vol. 26, p. 684.

86. William Loughton Smith to Alexander Hamilton, August 22, 1793, PAH, Vol. 15, pp. 262–264; Robert Gamble to Thomas Jefferson, August 23, 1793, PTJ, Vol. 26, pp. 746–747; Resolution on Franco-American Relations, c. August 27, 1793, PJM, Vol. 15, pp. 76–80.

11: "He is abandoned even by his votaries."

87. Viar and Jaudenes to Carondelet, *Correspondence of Clark and Genet,* p. 999; Thomas Jefferson to Josef Ignacio De Viar and Josef De Jaudenes, August 29, 1793, PTJ, Vol. 26, p. 786; d'Hauterive journal quoted in Bowman, *The Struggle for Neutrality,* p. 86.

88. Quoted in Richard Bienvenu, *The Ninth of Thermidor* (Oxford University Press, 1970), pp. 32–49.

89. Francois Louis Michel Chemin Deforgues to Edmond Charles Genet, July 30, 1793, quoted in Crandall, "Genet's Projected Attack," pp. 87–91.

90. Edmond Charles Genet to the Minister, October 7, 1793, quoted in Crandall, "Genet's Projected Attack," p. 98.

91. For the change in French policy, see Sheridan, "The Recall of Edmond Charles Genet," pp. 478–482.

92. Thomas Jefferson to Christopher Gore, September 2, 1793, PTJ, Vol. 27, pp. 13–14; Thomas Sim Lee to Thomas Jefferson, September 3, 1793, PTJ, Vol. 27, pp. 25–26.

93. Memorial from George Hammond, September 4, 1793, PTJ, Vol. 27, pp. 30–32; Thomas Jefferson to George Hammond, September 5, 1793, PTJ, Vol. 27, pp. 35–38; George Hammond to Thomas Jefferson, September 6, 1793, PTJ, Vol. 27, pp. 43–44; Thomas Jefferson to James Madison, September 8, 1793, JMP, Vol. 15, pp. 103–105.

94. Memorial from George Hammond, September 6, 1793, PTJ, Vol. 27, pp. 44–46.

95. Washington requested that Oliver Wolcott acquire evidence from Webster of Genet's accusations. See George Washington to Henry Knox, September 9, 1793, PGW, Presidential Series, Vol. 14, pp. 52–54; George Clinton to George Washington, September 8, 1793, PGW, Presidential Series, Vol. 14, pp. 47–49 (see editor's note 1 for Genet's reply to Clinton).

12: "The people began to speak out."

96. For examples of the memorials, see Thomas Griffin Peachy to Thomas Jefferson, September 3, 1793, PTJ, Vol. 27, pp. 28–29; Jeremiah Wadsworth to Thomas Jefferson, September 4, 1793, PTJ, Vol. 27, p. 35; Ludwell Lee and Roger West to George Washington, October 21, 1793, PGW, Presidential Series, Vol. 14, pp. 242–243; Address from Fairfax County, Virginia, Citizens, October 21, 1793, PGW, Presidential Series, Vol. 14, pp. 243–244; See also Ammon, *The Genet Mission,* 132–146. For a discussion of the public meetings that produced memorials

and addresses supporting the president, see Harry Ammon, "The Genet Mission and the Development of American Political Parties," *The Journal of American History,* Vol. 52, No. 4 (March 1966), pp. 725–741; see also Christopher J. Young, "Connecting the President and the People: Washington's Neutrality, Genet's Challenge, and Hamilton's Fight for Public Support," *Journal of the Early Republic,* Vol. 31, No. 3 (Fall 2011), pp. 435–466; Henry Lee to George Washington, September 17, 1793, PGW, Presidential Series, Vol. 14, pp. 108–111.

97. Thomas Jefferson to Edmond Charles Genet, September 7, 1793, PTJ, Vol. 27, pp. 52–53.

98. Translation, Edmond Charles Genet to Thomas Jefferson, September 18, 1793, ASP, Foreign Relations, Vol. 1, pp. 172–174.

99. Gouverneur Morris to George Washington, October 18, 1793, PGW, Presidential Series, Vol. 14, pp. 229–231; Gouverneur Morris to George Washington, October 19, 1793, PGW, Presidential Series, Vol. 14, pp. 233–235; Greg H. Williams, *The French Assault on American Shipping, 1793–1813: A History and Comprehensive Record of Merchant Marine Loss* (McFarland, 2009), p. 16.

13: "It is with extreme concern I have to inform you . . ."

100. Alexander Hamilton to Rufus King, August 13, 1793, PAH, Vol. 15, pp. 239–242 (see introductory note by editors, pp. 233–239); John Jay and Rufus King to Alexander Hamilton and Henry Knox, November 26, 1793, PAH, Vol. 15, pp. 411–412; Rufus King to Alexander Hamilton, November 26, 1793, PAH, Vol. 15, pp. 413–414; John Jay to Alexander Hamilton, November 26, 1793, PAH, Vol. 15, pp. 412–413; George Washington to Henry Knox, February 15, 1794, PGW, Presidential Series, Vol. 15, pp. 233–234; Alexander Dallas to Thomas Jefferson, December 4, 1793, PTJ, Vol. 27, p. 481; Thomas Jefferson to Edmond Charles Genet, December 18, 1793, PTJ, Vol. 27, p. 583.

101. AC, 3rd Congress, 1st Session, Senate, December 3, 1793, pp. 10–13.

102. AC, 3rd Congress, 1st Session, House of Representatives, Proceedings, December 5, 1793, pp. 136–137, 157; ASP, Foreign Relations, Vol. 1, pp. 140–188; AC, 3rd Congress, 1st Session, House of Representatives, December 6, 1793, pp. 138–140.

103. William Moultrie to George Washington, December 7, 1793, PGW, Presidential Series, Vol. 14, pp. 482–483; ASP, Foreign Relations, Vol. 1, pp. 309–311.

104. See Genet, *Washington, Jefferson, and "Citizen" Genet,* p. 39.

105. Quoted in Elkins and McKitrick, *Age of Federalism,* p. 372.

14: "I augur more good than evil."

106. Robert Troup to Alexander Hamilton, December 25, 1793, PAH, Vol. 15, pp. 587–588; Phillip Schuyler to Alexander Hamilton, December 15, 1793, PAH, Vol. 15, pp. 457–458; John Trumball to John Adams, January 16, 1794, FOL.

107. John Adams to Abigail Adams, December 20, 1793, FOL; John Quincy Adams, "Columbus," Part 4, *Columbian Centinel,* December 18, 1793; Thomas Boylston Adams to William Cranch, January 4, 1794, FOL; Abigail Adams to John Adams, December 31, 1793, FOL.

108. Alexander White to James Madison, December 28, 1793, JMP, Vol. 15, pp. 163–164.

109. AC, 3rd Congress, 1st Session, House of Representatives, January–April, 1794, pp. 155–159, 174–248, 256–349, 352–410, 413–432, 501, 505–522, 529–530, 561, 566–598, 600–603. For Madison's comment, see AC, 3rd Congress, 1st Session, House of Representatives, January 3, 1794, p. 157.

Epilogue

110. Ammon, *The Genet Mission*, pp. 171–179; for the comments on Genet's death, see Genet, *Washington, Jefferson, and "Citizen" Genet*, p. 52.

Part III: The XYZ Affair

1: "The conduct of the French Government is so much beyond calculation."

1. For the self-evaluation, see John Adams to Timothy Pickering, August 6, 1822, FOL.

2. "The Warning, No. I" [January 27, 1797], PAH, Vol. 20, pp. 490–495.

3. Wolcott's comments quoted in Bowman, *The Struggle for Neutrality*, p. 270; "The Answer" [December 8, 1796], PAH, Vol. 20, pp. 421–434. For a discussion of Adet's efforts to influence the election, see Michael F. Conlin, "The American Mission of Citizen Pierre-Auguste Adet: Revolutionary Chemistry and Diplomacy in the Early Republic," *Pennsylvania Magazine of History and Biography*, Vol. 124, No. 4 (October 2000), pp. 489–520. See also Bowman, *The Struggle for Neutrality*, pp. 262–278. For the *Aurora*'s publication of this letter and others by Adet, see James Tagg, *Benjamin Franklin Bache and the Philadelphia "Aurora"* (University of Pennsylvania Press, 1991), pp. 293–294; For the exchange of letters on the Jay Treaty between Adet and Secretary of State Pickering, see ASP, Foreign Relations, pp. 559–588.

4. For Monroe's letter criticizing the Jay Treaty, see [James Monroe], Enclosure: Sketch of the State of Affairs in France, June 23, 1795, PTJ, Vol. 28, pp. 392–398.

5. For Monroe's farewell address and the reply by Paul Barras, see ASP, Foreign Relations, Vol. 1, p. 747.

6. James Monroe, *A view of the conduct of the executive, in the foreign affairs of the United States, connected with the mission to the French Republic, during the years 1794, 5 & 6* (Benjamin Bache, 1797). For George Washington's detailed annotation of Monroe's publication, see Comments on Monroe's A View of the Conduct of the Executive of the United States, March 1798, PGW, Retirement Series, Vol. 2, pp. 169–217; for John Adams's view of Monroe's personal unpopularity in France, see John Adams to Elbridge Gerry, May 3, 1797, FOL.

7. For the documents relating to Pinckney's experiences in Paris, see AC, 5th Congress, 1797–1799, Appendix, pp. 3059–3095. See also James McHenry to George Washington, March 24, 1797, PGW, Retirement Series, Vol. 1, pp. 47–48; George Washington to James McHenry, April 3, 1797, PGW, Retirement Series,

Vol. 1, pp. 71–72; [Timothy Pickering], Enclosure: A Statement of Facts Relative to General Pinckney's Mission to France [March 30, 1797], PAH, Vol. 20, pp. 560–567.

8. Tagg, *Benjamin Franklin Bache*, p. 317; John Adams to Henry Knox, March 30, 1797, FOL; George Washington to James McHenry April 3, 1797, PGW, Retirement Series, Vol. 1, pp. 71–72; see also George Washington to Timothy Pickering, April 10, 1797, PGW, Retirement Series, Vol. 1, pp. 93–94.

9. Tagg, *Benjamin Franklin Bache*, p. 316.

10. John Adams to Timothy Pickering, March 14, 1797, FOL; Notes on Pinckney Case, March 19, 1797, FOL.

11. John Adams to William Heath, April 19, 1797, FOL; John Adams to John Quincy Adams, March 31, 1797, FOL.

2: "I have it much at heart to Settle all disputes with France."

12. For the Decree of the Executive Directory concerning the navigation of neutral vessels, loaded with merchandise belonging to the enemies of the republic, and the judgments on the trials relative to the validity of maritime prizes, 12th Ventose, 5th year, see AC, 5th Congress, Appendix, pp. 3076–3078; Rufus King to Timothy Pickering, March 12, 1797, AC, 5th Congress, Appendix, p. 3082. Pickering forwarded this dispatch from John Quincy Adams to Alexander Hamilton on April 29, 1797, PAH, Vol. 21, pp. 68–71. Pastoret quoted in Matthew Q. Dawson, *Partisanship and the Birth of America's Second Party, 1796–1800: Stop the Wheels of Government* (Greenwood Press, 2000), pp. 51–52.

13. Elbridge Gerry to John Adams, April 25, 1797, FOL; John Adams to Elbridge Gerry, May 3, 1797, FOL.

14. AC, 5th Congress, 1st Session, House of Representatives, May 16, 1797, pp. 54–59.

15. AC, 5th Congress, 1st Session, House of Representatives, May 22–June 3, 1797, pp. 67–237.

16. George Washington to Oliver Wolcott, May 29, 1797, PGW, Retirement Series, Vol. 1, pp. 161–162; John Adams to Elbridge Gerry, May 30, 1797, FOL.

17. AC, 5th Congress, 1st Session, House of Representatives, June 5–June 24, 1797, pp. 239–386.

18. Questions to be Proposed Concerning Negotiators to be Sent to France, May 27–28, 1797, FOL; Timothy Pickering to the Senate, February 27, 1797, ASP, Foreign Relations, Vol. 1, pp. 748–749. For a biography of Timothy Pickering, see Gerard H. Clarfield, *Timothy Pickering and the American Republic* (University of Pittsburgh Press, 1980).

19. Alexander Hamilton to Oliver Wolcott Jr., March 30, 1797, PAH, Vol. 20, pp. 567–568; Alexander Hamilton to Oliver Wolcott Jr., April 5, 1797, PAH, Vol. 21, pp. 22–23; Alexander Hamilton to Oliver Wolcott Jr., June 6, 1797, PAH, Vol. 21, pp. 98–101.

20. See Alexander Hamilton to Timothy Pickering, March 22, 1797, PAH, Vol. 20, pp. 545–547; Alexander Hamilton to Timothy Pickering, May 11, 1797, PAH, Vol. 21, pp. 81–84; see also Rufus King to Alexander Hamilton, April 2, 1797, PAH, Vol. 21, pp. 8–12.

21. John Adams to Elbridge Gerry, April 6, 1797, FOL.

22. For a biography of John Marshall, see Jean Edward Smith, *John Marshall: Definer of a Nation* (Henry Holt, 1996).

23. D'Hauterive's comments on Marshall and Pinckney quoted in Jean Edward Smith, *John Marshall,* p. 187.

24. On Adams's belief in Gerry's impartiality, see John Adams to Thomas Welsh, March 10, 1797, FOL; See Elkins and McKitrick, *The Age of Federalism,* pp. 556, 558; for a biography of Gerry, see George A. Billias, *Elbridge Gerry: Founding Father and Republican Statesman* (McGraw-Hill, 1976); for the Abigail Adams quote, see Richard Brookhiser, *What Would the Founders Do? Our Questions, Their Answers* (Basic Books, 2007), p. 148.

25. Quoted in Billias, *Elbridge Gerry,* p. 262, n. 70; Adams had nominated Dana, along with Pinckney and Marshall, in a letter to the Senate, May 31, 1797, FOL; see John Adams to Elbridge Gerry, June 20, 1797, FOL.

26. John Adams to Elbridge Gerry, July 17, 1797, FOL.

27. Elbridge Gerry to John Adams, July 14, 1797, FOL.

3: "Talleyrand . . . could not be for war with this country."

28. For the instructions to the commissioners, see AC, 5th Congress, Appendix, pp. 3324–3336.

29. Tagg, *Benjamin Franklin Bache,* p. 323.

30. For a discussion of French politics in 1797, see William Stinchcombe, "The Diplomacy of the WXYZ Affair," *The William and Mary Quarterly,* Vol. 34, No. 4 (October 1977), pp. 590–617; see also William Stinchcombe, "Talleyrand and the American Negotiations of 1797–1798," *The Journal of American History,* Vol. 62, No. 3 (December 1975), pp. 575–590.

31. Elkins and McKitrick, *The Age of Federalism,* p. 568.

32. For a study of Talleyrand's character, see Crane Brinton, *The Lives of Talleyrand* (W. W. Norton, 1963); see also Jack F. Bernard, *Talleyrand: A Biography* (Putnam, 1793); Jean Edward Smith, *John Marshall,* pp. 192–196.

33. Jean Edward Smith, *John Marshall,* p. 198; Billias, *Elbridge Gerry,* p. 267.

34. Elbridge Gerry to Charles Cotesworth Pinckney, September 20, 1797, in *Elbridge Gerry's Letterbook: Paris 1797–1798,* ed. Russell W. Knight (Essex Institute, 1966), p. 7; Billias, *Elbridge Gerry,* p. 263.

35. Jean Edward Smith, *John Marshall,* p. 200.

36. There are numerous accounts of the meetings between the Americans and the French agents sent by Talleyrand. The account that follows below relies on John Marshall's record of the meetings, found in PJM, Vol. 3; and in abbreviated form in Smith, *John Marshall;* but see also Elkins and McKitrick, *The Age of Federalism,* pp. 571–579; and Stinchcombe, "The Diplomacy of the WXYZ Affair."

37. John Adams to Timothy Pickering, October 31, 1797, FOL.

38. Jean Edward Smith, *John Marshall,* p. 205.

4: "We experience a haughtiness . . . unexampled in the history and practice of nations."

39. PJM, Vol. 3, p. 251; Knight, *Elbridge Gerry's Letterbook,* pp. 18–19; PJM, Vol. 3, p. 254.

40. Jean Edward Smith, *John Marshall,* p. 209–210; PJM, Vol. 3, p. 171.

41. PJM, Vol. 3, p. 173.

42. Ibid., pp. 176–177.

43. Ibid., pp. 182–183.

44. Jean Edward Smith, *John Marshall,* p. 213.

45. Jean Edward Smith, *John Marshall,* p. 221.

46. Elbridge Gerry to Mrs. Gerry, November 28, 1797, in Knight, *Elbridge Gerry's Letterbook,* p. 21; John Marshall to Rufus King, quoted in Jean Edward Smith, *John Marshall,* p. 220; Rufus King to Messrs. Pinckney, Marshall, and Gerry, December 23, 1797, in *The Life and Correspondence of Rufus King: Comprising his letters, private and official, his public documents and speeches,* ed. Charles R. King, MD, Vol. 2 (G. P. Putnam's Sons, 1895), pp. 262–263.

5: "Shall an immediate declaration of war be recommended?"

47. John Adams to the US Congress, November 22, 1797, AC, 5th Congress, 2nd Session, House of Representatives, November 23, 1797, pp. 630–634, November 27, 1797, pp. 645–648.

48. George Washington to Oliver Wolcott Jr., January 22, 1798, PGW, Retirement Series, Vol. 2, pp. 39–40; John Adams to James McHenry, Timothy Pickering, Oliver Wolcott Jr., and Charles Lee, January 24, 1798, as an enclosure in PAH, Vol. 21, pp. 339–341.

49. Jean Edward Smith, *John Marshall,* p. 222.

50. PJM, Vol. 3, p. 205.

51. Ibid., p. 223.

52. Ibid., p. 232.

53. See Elbridge Gerry to Mrs. Gerry, March 26, 1798, in Knight, *Elbridge Gerry's Letterbook,* pp. 33–34.

54. PJM, Vol. 3, pp. 236–237.

55. See Talleyrand [to John Marshall], April 13, 1798, PJM, Vol. 3, p. 461; John Marshall to Talleyrand, April 13, 1798, PJM, Vol. 3, p. 462; John Marshall to Charles Cotesworth Pinckney, April 21, 1798, PJM, Vol. 3, p. 463; John Marshall to Timothy Pickering, June 18, 1798, PJM, Vol. 3, p. 467.

6: "He . . . was the dupe of *Diplomatic Skill.*"

56. For Elbridge Gerry's rebuttal to Marshall's account in his dispatches, see his letters to President John Adams in Knight, *Elbridge Gerry's Letterbook,* pp. 44–74; Charles Cotesworth Pinckney to Rufus King, April 4, 1798, in *Life and Correspondence of Rufus King,* Vol. 2, pp. 303–304; John Quincy Adams to John Adams, September 25, 1798, FOL; George Washington to Thomas Pinckney, February 10, 1799, PGW, Retirement Series, Vol. 3, pp. 365–366.

7: "Is this the language of an American who loves his country?"

57. AC, 5th Congress, 2nd Session, House of Representatives, March 19, 1798, pp. 1271–1272; Thomas Jefferson to James Madison, March 21, 1798, JMP, Vol. 17, pp. 99–100.

58. Tagg, *Benjamin Franklin Bache,* pp. 336–337.

59. For the House debates, see AC, 5th Congress, 2nd Session, March 26–April 2, 1798, pp. 1314–1371.

60. AC, 5th Congress, 2nd Session, House of Representatives, April 2, 1798, pp. 1370–1371.

61. AC, 5th Congress, 2nd Session, House of Representatives, April 3, 1798, pp. 1374–1375, and April 6, 1798, pp. 1377–1380.

62. "The Warning, No. IV," PAH, Vol. 20, pp. 524–527; for Allen's comments, see AC, 5th Congress, 2nd Session, House of Representatives, April 20, 1798, pp. 1483–1485; for the newspaper attacks on Republicans that followed the publication of the transcripts, see James Morton Smith, "Background for Repression: America's Half-War with France and the Internal Security Legislation of 1798," *Huntington Library Quarterly,* Vol. 18, No. 1 (November 1954), pp. 50–51.

63. AC, 5th Congress, 2nd Session, House of Representatives, April 26, 1798, p. 1554.

64. Tagg, *Benjamin Franklin Bache,* pp. 339–342.

65. George Washington to Timothy Pickering, April 16, 1798, PGW, Retirement Series, Vol. 2, pp. 242–243; see also Timothy Pickering to Alexander Hamilton, April 9, 1798, PAH, Vol. 21, pp. 408–410.

66. For the act suspending commercial intercourse with France, see *The Avalon Project;* AC, 5th Congress, 2nd Session, Senate, June 25, 1798, p. 588; for the abrogation of the treaties of 1778, see AC, 5th Congress, 2nd Session, House of Representatives, June 25, 1798, pp. 2035–2037, June 30, 1798, p. 2063, July 6, 1798, pp. 2116–2128.

67. AC, 5th Congress, 2nd Session, Senate, June 21, 1798, pp. 585–586; for the popularity of John Adams, see James Morton Smith, "Background for Repression," pp. 37–58.

8: "Millions for defense but not one cent for tribute."

68. For examples of these memorials, see Ebenezer Tucker to John Adams [Address of the Citizens of the Township of Little Eggharbour], April 23, 1798, FOL; Jacob Rahm to John Adams [The Address of the Inhabitants of Shippensburg and Its Vicinity], April 28, 1798, FOL; John Edwards to John Adams [The Address & Memorial of the Citizens of Charleston], May 1798, FOL; Young Men of Philadelphia to John Adams, May 7, 1798, FOL; Joseph G. Wright to John Adams [The Address of the Inhabitants of the Town of Wilmington], May 1798, FOL; see also James Morton Smith, "Background for Repression," pp. 39, 50. For an analysis of the themes of these memorials, see Thomas M. Ray, "'Not One Cent for Tribute': The Public Addresses and American Popular Reaction to the

XYZ Affair, 1798–1799," *Journal of the Early Republic,* Vol. 3, No. 4 (Winter 1983), pp. 389–412.

69. John Adams to Maxwell Armstrong, August 13, 1798, FOL; John Adams to Robert Wharton, April 23, 1798, FOL; James Madison to Thomas Jefferson, June 10, 1798, JMP, Vol. 17, pp. 150–151; John Lathrop Jr., *An Oration pronounced on the 4th Day of July 1798 at the Request of the Inhabitants of Dedham and its Vicinity, in Commemoration of the Anniversary of American Independence* (Minerva Press, 1798); Cabot comment quoted in Stephen G. Kurtz, *The Presidency of John Adams: The Collapse of Federalism, 1795–1800* (University of Pennsylvania Press, 1957), p. 301.

70. John W. Kuehl, "Southern Reaction to the XYZ Affair: An Incident in the Emergence of American Nationalism," *The Register of the Kentucky Historical Society,* Vol. 70, No. 1 (January 1972), pp. 21–49, quote on p. 23.

71. George Washington to John Adams, July 4, 1798, FOL.

72. AC, 5th Congress, 2nd Session, House of Representatives, April 24, 1798, pp. 1525–1526, May 18, 1798, pp. 1771–1772; see also Elkins and McKitrick, *The Age of Federalism,* p. 598.

73. For an excellent discussion of the maneuvers to make Hamilton inspector general, see the editor's "Introductory Note: From George Washington" [July 14 1798], PAH, Vol. 22, pp. 4–17.

74. John Adams to Harrison Gray Otis, May 9, 1823, FOL.

75. Fisher Ames to Timothy Pickering, quoted in Elkins and McKitrick, *The Age of Federalism,* p. 597.

9: "There is reason to believe that the XYZ delusion is wearing off."

76. *Memoir of Dr. George Logan of Stenton,* ed. Deborah Norris Logan (Historical Society of Pennsylvania, 1899), pp. 56, 67.

77. "To the Citizens of the United States," and the introductory note to it by the editor of the *Aurora,* in Logan, *Memoir,* pp. 55–56, 89–93; William Vans Murray to Timothy Pickering, August 13, 1798, and William Vans Murray to John Quincy Adams, August 24, 1798, in Ford, *Letters of William Vans Murray,* pp. 454–455. For An Act for the Punishment of Certain Crimes therein Specified, see 18 U.S. Code 953.

78. For the Fries Rebellion, see Proclamation on Insurrection in Pennsylvania, March 12, 1799, FOL; for a full account of Fries's Rebellion, see Paul Douglas Newman, *Fries's Rebellion: The Enduring Struggle for the American Revolution* (University of Pennsylvania Press, 2005); see also W. W. H. Davis, *The Fries Rebellion, 1798–99; an armed resistance to the House tax law, passed by Congress, July 9, 1798, in Bucks and Northampton Counties, Pennsylvania* (Kessinger, 2010); see also Harlow Giles Ungar, *The French War Against America: How a Trusted Ally Betrayed Washington and the Founding Fathers* (John Wiley & Sons, 2005), p. 208.

79. See Thomas Jefferson to Edmund Pendleton, January 29, 1799, PTJ, Vol. 30, pp. 661–663. For a discussion of the legislation to suppress criticism of the administration, see Part 4 of this volume.

80. John Adams to James McHenry, October 22, 1798, FOL; Enclosure on Relations Between United States and France, September 28, 1798, PTJ, Vol. 31, pp. 46–47; John Quincy Adams to John Adams, September 25, 1798, FOL; for Jefferson's view on the Talleyrand letter, see Thomas Jefferson to James Madison, February 19, 1799, PTJ, Vol. 31, pp. 44–46. For a full discussion of Talleyrand's new diplomacy efforts, see Bowman, *The Struggle for Neutrality*, pp. 334–359. See also Elkins and McKitrick, *The Age of Federalism*, pp. 643–690.

81. AC, 5th Congress, 3rd Session, House of Representatives, December 8, 1798, pp. 2420–2422. For the message of February 18, 1799, and a translation of the Talleyrand letter to Pichon, see *The Avalon Project*.

82. Timothy Pickering to Alexander Hamilton, February 25, 1799, PAH, Vol. 22, pp. 500–503; Thomas Jefferson to James Madison, February 19, 1799, PTJ, Vol. 31, pp. 44–46.

83. For a discussion of the Convention of 1800 negotiations, see Bowman, *The Struggle for Neutrality*, pp. 386–411. For the nomination of Murray, Ellsworth, and Davie as commissioners or "envoys extraordinary" to France, see John Adams to United States Senate, February 25, 1799, FOL.

Part IV: The Alien and Sedition Acts

1. *The Debates in the Several State Conventions on the Adoption of the Federal Constitution*, ed. Jonathan Elliot (Philadelphia, 1891), Vol. 4, May 14, 1788, p. 330.

1: "Many Jacobins and vagabonds."

2. See Michael Durey, "Thomas Paine's Apostles: Radical Emigrés and the Triumph of Jeffersonian Republicanism," *The William and Mary Quarterly*, 3rd series, Vol. 44, No. 4 (October 1987), pp. 661–688.

3. For the first naturalization law, see AC, 1st Congress, 2nd Session, March 26, 1790, p. 103; for the debate on the second naturalization bill, see AC, 3rd Congress, 2nd Session, December 22, 1794–January 8, 1795, pp. 1004–1009, 1021–1023, 1026–1030, 1033–1058, 1061, 1064–1066.

4. For the debates in the House, see AC, 5th Congress, 2nd Session, May 3–May 22, 1798, pp. 1570–1582; 1725; 1776–1784.

5. An Act Supplementary to and to amend the act entitled An Act to establish a uniform rule of naturalization, and to repeal the act heretofore passed on that subject. *Statutes at Large*, 5th Congress, Library of Congress American Memory, p. 566.

6. AC, 5th Congress, 2nd Session, Senate, April 25, 1798–June 8, 1798, pp. 548–549, 554–559; 564–571, 573, 575.

7. For this debate in the House see AC, 5th Congress, 2nd Session, House of Representatives, June 19–21, 1798, pp. 1973–2029.

8. Constitution, article 1, section 9, clause 1. For Gallatin's argument, see AC, 5th Congress, 2nd Session, House of Representatives, June 19, 1798, pp. 1973–1983.

9. See, for example, Harrison Gray Otis's argument on June 19, 1798, AC, 5th Congress, 2nd Session, House of Representatives, pp. 1986–1989.

10. AC, 5th Congress, 2nd Session, June 16, 1798, pp. 1967–1968.

11. For Otis's comments, see AC, 5th Congress, 2nd Session, June 21, 1798, pp. 1986–1989.

12. For Livingston's comments, see AC, 5th Congress, 2nd Session, June 21, 1798, pp. 2005–2015; for Kittera's comment, see AC, 5th Congress, 2nd Session, June 21, 1798, p. 2016.

13. *Statutes at Large*, Vol. 1, Library of Congress, American Memory, pp. 570–572.

14. AC, 5th Congress, 2nd Session, Senate, July 3, p. 598; House of Representatives, July 3, 1798, p. 2088.

15. An Act Respecting Alien Enemies, *The Avalon Project*.

16. President Woodrow Wilson used the Alien Enemies Act during World War I to require all enemy aliens to register and be detained if there was reasonable cause to believe they were aiding and abetting the enemy. President Franklin D. Roosevelt applied the act against Japanese, Italian, and German nationals during World War II. For a discussion of the use of this act in the twentieth century, see Robert H. Wagstaff, *Terror Detentions and the Rule of Law: US and UK Perspectives* (Oxford University Press, 2013), Chapter 2, pp. 39–60.

2: "Deliver us from . . . the public floods of falsehood and hatred."

17. AC, 5th Congress, 2nd Session, Senate, June 23, 1798, p. 588.

18. Quoted in James Morton Smith, "Background for Repression," p. 44; Katherine Ann Brown and Todd Gitlin, "Partisans, Watchdogs, and Entertainers: The Press for Democracy and Its Limits," in *The Oxford Handbook of American Public Opinion and the Media,* ed. Robert Y. Shapiro and Lawrence R. Jacobs (Oxford University Press, 2013), p. 76; Jon R. Bond and Kevin B. Smith, *Analyzing American Democracy: Politics and Political Science* (Routledge, 2013), p. 287.

19. *New Letters of Abigail Adams, 1788–1804,* ed. Stewart Mitchell (Houghton Mifflin, 1947), pp. 96–97.

20. Walter Berns, "Freedom of the Press and the Alien and Sedition Laws: A Reappraisal," *Supreme Court Review,* Vol. 109 (1970), 112.

21. For the full documentation on William Cobbett's legal troubles, see Richard Ingrams, *The Life and Adventures of William Cobbett* (Harper Perennial, 2006).

22. AC, 5th Congress, 2nd Session, House of Representatives, July 5, 1798, p. 2098. For Allen's full comments that day, see pp. 2093–2101.

23. George Washington to Oliver Wolcott Jr., May 29, 1797, PGW, Retirement Series, Vol. 1, p. 162; George Washington to Timothy Pickering, February 6, 1798, PGW, Retirement Series, Vol. 2, pp. 76–77; "Virginiensis" [Charles Lee], *Defense of the Alien and Sedition Act* (Philadelphia, 1798), quoted in Marc Lendler, "'Equally Proper at All Times and at All Times Necessary': Civility, Bad Tendency, and the Sedition Act," *Journal of the Early Republic,* Vol. 24, No. 3 (Autumn 2004), p. 428.

24. AC, 5th Congress, 2nd Session, Senate, June 23–27, 1798, pp. 588–592; July 2–4, 1798, pp. 596–599.

25. For the complete House of Representatives debate on sedition, see AC, 5th Congress, 2nd Session, July 5–6, 1798, p. 2093; July 9–10, pp. 2133–2171.

26. AC, 5th Congress, 2nd Session, House of Representatives, July 5, 1798, pp. 2093–2101.

27. Ibid., pp. 2103–2104.

28. AC, 5th Congress, 2nd Session, House of Representatives, July 10, 1798, pp. 2151–2152.

29. Ibid., p. 2152.

30. AC, 5th Congress, 2nd Session, House of Representatives, July 5, 1798, p. 2112.

31. AC, 5th Congress, 2nd Session, House of Representatives, July 10, 1798, p. 2158.

32. Ibid., p. 2171.

33. For the vote, see AC, 5th Congress, 2nd Session, House of Representatives, July 10, 1798, pp. 2171–2172; An Act in Addition to the Act, Entitled An Act for the Punishment of Certain Crimes Against the United States, *The Avalon Project.*

3: "Much good may . . . result from the investigation of Political heresies."

34. Thomas Jefferson to James Madison, June 7, 1798, JMP, Vol. 30, pp.143–145; George Washington to Alexander Addison, June 3, 1798, PGW, Retirement Series, Vol. 2, pp. 310–311.

35. Boston *Gazette* of July 9, 1798, quoted in Vanessa B. Beasley, *Who Belongs in America? Presidents, Rhetoric, and Immigration* (Texas A&M Press, 2006), 50; Craig R. Smith, "The Alien and Sedition Crisis," in *Silencing the Opposition: How the US Government Suppressed Freedom of Expression During Major Crises* (State University of New York Press, 2011), p. 15.

36. For the Bache case, see Bruce A. Ragsdale, "The Sedition Act Trials," *Federal Judicial Center* (Federal Judicial History Office, 2005), p. 20; and Gordon T. Belt, "The Sedition Act of 1798: A Brief History of Arrests, Indictments, Mistreatments, and Abuse," online publication of *The First Amendment Center, Newseum Institute*, Washington, DC, p. 2.

37. See Belt, "The Sedition Act," pp. 11–12; Ragsdale, "The Sedition Act Trials," p. 21.

38. Belt, "The Sedition Act," pp. 1–2.

39. Terri Diane Halperin, *The Alien and Sedition Acts of 1798: Testing the Constitution* (Johns Hopkins University Press, 2016), pp. 92–94. For this letter, see George Gibbs, *Memoirs of the Administrations of Washington and John Adams, Edited from the Papers of Oliver Wolcott*, Vol. 1 (William Van Norden, Printer, 1845), pp. 424–425. In 1800, Adams wrote an apology to Thomas Pinckney, admitting that he had come to a conclusion in his letter to Coxe that was wholly unfounded. See Adams's explanation of the letter, John Adams to Thomas Pinckney, October 27, 1800, in Gibbs, *Memoirs of the Administrations of Washington and John Adams*, 425–426.

40. George Washington to Charles Cotesworth Pinckney, August 10, 1799, PGW, Retirement Series, Vol. 3, pp. 233–235; George Washington to Timothy Pickering, August 4, 1799, PGW, Retirement Series, Vol. 3, pp. 221–223.

41. Allan C. Clark, "William Duane," *Records of the Columbia Historical Society, Washington DC,* Vol. 9 (The Society, 1906), pp. 14–62, quote on p. 14.

42. Alice J. Retzer, "The Virginia Resolutions of 1798: A Study of the Contemporary Debate" (Honors Thesis, University of Richmond, 1969), p. 9.

43. Ibid., pp. 30–31.

44. Benjamin Michael Gies, "Kentucky's First Statesman: George Nicholas and the Founding of the Commonwealth" (Master's Thesis, University of Louisville, 2016), p. 100; *Kentucky Gazette* (Lexington), August 1, 1798; see also Nicholas's accusation that Representative Robert Harper had disgraced himself by voting for the Sedition Act, in *First American West: Correspondence between George Nicholas Esq. of Kentucky and the Hon. Robert G. Harper, member of congress from the district of 96, state of South Carolina,* Library of Congress, American Memory; Clark County resolutions quoted in Ethelbert Dudley Warfield, *The Kentucky Resolutions of 1798: An Historical Study* (G. P. Putnam's Sons, 1887), p. 42.

45. Warfield, *The Kentucky Resolutions,* pp. 17, 41–42; Douglass Bradburn, *The Citizenship Revolution: Politics and the Creation of the Union 1774–1804* (University of Virginia Press, 2009), 171; *Kentucky Gazette* (Lexington), November 10, 1798, quoted in Gies, "Kentucky's First Statesman," p. 100.

46. Gies, "Kentucky's First Statesman," pp. 100–101; *Kentucky Gazette* (Lexington), November 10, 1798; Bradburn, *The Citizenship Revolution,* p. 169.

47. *Kentucky Gazette* (Lexington), November 10, 1798, quoted in Gies, "Kentucky's First Statesman," 100.

4: "I do not care if they fire thro' his arse!"

48. Belt, "The Sedition Act of 1798," pp. 2–3, quoted in James Morton Smith, *Freedom's Fetters: The Alien and Sedition Laws and American Civil Liberties* (Cornell University Press, 1956), pp. 251–252, 255.

49. See S. Mintz and S. McNeil, "The Alien and Sedition Acts, ID 245," *Digital History,* 2016; Belt, "The Sedition Act of 1798," p. 9; James Morton Smith, *Freedom's Fetters,* 271.

50. For the House discussions of the Lyon-Griswold controversy, see AC, 5th Congress, 2nd Session, House of Representatives, January 30, 1798, pp. 955–957, February 1, 1798, pp. 958–960, February 2, 1798, pp. 961–962, February 5, 1798, pp. 964–965, February 6, 1798, pp. 965–968, February 7, 1798, pp. 969–970, February 8, 1798, pp. 970–980, February 9, 1798, pp. 981–1000, February 12, 1798, pp. 1000–1029, February 15, 1798, pp. 1034–1035, February 16, 1798, pp. 1036–1043, February 20, 1798, pp. 1048–1058, February 23, 1798, pp. 1063–1068.

51. For a brief account of Matthew Lyon's trial, see Aleine Austin, "Matthew Lyon's Trial for Sedition," in *Retracing the Past,* Third Edition, Vol. 1, ed. Gary B. Nash and Ronald Schultz (Harper Collins, 1994), pp. 128–129; see also Aleine Austin, *Matthew Lyon, "New Man" of the Democratic Revolution, 1749–1822*

(Pennsylvania State University Press, 1981); Ragsdale, "The Sedition Act Trials," pp. 53–54, 56; Maeva Marcus, ed., *Documentary History of the Supreme Court of the US, 1789–1800,* Vol. 3 (Columbia University Press, 1990), pp. 292–294.

52. *The Aurora and General Advertiser,* as quoted in *Porcupine's Gazette* (Philadelphia), November 3, 1798; James Morton Smith, *Freedom's Fetters,* p. 246.

53. For biographies of Matthew Lyon, see J. Fairfax McLaughlin, *Matthew Lyon, the Hampden of Congress, a Biography* (1900; reprint by Forgotten Books, 2012); and Aleine Austin, *Matthew Lyon, "New Man" of the Democratic Revolution, 1749–1822* (Pennsylvania State University Press, 1981).

5: "The nullification of all unauthorized acts . . . is the rightful remedy."

54. *Centinel of Freedom* (Newark, NJ), December 18, 1798; See Douglas Bradburn, "A Clamor in the Public Mind: Opposition to the Alien and Sedition Acts," *The William and Mary Quarterly,* 3rd series, Vol. 65, No. 3 (July 2008), pp. 565–600; for a discussion of newspaper and petition opposition to the Alien and Sedition Acts, see also James Morton Smith, "The Grass Roots Origins of the Kentucky Resolutions, *The William and Mary Quarterly,* Vol. 27, No. 2 (April 1970), pp. 221–245.

55. James Morton Smith, *Freedom's Fetters,* p. 236; see also Warfield, *The Kentucky Resolutions.*

56. Draft of the Kentucky Resolutions 1798, *The Avalon Project.* See the Editorial Note to The Kentucky Resolutions of 1798, PTJ, Vol. 30, pp. 529–556.

57. James Morton Smith, *Freedom's Fetters,* pp. 240–241; Adrienne Koch and Harry Ammon, "The Virginia and Kentucky Resolutions: An Episode in Jefferson's and Madison's Defense of Civil Liberties," *The William and Mary Quarterly,* Vol. 5, No. 2 (April 1948), pp. 145–176; see also the Editorial Note to The Kentucky Resolutions of 1798, PTJ, Vol. 30, pp. 529–556.

58. Virginia Resolution, *The Avalon Project.* For an excellent analysis of Madison's approach in the Virginia Resolutions, see the Editorial Note to Virginia Resolutions, December 21, 1798, PJM, Vol. 17, pp. 185–191; see also Koch and Ammon, "The Virginia and Kentucky Resolutions."

59. Quoted in Frank Maloy Anderson, "Contemporary Opinion of the Virginia and Kentucky Resolutions," *American Historical Review,* Vol. 5, No. 1 (October 1899), pp. 45–63; No. 2 (December 1899), pp. 225–244.

60. For the Kentucky Resolutions of 1799, see *The Avalon Project.*

6: "No Stamp Act, No Sedition Act. No Alien Bills, No Land Tax, downfall to the Tyrants of America."

61. For the Brown case, see Belt, "The Sedition Act of 1798," pp. 8–9.

62. For the cases of Charles Holt and Jedidiah Peck, see Belt, "The Sedition Act of 1798," pp. 9–11.

63. For a full account of the Cooper trial, see Peter Hoffer, *The Free Press Crisis of 1800: Thomas Cooper's Trial for Seditious Libel* (University Press of Kansas, 2011); Halperin, *The Alien and Sedition Acts of 1798,* pp. 85–87. See Cooper's own account of his trial, *An Account of the Trial of Thomas Cooper, of*

Northumberland; on a charge of libel against the president of the United States; taken in short hand. With a preface, notes, and appendix, by Thomas Cooper (April 1800; reprinted by Gale ECCO, 2010). For Hamilton's 1800 evaluation of John Adams, see Letter from Alexander Hamilton, Concerning the Public Conduct and Character of John Adams, Esq. President of the United States (October 24, 1800), PAH, Vol. 25, pp. 186–234.

64. See Ragsdale, "The Sedition Act Trials," pp. 28–29, 62; Halperin, *The Alien and Sedition Acts,* pp. 87–91; for a biography of Callender, see Michael Durey, *"With the Hammer of Truth": James Thomson Callender and America's Early National Heroes* (University of Virginia Press, 1990).

Conclusion

1. Alexander Hamilton, Conversation with George Beckwith (October 1789), PAH, Vol. 5, pp. 482–490.

BIBLIOGRAPHY

Primary Sources

American State Papers. Foreign Relations. Vol. 1. Library of Congress, American Memory.

American State Papers. Indian Affairs. Vol. 1. Library of Congress, American Memory.

Annals of Congress. Debates and Proceedings, 1789–1824. Library of Congress, American Memory.

The Avalon Project. Documents in Law, History, and Diplomacy. Yale University.

Bickford, Charlene Bangs, Kenneth R. Bowling, William Charles diGiacomantonio, and Helen E. Veit, eds. *Documentary History of the First Federal Congress, 1789–1791*, Vol. 15. Johns Hopkins Universtiy Press, 2004.

Cooper, Thomas. *An Account of the Trial of Thomas Cooper, of Northumberland; on a charge of libel against the president of the United States; taken in short hand. With a preface, notes, and appendix, by Thomas Cooper*. April 1800. Reprinted by Gale ECCO, 2010.

Correspondence of Clark and Genet, Selections from the Draper Collection in the Possession of the State Historical Society of Wisconsin, To Elucidate the Proposed French Expedition under George Rogers Clark Against Louisiana in the Years, 1793–94. Government Printing Office, 1897.

The Diaries of George Washington. Vol. 6. Ed. Donald Jackson and Dorothy Twohig. The University of Virginia Press.

The Diary and Letters of Gouverneur Morris: Minister of the United States to France, Member of the Constitutional Convention, Etc. Vol. 1, ed. Anne Cary Morris. Charles Scribner's Sons, 1888.

Documentary History of the First Federal Congress, 1789–1791. Vol. 15. Ed. Charlene Bangs et al. Johns Hopkins University Press, 2004.

Elbridge Gerry's Letterbook: Paris 1797–1798. Ed. Russell W. Knight. Essex Institute, 1966.

Findley, William. *History of the Insurrection in the Four Western Counties of Pennsylvania in the Year MDCCXCIV; with a Recital of the Circumstances Specially Connected therewith, and an Historical Review of the Previous Situation of the Country.* Philadelphia 1796.

First American West: Correspondence between George Nicholas Esq. of Kentucky and the Hon. Robert G. Harper, member of congress from the district of 96, state of South Carolina. Library of Congress, American Memory.

The Gilder Lehrman Institute of American History. New-York Historical Society, GLCO2437.05942. October 11, 1793.

Lathrop, John, Jr. *An Oration pronounced on the 4th Day of July 1798 at the Request of the Inhabitants of Dedham and its Vicinity, in Commemoration of the Anniversary of American Independence.* Minerva Press, 1798.

Letters of William Vans Murray to John Quincy Adams, 1797–1803. Ed. Worthington C. Ford. Government Printing Office, 1914.

The Life and Correspondence of Rufus King: Comprising his letters, private and official, his public documents and speeches. Vol. 2, *1795–1799.* Ed. Charles R. King, MD. G. P. Putnam's Sons, 1895.

Letters of William Vans Murray to John Quincy Adams, 1797–1803. Ed. Worthington C. Ford. Government Printing Office, 1914.

Memoir of Dr. George Logan of Stenton. Ed. Deborah Norris Logan Historical Society of Pennsylvania, 1899.

Monroe, James. *A view of the conduct of the executive, in the foreign affairs of the United States, connected with the mission to the French Republic, during the years 1794, 5 & 6.* Benjamin Bache, 1797.

Muter, George. *On Saturday the 24th instant a numerous meeting of respectable citizens from different parts of this state assembled in Lexington.* Printed by John Bradford, 1794.

New Letters of Abigail Adams, 1788–1804. Ed. Stewart Mitchell. Houghton Mifflin, 1947.

The Papers of John Adams. Massachusetts Historical Society.

The Papers of Alexander Hamilton. Ed. Harold C. Syrett. 27 Vols. Columbia University Press.

The Papers of James Madison. Congressional Series, 1751–1801.

The Papers of John Marshall. Vol. 3, *Correspondence and Papers, January 1796-December 1798.* Ed. William Stinchcombe, Charles T. Cullen, Leslie Tobias. University of North Carolina Press, 1979.

The Papers of George Washington. Presidential Series, 1788–1797. 17 Vols. University of Virginia Press.

The Papers of George Washington. Retirement Series, 1797–1799. 4 Vols. University of Virginia Press.

The Papers of George Washington. Revolutionary War Series, 1775–1780. 24 Vols. University of Virginia Press.

The Papers of Thomas Jefferson. Vols. 16–33. Princeton University Press.

"Papers Relating to What is Known at the Whiskey Rebellion in Western Pennsylvania, 1794." *Pennsylvania Archives.* Second Series. Ed. John B. Linn and

William H. Egle, MD, Vol. 4. Clarence M. Busch, State Printer of Pennsylvania, 1896.

The Public Statutes at Large of the United States of America. Vol. 1. Ed. Richard Peters, Esq. Charles C. Little and James Brown, 1850.

US Statutes at Large, Vol. 1, Library of Congress.

State Trials of the United States during the Administration of Washington and Adams, With References, Historical and Professional, and Preliminary Notes on the Politics of the Times. Ed. Francis Wharton. Carey and Hart, 1849.

The Works of Thomas Jefferson. Ed. Paul Leicester Ford. G. P. Putnam's Sons, 1904.

Writings of John Quincy Adams. Vol. 2, 1796–1801. Ed. Worthington C. Ford. MacMillan, 1913.

Secondary Sources

Articles

Aldrich, John H., and Ruth W. Grant. "The Antifederalists, the First Congress, and the First Parties." *The Journal of Politics,* Vol. 55, no. 2 (May 1993), pp. 295–326.

Ammon, Harry. "The Genet Mission and the Development of American Political Parties." *The Journal of American History,* Vol. 52, No. 4 (March 1966), pp. 725–741.

Anderson, Frank Maloy. "Contemporary Opinion of the Virginia and Kentucky Resolutions." *American Historical Review,* Vol. 5, No. 1 (October 1899), pp. 45–63; No. 2 (December 1899), pp. 225–244.

Austin, Aleine. "Matthew Lyon's Trial for Sedition." In *Retracing the Past,* Third Edition, Vol. 1, ed. Gary B. Nash and Ronald Schultz. Harper Collins, 1994, pp. 128–129.

Banning, Lance. "Republican Ideology and the Triumph of the Constitution, 1789–1793." *The William and Mary Quarterly,* 3rd series, Vol. 31, No. 2 (April 1974), pp. 168–188.

Barber, William D. "'Among the Most Techy Articles of Civil Police': Federal Taxation and the Adoption of the Whiskey Excise." *The William and Mary Quarterly,* 3rd series, Vol. 25, No. 1 (January 1968), pp. 58–84.

Belt, Gordon T. "The Sedition Act of 1798: A Brief History of Arrests, Indictments, Mistreatments, and Abuse." Online publication of *The First Amendment Center, Newseum Institute,* Washington, DC.

Berns, Walter. "Freedom of the Press and the Alien and Sedition Laws: A Reappraisal." *The Supreme Court Review,* Vol. 109 (1970), pp. 109–159.

Bonsteel Tachau, Mary K. "The Whiskey Rebellion in Kentucky: A Forgotten Episode of Civil Disobedience." *Journal of the Early Republic,* Vol. 2, No. 3 (Autumn 1982), pp. 239–259.

Bradburn, Douglas. "A Clamor in the Public Mind: Opposition to the Alien and Sedition Acts." *The William and Mary Quarterly,* 3rd series, Vol. 65, No. 3 (July 2008), pp. 565–600.

Brown, Katherine Ann, and Todd Gitlin. "Partisans, Watchdogs, and Entertainers: The Press for Democracy and Its Limitations." In *The Oxford Handbook of American Public Opinion and the Media*, ed. Robert Y. Shapiro and Lawrence R. Jacobs (Oxford University Press, 2013), pp. 74–88.

Campbell, Wesley J. "The French Intrigue of James Cole Mountflorence." *The William and Mary Quarterly*, 3rd series, Vol. 65, No. 4 (October 2008), pp. 779–796.

———. "The Origins of Citizen Genet's Projected Attack on Spanish Louisiana: A Case Study in Girondin Politics." *French Historical Studies*, Vol. 33, No. 4 (Fall 2010), pp. 515–544.

Clark, Allan C. "William Duane." *Records of the Columbia Historical Society, Washington, DC*. Vol. 9 (The Society, 1906).

Coleman, Aaron N. "'A Second Bounaparty?' A Reexamination of Alexander Hamilton During the Franco-American Crisis, 1796–1801." *Journal of the Early Republic*, Vol. 28, No. 2 (Summer 2008), pp. 183–214.

Conlin, Michael F. "The American Mission of Citizen Pierre-Auguste Adet: Revolutionary Chemistry and Diplomacy in the Early Republic." *Pennsylvania Magazine of History and Biography*, Vol. 124, No. 4 (October 2000), pp. 489–520.

Crandall, Regina Katharine. "Genet's Projected Attack on Louisiana and the Floridas, 1793–94." PhD Dissertation, University of Chicago, 1902.

Crews, Ed. "Rattle-Skull, Stonewall, Bogus, Blackstrap, Bombo, Mimbo, Whistle Belly, Syllabub, Sling, Toddy, and Flip: Drinking in Colonial America." Online in *Colonial Williamsburg Journal* (Holiday 2007).

Davis, Jeffrey A. "Guarding the Republican Interest: The Western Pennsylvania Democratic Societies and the Excise Tax." *Pennsylvania History: A Journal of Mid-Atlantic Studies*, Vol. 67, No. 1 (Winter 2000), pp. 43–62.

Durey, Michael. "Thomas Paine's Apostles: Radical Emigrés and the Triumph of Jeffersonian Republicanism." *The William and Mary Quarterly*, 3rd series, Vol. 44, No. 4 (October 1987), pp. 661–688.

Forkosch, Morris D. "Freedom of the Press: Croswell's Case," *Fordham Law Review*, Vol. 33, No. 3 (1965), pp. 415–448.

Gies, Benjamin Michael. "Kentucky's First Statesman: George Nicholas and the Founding of the Commonwealth." Master's Thesis, University of Louisville, 2016.

Holt, Wythe. "The Whiskey Rebellion of 1794: A Democratic Working-Class Insurrection." Unpublished essay, Georgia Workshop in Early American History and Culture, University of Georgia.

Howe, John R., Jr. "Republican Thought and the Political Violence of the 1790s." *American Quarterly*, Vol. 19, No. 2, Part 1 (Summer 1967), pp. 147–165.

Hughes, Gerard. "Norms for a Misuse of Authority: The Alien and Sedition Acts." *Revue Française D'Études Americaines*, No. 74 (October 1997), pp. 93–102.

Jones, Robert F. "George Washington and the Politics of the Presidency." *Presidential Studies Quarterly*, Vol. 10, No. 1 (Winter 1980), pp. 28–35.

Ketcham, Ralph l. "France and American Politics, 1763–1793." *Political Science Quarterly*, Vol. 78, No. 2 (June 1963), pp. 198–223.

Koch, Adrienne, and Harry Ammon. "The Virginia and Kentucky Resolutions: An Episode in Jefferson's and Madison's Defense of Civil Liberties." *The William and Mary Quarterly*, Vol. 5, No. 2 (April 1948), pp. 145–176.

Kohn, Richard H. "The Washington Administration's Decision to Crush the Whiskey Rebellion." *The Journal of American History*, Vol. 59, No. 3 (December 1972), pp. 567–584.

Koschnik, Albrecht. "The Democratic Societies of Philadelphia and the Limits of the American Public Sphere, Circa 1793–1795." *The William and Mary Quarterly*, Vol. 58, No. 3 (July 2001), pp. 625–636.

Kramer, Eugene F. "Some New Light on the XYZ Affair: Elbridge Gerry's Reasons for Opposing War with France." *New England Quarterly*, Vol. 29, No. 4 (December 1956), pp. 509–513.

Krom, Cynthia L., and Stephanie Krom. "The Whiskey Tax of 1791 and the Consequent Insurrection: 'A Wicked and Happy Tumult.'" *Accounting Historians Journal*, Vol. 40, No. 2, (December 2013), pp. 91–114.

Kuehl, John W. "Southern Reaction to the XYZ Affair: An Incident in the Emergence of American Nationalism." *The Register of the Kentucky Historical Society*, Vol. 70, No. 1 (January 1792), pp. 21–49.

Landis, Charles I. "Jasper Yeates and His Times." *The Pennsylvania Magazine of History and Biography*, Vol. 46, No. 3 (1922), pp. 199–231.

Lendler, Marc. "'Equally Proper at All Times and at All Times Necessary': Civility, Bad Tendency, and the Sedition Act." *Journal of the Early Republic*, Vol. 24, No. 3 (Autumn 2004), pp. 419–444.

Marsh, Philip M. "John Beckley: Mystery Man of the Early Jeffersonians." *The Pennsylvania Magazine of History and Biography*, Vol. 72, No. 1 (January 1948), pp. 54–69.

Mayo, Bernard, ed. "Instructions to the British Ministers to the United States, 1791–1812." No. 3, American Historical Association, 1941, pp. 37–39.

Mintz, S., and S. McNeil. "The Alien and Sedition Acts, ID 245." *Digital History*, University of Houston. Online publication at http://www.digitalhistory.uh.edu, 2016.

Parton, James. "The Exploits of Edmond Genet in the United States," *The Atlantic Monthly: A Magazine of Literature, Science, Art and Politics*, Vol. 31 (April 1873), pp. 390–405.

Pasley, Jeffrey L. "The Cheese and the Words: Popular Political Culture and Participatory Democracy in the Early American Republic." In *Beyond the Founders: New Approaches to the Political History of the Early American Republic*, ed. Jeffrey L. Pasley, Andrew W. Robertson, and David Waldstreicher. University of North Carolina Press, 2004, pp. 31–56.

Ragsdale, Bruce A. "The Sedition Act Trials." *Federal Judicial Center*. Federal Judicial History Office, 2005.

Ray, Thomas M. "'Not One Cent for Tribute': The Public Addresses and American Popular Reaction to the XYZ Affair, 1798–1799." *Journal of the Early Republic*, Vol. 3, No. 4 (Winter 1983), pp. 389–412.

Retzer, Alice J. "The Virginia Resolutions of 1798: A Study of the Contemporary Debate." Honors Thesis, University of Richmond, 1969.

Sheridan, Eugene R. "The Recall of Edmond Charles Genet: A Study in Transatlantic Politics and Diplomacy." *Diplomatic History,* Vol. 18 (Fall 1994), pp. 463–488.

Sioli, Marco. "Citizen Genet and Political Struggle in the Early Republic." In "Crise et Crises." Special issue, *Revue Française D'Études Americaines,* No. 64 (May 1995), pp. 259–267.

Smelser, Marshall. "George Washington and the Alien and Sedition Acts." *The American Historical Review,* Vol. 59, No. 2 (January 1954), pp. 322–334.

Smith, Craig R. "The Alien and Sedition Crisis." In *Silencing the Opposition: How the US Government Suppressed Freedom of Expression During Major Crises.* State University of New York Press, 2011, pp. 1–21.

Smith, James Morton. "Background for Repression: America's Half-War with France and the Internal Security legislation of 1798." *Huntington Library Quarterly,* Vol. 18, No. 1 (November 1954), pp. 37–58.

———. "The Grass Roots Origins of the Kentucky Resolutions." *The William and Mary Quarterly,* Vol. 27, No. 2 (April 1970), pp. 221–245.

Stinchcombe, William. "The Diplomacy of the WXYZ Affair." *The William and Mary Quarterly,* Vol. 34, No. 4 (October 1977), pp. 590–617.

———. "Talleyrand and the American Negotiations of 1797–1798." *The Journal of American History,* Vol. 62, No. 3 (December 1975), pp. 575–590.

Warren, Jack D. "'The Line of My Official Conduct': George Washington and Congress, 1789–1797." In *Neither Separate nor Equal: Congress in the 1790s,* ed. Kenneth R. Bowling and Donald R. Kennon. Ohio University Press, 2000, pp. 238–268.

White, Kenneth A. "'Such Disorder Can Only Be Cured by Copious Bleedings': The Correspondence of Isaac Craig during the Whiskey Rebellion." *The Western Pennsylvania Historical Magazine,* Vol. 67, no. 3 (July 1984), pp. 213–242.

Wood, Gordon S. "Conspiracy and the Paranoid Style: Causality and Deceit in the Eighteenth Century." *The William and Mary Quarterly,* 3rd series, Vol. 39, No. 3 (July 1982), pp. 401–441.

———. "Ideology and the Origins of Liberal America," *The William and Mary Quarterly,* 3rd series, Vol. 44, No. 3 (July 1987), pp. 628–640.

"Yellow Fever Attacks Philadelphia, 1793." *EyeWitness to History,* www.eye witnesstohistory.com (2005).

Young, Christopher J. "Connecting the President and the People: Washington's Neutrality, Genet's Challenge, and Hamilton's Fight for Public Support." *Journal of the Early Republic,* Vol. 31, No. 3 (Fall 2011), pp. 435–466.

Books

Ammon, Henry. *The Genet Mission.* W. W. Norton, 1973.

Austin, Aleine. *Matthew Lyon, "New Man" of the Democratic Revolution, 1749–1822.* Pennsylvania State University Press, 1981.

Baldwin, Leland. *Whiskey Rebels: The Story of a Frontier Uprising.* University of Pittsburgh Press, 1939.

Beasley, Vanessa B. *Who Belongs in America? Presidents, Rhetoric, and Immigration*. Texas A&M Press, 2006.

Bernard, Jack F. *Talleyrand: A Biography*. Putnam, 1793.

Bienvenu, Richard. *The Ninth of Thermidor*. Oxford University Press, 1970.

Billias, George A. *Elbridge Gerry: Founding Father and Republican Statesman*. McGraw-Hill, 1976.

Bond, Jon R., and Kevin B. Smith. *Analyzing American Democracy: Politics and Political Science*. Routledge, 2013.

Bowman, Albert Hall. *The Struggle for Neutrality: Franco-American Diplomacy During the Federal Era*. University of Tennessee Press, 1974.

Boyd, Steven R., ed. *The Whiskey Rebellion: Past and Present Perspectives*. Greenwood Press, 1985.

Brackenridge, H. H. *Incidents of the Insurrection in the Western Parts of Pennsylvania*. Classic Reprint. Forgotten Books, 2016.

Brackenridge, H. M. *History of the Western Insurrection in Western Pennsylvania Commonly Called the Whiskey Insurrection, 1794*. 1859 . . . reprint Heritage Books, 2009.

Bradburn, Douglas. *The Citizenship Revolution: Politics and the Creation of the American Union, 1774–1804*. University of Virginia Press, 2009.

Bragg, C. L. *Crescent Moon over Carolina: William Moultrie & American Liberty*. University of South Carolina Press, 2013.

Brinton, Crane. *The Lives of Talleyrand*. W. W. Norton, 1963.

Brookhiser, Richard. *What Would the Founders Do? Our Questions, Their Answers*. Basic Books, 2007.

Chernow, Ron. *Alexander Hamilton*. Penguin Press, 2004.

Clarfield, Gerard H. *Timothy Pickering and American Diplomacy, 1795–1800*. University of Missouri Press, 1969.

———. *Timothy Pickering and the American Republic*. University of Pittsburgh Press, 1980.

Cunningham, Noble E., Jr. *The Early Republic, 1789–1828*. University of South Carolina Press, 1968.

Davis, W. W. H. *The Fries Rebellion, 1798–99; an armed resistance to the House tax law, passed by Congress, July 9, 1798, in Bucks and Northampton Counties, Pennsylvania*. 1899, reprint Kessinger, 2010.

Dawson, Matthew Q. *Partisanship and the Birth of America's Second Party, 1796–1800: Stop the Wheels of Government*. Greenwood Press, 2000.

Dungan, Nicholas. *Gallatin: America's Swiss Founding Father*. New York University Press, 2010.

Durey, Michael. *"With the Hammer of Truth": James Thomson Callender and America's Early National Heroes*. University of Virginia Press, 1990.

Egle, William H. *An Illustrated History of the Commonwealth of Pennsylvania*. RareBooksClub.com. March 6, 2012.

Elkins, Stanley, and Eric McKitrick. *The Age of Federalism: The Early American Republic, 1788–1800*. Oxford University Press, 1993.

Eliot, Jonathan, ed. *The Debates in the Several State Conventions on the Adoption of the Federal Constitution*. Philadelphia 1891.

Genet, George Clinton. *Washington, Jefferson, and "Citizen" Genet, 1793.* New York Public Library, 1905.

Gibbs, George. *Memoirs of the Administrations of Washington and John Adams, Edited from the Papers of Oliver Wolcott.* Vol. 1. William Van Norden, Printer, 1845.

Halperin, Terri Diane. *The Alien and Sedition Acts of 1798: Testing the Constitution.* Johns Hopkins University Press, 2016.

Hoffer, Peter Charles. *The Free Press Crisis of 1800: Thomas Cooper's Trial for Seditious Libel.* University Press of Kansas, 2011.

Hofstadter, Richard. *The Idea of a Party System: The Rise of Legitimate Opposition in the United States, 1780–1840.* University of California Press, 1969.

Hogeland, William. *The Whiskey Rebellion: George Washington, Alexander Hamilton and the Frontier Rebels Who Challenged America's Newfound Sovereignty.* Simon and Schuster, 2010.

Ingrams, Richard. *The Life and Adventures of William Cobbett.* Harper Perennial, 2006.

Kurtz, Stephen G. *The Presidency of John Adams: The Collapse of Federalism, 1795–1800.* University of Pennsylvania Press, 1957.

Marcus, Maeva, ed. *Documentary History of the Supreme Court of the US, 1789–1800.* Vol. 3. Columbia University Press, 1990.

McLaughlin, J. Fairfax. *Matthew Lyon, the Hampden of Congress, a Biography.* 1900, reprint Forgotten Books, 2012.

Miller, John C. *Crisis in Freedom: The Alien and Sedition Acts.* Little, Brown, 1951.

Newman, Paul Douglas. *Fries Rebellion: The Enduring Struggle for the American Revolution.* University of Pennsylvania Press, 2005.

Nichols, Roy. F. *The Invention of the American Political Parties: A Study of Political Improvisation.* Free Press, 1967.

Pasley, Jeffrey L. *The Tyranny of Printers: Newspaper Politics in the Early American Republic.* University of Virginia Press, 2001.

Powell, J. M. *Bring Out Your Dead: The Great Plague of Yellow Fever in Philadelphia in 1793.* Reprint, University of Pennsylvania Press, 1993.

Rosenfeld, Richard N. *American Aurora: A Democratic-Republican Returns.* St. Martin's Griffin, 1997.

Sharp, James Roger. *American Politics in the Early Republic: The New Nation in Crisis.* Yale University Press, 1993.

Shaw, Peter. *The Character of John Adams.* University of North Carolina Press, 1976.

Slack, Charles. *Liberty's First Crisis: Adams, Jefferson, and the Misfits Who Saved Free Speech.* Grove Press, 2015.

Slaughter, Thomas P. *The Whiskey Rebellion: Frontier Epilogue to the American Revolution.* Oxford University Press 1988.

Smith, James Morton. *Freedom's Fetters: The Alien and Sedition Laws and American Civil Liberties.* Cornell University Press, 1956.

Smith, Jean Edward. *John Marshall: Definer of a Nation.* Henry Holt, 1996.

Smith, Jeffery A. *Printers and Press Freedom: The Ideology of Early American Journalism.* Oxford University Press, 1988.

———. *War and Press Freedom: The Problem of Prerogative Power.* Oxford University Press, 1999.

Tagg, James. *Benjamin Franklin Bache and the Philadelphia "Aurora."* University of Pennsylvania Press, 1991.

Tolles, Frederick B. *George Logan of Philadelphia.* Oxford University Press, 1953.

Ungar, Harlow Giles. *The French War Against America: How a Trusted Ally Betrayed Washington and the Founding Fathers.* John Wiley & Sons, 2005.

Wagstaff, Robert H. *Terror Detentions and the Rule of Law: US and UK Perspectives.* Oxford University Press, 2013.

Warfield, Ethelbert Dudley. *The Kentucky Resolutions of 1798: An Historical Study.* G. P. Putnam's Sons, 1887.

Wharton, Francis. *State Trials of the United States during the Administration of Washington and Adams, With References, Historical and Professional, and Preliminary Notes on the Politics of the Times.* Cary and Hart, 1849.

Williams, Greg H. *The French Assault on American Shipping, 1793–1813: A History and Comprehensive Record of Merchant Marine Loss.* McFarland, 2009.

INDEX